The Best of

Navigation

Edited by Charles Mason

The Best of

Navigation

SAIL Books
34 Commercial Wharf
Boston, Massachusetts

SAIL Books are published by Sail Publications, Inc.

The Best of SAIL Navigation
    1. Navigation—Addresses, essays, lectures.
2. Sailing—Addresses, essays, lectures.
I. Mason, Charles   II. Sail
VK555.B5   623.89   81-21337
ISBN 0-914814-27-3   AACR2
Printed in the U.S.A.

Foreword

The navigator has always been accorded a special place on board a sailing ship. It is the navigator who must guide his vessel to a distant shore and then back home. Take the epic Mediterranean travels of Odysseus, the Vikings' arduous open sea voyages, or the spectacular renaissance discoveries of new worlds and opportunities. All were accomplished because a navigator knew, after the fashion of his epoch, how to use the sun, stars and moon together with some common sense and judgement.

The navigator remains crucial today whether he is aboard a top flight ocean racer looking for a way to save seconds on a long beat to windward or aboard a cruising boat sailing across some sun-flecked body of water. The knowledge available to the modern navigator is far more complete than that available to his ancient predecessors, but the process of directing a boat of any size still depends on an unavoidable alternative: either you know how to get where you are going or you don't. Today's ignorance produces results identical to those of any other century you care to pick. Unless blind luck intercedes on your behalf, the chance of a safe arrival, or return, can become dramatically small.

For the real sailor then, there is a fascination and a challenge in knowing where he is, no matter whether he is in the middle of a vast ocean, trying to locate a buoy at night or in the fog, or just poking along a shoreline near home while looking for a good place to stop for lunch. Each situation requires you to know where you are, and each situation requires the use of one or more techniques possessed by every good navigator.

SAIL Magazine has published many articles on navigation over the years, but the aim has always been to offer practical material that can be used by every small-boat sailor. A compilation of these many articles has created its own challenge, namely how best to present a wide range of subject material. The solution has been to group the articles into seven general categories and then present a collection of thought-provoking articles about each one of them.

Having been involved in the original preparation of this material for SAIL, I would like to thank Stan Grayson and Anne Wieschhoff of SAIL Books for their expertise in making all the necessary course corrections to bring the articles to final book form. And, of course, my deep appreciation goes to the authors — experts all — who sat down in the first place to give the rest of us the wisdom they have acquired from many, many years' experience.

Navigators have always been part of adventure and exploration. And even though the great frontiers have all but vanished, the challenge and exhilaration of confidently charting our own courses is something we all can still enjoy. After all, if you know where you are right now, you know how to project, pretty precisely, where you ought to be in the future.

Charles Mason
Boston, Massachusetts

Contents

1. PILOTING

15 DR, EP and the Running Fix
James B. Kane

19 Piloting: Keep Up with the Problem
Robert H. Gulmon

25 Selecting Visual Aids to Navigation
John Ellsworth

29 How Far Can You See?
Ed Bergin

33 Running Fixes and Night Approaches
Mike Saunders

38 Halving Your Trouble by Doubling the Angle
Charles Mason

40 Boat Speed and the Current
James B. Kane

43 Understanding Apparent Current
Robert H. Gulmon

49 Fighting the Currents
James B. Kane

52 Anticipating Collisions
Ray A. Fletcher

2. FOG

57   Fighting through Fog
Earl B. Rubell

61   When Visibility is Reduced
John Mellor

66   Pre-navigation is What Gets You Home
Burt Sauer

71   Stand-off Strategy for Fog
Burt Sauer

75   Using the Radio Direction Finder
Burt Sauer

3. CELESTIAL

85   Celestial Navigation Simplified
Bill Thomte

88   Dusting off the Sextant
John Ellsworth

92   The Noon Sight
Paul Dodson

95   Getting Down to Sight Reduction
James B. Kane

100   Sunlines . . . Valuable Checks
Paul Dodson

104   Precomputed Sun Sights
Crocker Wight

107   Precomputed Star Sights
Robert Silverman

112   Latitude by Polaris and Mintaka
William V. Kielhorn

116   Set Your Sights on Celestial
Ralph Naranjo

4. RACING

123   Good Navigation Begins at Home
Richard T. du Moulin

126   Keeping on Top of the Situation
       Michel G. Emmanuel

130   The Racing Navigator
       Richard T. du Moulin

133   The Navigator's Worksheets
       Richard T. du Moulin

137   The Best Course to Windward
       Alan J. Adler

142   Beating to Windward
       William R. Knowlton

148   When There's Current on the Windward Leg
       William R. Knowlton

153   Tacking Downwind
       Jack Nelson

5. CHARTS & AIDS

159   Charts Can Help You Plan Ahead
       Robert H. Gulmon

163   Don't Forget the Fine Print
       James B. Kane

167   Avoiding Terra Incognita
       Murray Lesser

170   Setting Up the Universal Plotting Sheet
       Ed Bergin

175   Detailing Special Charts
       Lou Hohenstein

178   Understanding Mercator's Chart
       William V. Kielhorn

183   The Pelorous
       James B. Kane

186   Mylar as an Aid for Navigators
       John Ellsworth

190   Homemade Instruments
       James B. Kane

192   Utilizing the Almanacs
          Joe Consolmagno

6. EQUIPMENT

197   Plan Ahead for Safety
          William V. Kielhorn

202   What Equipment Should You Have?
          Lou Hohenstein

207   Understanding the Radio Direction Finder
          Burt Sauer

215   Correcting the RDF
          Burt Sauer

224   Operating Your Magnetic Compass
          William V. Kielhorn

230   Compensate Your Compass
          William V. Kielhorn

238   Determining Your Speed
          William V. Kielhorn

243   Electronic Depthsounders: The Versatile Helpers
          James B. Kane

249   The Lead Is Not Dead
          Dag Pike

253   Get the Most Out of Your Loran-C
          Parker Boggs

7. CALCULATORS

263   Try a Programmable Calculator
          Jim Abbott

266   Dead Reckoning Without Having to Plot
          Joe Consolmagno

271   Another Way to Solve the Navigational Triangle
          M.A. Schultz

274   Calculators: Keeping Them Going
          Ed Bergin & Jack Buchanek

8. CONTRIBUTORS

279

1

PILOTING

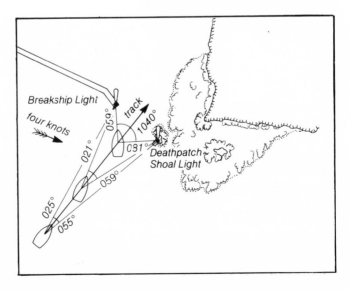

DR, EP and the Running Fix

By James B. Kane

Suppose, because of fog or a lack of instruments, you have no means of precisely fixing your position. What would you do? You probably would use dead reckoning (DR).

When you plot your courses and distances from your last *well-determined* position to get your present position, you are using the simplest form of dead reckoning. Naturally, you get your distance by multiplying

your speed by the time you've sailed at that speed.

Let's say you get a fix at 1018 (10:18 AM) which puts you 2.5 miles off Grassy Point Lighthouse when you are abeam (Fig. 1). You intend to pass 2.0 miles off Rocky Point, then head for Sandy Point. By drawing a line between these two positions, then parallelling it to a compass rose, you find your course to be 020° magnetic, and you steer 020°. But before you sight Rocky Point light-

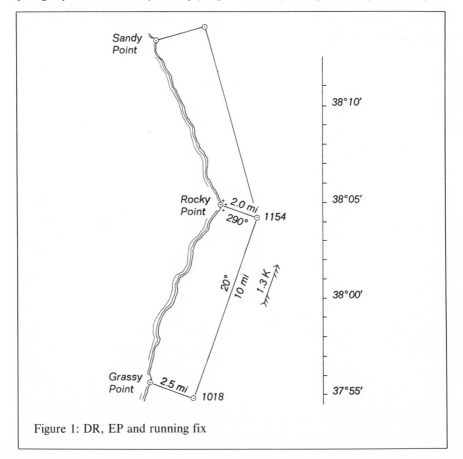

Figure 1: DR, EP and running fix

house, a heavy rain squall obscures it. Because you're unable to see Rocky Point, you want to know what time you'll be abeam so that you will know when to change course.

The first thing to do is to measure the distance on your course line between the two points; you find it is 10 miles. Now estimate your speed through the water; let's say it's five knots. Ten miles at five knots will take you two hours. Therefore, at 1218 your DR is 290°, 2.0 miles off Rocky Point lighthouse.

But the Tidal Current Tables show that you also have a 1.3-knot fair current and your boat, therefore, is doing 6.3 knots over the ground. Ten miles divided by 6.3 knots gives you 1.6 hours or one hour and 36 minutes (each tenth of an hour is six minutes). One hour and 36 minutes added to 1018 equals 1154. Accordingly, your 1218 DR position now becomes your 1154 estimated position (EP).

You determine a DR by measuring the distance sailed through the water on course from a fix. You determine

your EP by considering the disturbing elements (wind and current) and applying their effect to the DR. If a current is unpredictable or uncertain, you're better off using a DR position.

Unfortunately, the terms DR and EP aren't standard, and even some textbooks use DR when they really mean EP; the U.S. Naval Oceanographic Office, however, agrees with the meanings of DR and EP I have given you.

But I have said only what a DR and EP are. Generally, when you are making a course change, as you did at Rocky Point, you estimate your speed to be the *least* you think you're making. Otherwise you may make the course change too early, and the next thing you know they will be naming one of those rocks off Rocky Point after you or your boat.

Conversely, when you are making a landfall using both DR and EP, estimate your speed to be the *maximum* you could make. This way you won't run on the beach while you're still below eating supper. There is an

TABLE 19

Speed, Time, and Distance

Min-utes	Speed in knots																Min-utes
	0.5	1.0	1.5	2.0	2.5	3.0	3.5	4.0	4.5	5.0	5.5	6.0	6.5	7.0	7.5	8.0	
	Miles	Miles	Miles	Miles	Miles	Miles	Miles	Miles	Miles	Miles	Miles	Miles	Miles	Miles	Miles	Miles	
1	0.0	0.0	0.0	0.0	0.0	0.0	0.1	0.1	0.1	0.1	0.1	0.1	0.1	0.1	0.1	0.1	1
2	0.0	0.0	0.0	0.1	0.1	0.1	0.1	0.1	0.1	0.2	0.2	0.2	0.2	0.2	0.2	0.3	2
3	0.0	0.0	0.1	0.1	0.1	0.2	0.2	0.2	0.2	0.3	0.3	0.3	0.3	0.4	0.4	0.4	3
4	0.0	0.1	0.1	0.1	0.2	0.2	0.2	0.3	0.3	0.3	0.4	0.4	0.4	0.5	0.5	0.5	4
5	0.0	0.1	0.1	0.2	0.2	0.2	0.3	0.3	0.4	0.4	0.5	0.5	0.5	0.6	0.6	0.7	5
6	0.0	0.1	0.2	0.2	0.2	0.3	0.4	0.4	0.4	0.5	0.6	0.6	0.6	0.7	0.8	0.8	6
7	0.1	0.1	0.2	0.2	0.3	0.4	0.4	0.5	0.5	0.6	0.6	0.7	0.8	0.8	0.9	0.9	7
8	0.1	0.1	0.2	0.3	0.3	0.4	0.5	0.5	0.6	0.7	0.7	0.8	0.9	0.9	1.0	1.1	8
9	0.1	0.2	0.2	0.3	0.4	0.4	0.5	0.6	0.7	0.8	0.8	0.9	1.0	1.0	1.1	1.2	9
10	0.1	0.2	0.2	0.3	0.4	0.5	0.6	0.7	0.8	0.8	0.9	1.0	1.1	1.2	1.2	1.3	10
11	0.1	0.2	0.3	0.4	0.5	0.6	0.6	0.7	0.8	0.9	1.0	1.1	1.2	1.3	1.4	1.5	11
12	0.1	0.2	0.3	0.4	0.5	0.6	0.7	0.8	0.9	1.0	1.1	1.2	1.3	1.4	1.5	1.6	12
13	0.1	0.2	0.3	0.4	0.5	0.6	0.7	0.8	0.9	1.1	1.2	1.3	1.4	1.5	1.6	1.7	13
14	0.1	0.2	0.4	0.5	0.6	0.7	0.8	0.9	1.0	1.2	1.3	1.4	1.5	1.6	1.8	1.9	14
15	0.1	0.2	0.4	0.5	0.6	0.8	0.9	1.0	1.1	1.2	1.4	1.5	1.6	1.8	1.9	2.0	15
16	0.1	0.3	0.4	0.5	0.7	0.8	0.9	1.1	1.2	1.3	1.5	1.6	1.7	1.9	2.0	2.1	16
17	0.1	0.3	0.4	0.6	0.7	0.8	1.0	1.1	1.3	1.4	1.6	1.7	1.8	2.0	2.1	2.3	17
18	0.2	0.3	0.4	0.6	0.8	0.9	1.0	1.2	1.4	1.5	1.6	1.8	2.0	2.1	2.2	2.4	18
19	0.2	0.3	0.5	0.6	0.8	1.0	1.1	1.3	1.4	1.6	1.7	1.9	2.1	2.2	2.4	2.5	19
20	0.2	0.3	0.5	0.7	0.8	1.0	1.2	1.3	1.5	1.7	1.8	2.0	2.2	2.3	2.5	2.7	20
21	0.2	0.4	0.5	0.7	0.9	1.0	1.2	1.4	1.6	1.8	1.9	2.1	2.3	2.4	2.6	2.8	21
22	0.2	0.4	0.6	0.7	0.9	1.1	1.3	1.5	1.6	1.8	2.0	2.2	2.4	2.6	2.8	2.9	22
23	0.2	0.4	0.6	0.8	1.0	1.2	1.3	1.5	1.7	1.9	2.1	2.3	2.5	2.7	2.9	3.1	23
24	0.2	0.4	0.6	0.8	1.0	1.2	1.4	1.6	1.8	2.0	2.2	2.4	2.6	2.8	3.0	3.2	24
25	0.2	0.4	0.6	0.8	1.0	1.2	1.5	1.7	1.9	2.1	2.3	2.5	2.7	2.9	3.1	3.3	25
26	0.2	0.4	0.6	0.9	1.1	1.3	1.5	1.7	2.0	2.2	2.4	2.6	2.8		3.2	3.5	26
27	0.2	0.4	0.7	0.9	1.1	1.4		1.8	2.0	2.2	2.5	2.7			3.4	3.6	27
28	0.2	0.5	0.7	0.9	1.2	1.				3.	2.6	2.8			3.5	3.7	28
29	0.2		0.7	1.0	1.						2.7	2.9			3.9		29
30																	30

Figure 2

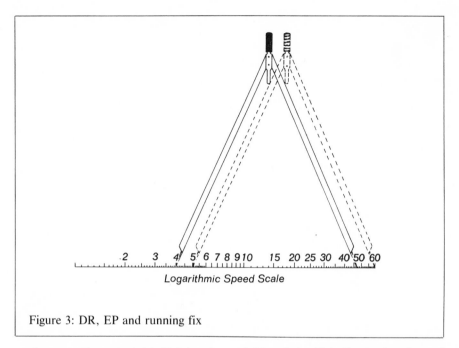

.2   3   4 5 6 7 8 9 10   15 20 25 30 40 50 60

Logarithmic Speed Scale

Figure 3: DR, EP and running fix

easier way than straight division to find your distance run: use a Time, Speed, and Distance table. You'll find one in Bowditch (HO) Table 19. Crank in any two quantities and reel the third one out of the table (Fig. 2).

If you have no Bowditch aboard you can use the logarithmic speed scale found on most National Ocean Survey charts. Here's how it works.

To find speed place one point of your dividers on the elapsed time and the other point on the distance (in miles) sailed during this time. Without changing the spread of your dividers, put the right point on 60 and the left point will indicate your speed in knots (Fig. 3).

To find distance place one point of your dividers on 60 and the other point on your speed in knots. Without changing the spread of your dividers or the right-left relationship of the points, stick the right point on the elapsed time. The left point will indicate your distance in miles. Or you can place the left point of your dividers on the distance in miles and the

right point will indicate the elapsed time.

Let's assume you sail four miles in 48 minutes. How many knots are you making? Place the right point of your dividers on 48 and the left point on four (Fig. 3). Without changing the spread, put the right point on 60 and the left point shows five. You're making five knots.

If you need help in remembering which point goes where, remember the right point always indicates *time*; the left point indicates *speed* or *distance*.

If you have neither a set of dividers nor a Time, Speed, and Distance table, you'll have to compute your speed on paper. To get your distance in nautical miles, multiply your speed (in knots) by your elapsed time in minutes, then divide by 60.

Your elapsed time equals *distance* multiplied by 60, divided by your speed. To get your *speed*, divide your distance times 60 by the elapsed time.

Of course, you can solve time,

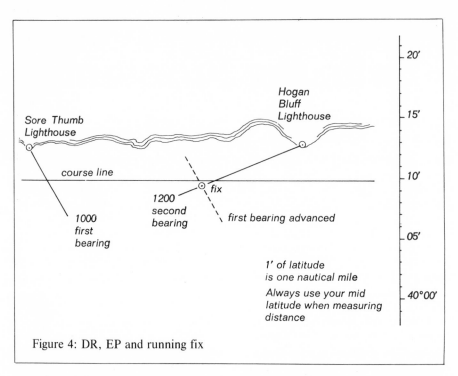

Figure 4: DR, EP and running fix

Inside figure, the following labels appear:

20'

Hogan
Bluff
Lighthouse

15'

Sore Thumb
Lighthouse

course line

10'

1200
second
bearing

fix

1000
first
bearing

first bearing advanced

05'

1' of latitude
is one nautical mile

Always use your mid
latitude when measuring
distance

40°00'

speed, and distance problems with a slide rule, and nautical instrument stores sell several kinds of circular slide rules especially for these time, speed, and distance problems.

When someone says "running fix," many of us think of celestial navigation, but you can use a running fix with coastwise piloting, too. To work a running fix, though, you must use DR or EP.

Here is an example. You take a bearing on Sore Thumb lighthouse at 1000 (10:00 AM) and plot it on your chart (Fig. 4). Later, at 1200 you take a bearing on Hogan Bluff lighthouse and you plot it on your chart. Let's assume you're making 6.5 knots. Now compute the distance you ran between the two bearings. Two hours at 6.5 knots is 13 miles. With either parallel rulers or a pair of

triangles, advance your first bearing 13 miles along your course line. The spot at which the 1200 second bearing and your 1000 advanced first bearing intersect is your running fix. Of course, the accuracy of any running fix depends on how well you've kept track of your course and distance.

Seldom is a DR or even an EP exactly where you are, and you must use them very carefully in shoal water. On the other hand, if you rely completely on instruments, you're also risking a grounding. So practice DRs and EPs. Run your DR ahead of you so you can predict when you'll pick up the lights, landmarks and other aids to navigation you are looking for.

A good navigator always keeps ahead of his boat.

Piloting: Keep Up with the Problem

By Robert H. Gulmon

Virtually all groundings take place within sight of land or within what I call *piloting waters*. In fact, many navigators agree that entering and leaving port can be the most hazardous parts of any voyage — assuming normal weather conditions en route.

The principles of piloting are deceptively simple. In the case of visual piloting, the true bearing of an identifiable fixed object, plotted on the chart as a line to the object, constitutes a *line of position* — a line upon which the vessel is presumed to be located. Two or more such lines, obtained by near-simultaneous bearings of different objects, intersect to define the boat's position at the time the bearings were taken. Then the information obtained from several such fixes taken at frequent intervals is used to direct the boat's progress along a safe track to the desired destination. This is the aspect of piloting that demands the highest order of experience, skill, and judgment.

The main difficulty stems from the fact that by the time a fix is plotted on a chart, it is already outdated. If a boat is making six knots, and you take five minutes to plot a round of bearings on the chart, the fix position is a half-mile astern of where the boat actually is. So, when you are in piloting waters, usually it is not sufficient for a navigator merely to know where he *was*. He also must know where he *is*, and where he is *going to be* in the near future. This requires developing techniques for rapidly projecting past fix information into the present and future. In other words, you have to learn how to keep up with the problem.

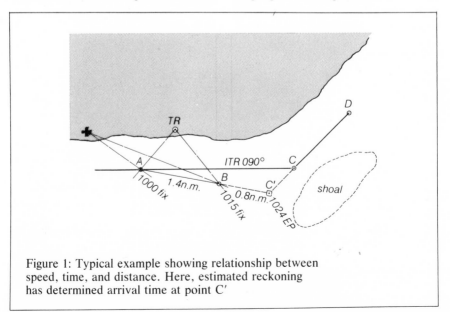

Figure 1: Typical example showing relationship between speed, time, and distance. Here, estimated reckoning has determined arrival time at point C′

By way of illustration, let's consider a simplified but typical situation of a boat sailing parallel to a coastline on a course of 090° (Fig. 1). The intended track (ITR) is shown as a heavy, solid line passing through points A, C, and D. The planned course change at C is necessary to avoid the unmarked shoal area that lies to the east. You have obtained fixes at points A and B, at the times indicated, by taking bearings on landmarks. The problem facing you, the navigator, is how to determine when you have arrived at the turning point. In the absence of an identifiable object that could be used to mark your arrival at this point, you must rely on the information provided by the fixes taken at points A and B.

The first fact that the fixes reveal is that the boat is not making good the intended track of 090°. Although she is steering 090°, the boat is being set to the south by current and is actually making 100° over the ground. Because you have estimated this fact, you might choose to maintain your present course of 090° and simply select a new turning point, C', which lies on the extension of the track you have been making good. What you need is the time of arrival at point C'.

By measuring the distance from A to B, you see you have made 1.4 miles over the ground during the elapsed time of 15 minutes between fixes: an average speed of 5.6 knots. Next you measure the distance from B to C' and determine this distance to be 0.8 miles. Assuming no significant change in speed, you can then compute that it will take almost nine minutes to go from B to C', making the arrival time at the turning point 1024.

This simplified example illustrates the kinds of computations a navigator must perform in order to find out where he or she is, when he will ar-

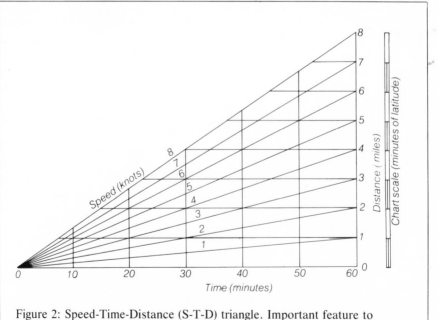

Figure 2: Speed-Time-Distance (S-T-D) triangle. Important feature to remember is that distance scale should conform to scale on chart

rive at a given point, or where he will be at some specified future time. All these are *speed-time-distance* problems which are solved by employing some form of the basic relationship: distance (D) is the product of speed (S) and time (T), or (D = ST). To solve either for speed or for time, the equation is transposed to the forms $S = \dfrac{D}{T}$ or $T = \dfrac{D}{S}$. If you want to express D in nautical miles, S in knots, and T in minutes, the equations become: $D = \dfrac{ST}{60}$, $S = \dfrac{60D}{T}$, and $T = \dfrac{60D}{S}$.

An experienced navigator is always conscious of the inherent lag in any plotted position, and he or she acquires considerable proficiency in assessing mentally the approximate extent of this lag. In his mind's eye he sees a point down-course from his last plotted fix that represents his position at the moment. You learn to do this by memorizing certain basic relationships that can be used for making rapid mental estimates: three knots is roughly equivalent to 100 yards per minute; 60 divided by the speed in knots yields the time in min-

utes to go one mile; and in six minutes you travel a distance in miles equal to one-tenth your speed in knots.

Although such techniques are useful for keeping mentally abreast of a problem, they do not replace the need for more precise methods, such as dead reckoning or estimated reckoning, to predict a vessel's future progress. Dead reckoning is commenced, or recommenced, each time a boat's position has been accurately established, and it consists of projecting a track, based on the true course steered and speed by the log, that shows where the vessel will be at specified intervals of future time. Estimated reckoning is performed in a similar manner but is based on the course and speed made good over the ground, as in the example of Figure 1, or by correcting dead reckoned positions for the effects of known currents. Both methods involve the use of the time-speed-distance formulas previously discussed.

Although applying these formulas requires nothing more complicated than straight arithmetic, the need for speed and accuracy in piloting dictates using some kind of computa-

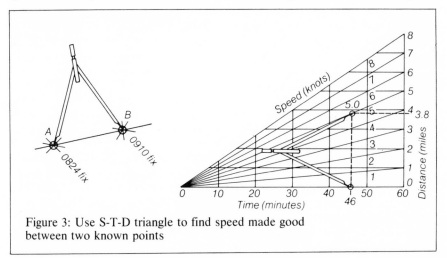

Figure 3: Use S-T-D triangle to find speed made good between two known points

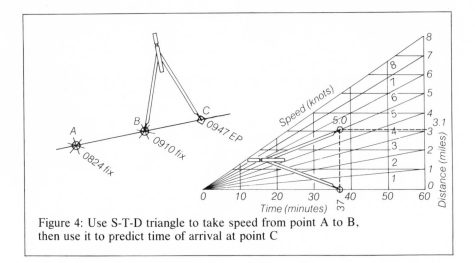

Figure 4: Use S-T-D triangle to take speed from point A to B,
then use it to predict time of arrival at point C

tional aid to replace longhand calculations. Among the devices commonly used are ordinary slide rules,
special navigational computers, and
more recently, the ubiquitous bat-
tery-powered pocket calculator.
Though all are superior to longhand
methods, there is another device that
can be used with small-craft charts,
as well as many Coast and Harbor
Charts, that is faster and I think more
convenient than any of the above:
the Speed-Time-Distance triangle—
a gadget you can make yourself in
about five minutes.

The Speed-Time-Distance (S-T-
D) triangle is nothing more than a
graph of distance versus time for a
range of speeds. Its particular advantage stems from the fact that, for
appropriately scaled charts, the distance scale of the graph can be made
to correspond with the scale of the
chart. The S-T-D triangle can be constructed to scale on a piece of graph
paper and taped to the chart being
used or it can be drawn on the chart
itself where it is permanently available for future use. You construct
the graph by first laying off a distance scale on the right-hand ordi-
nate. The scale is in nautical miles,
numbered from bottom to top, and

each scale division corresponds in
length to one minute of arc on the
latitude scale of the chart. The number of divisions does not need to exceed the top speed of your boat in
knots. The time scale is marked off
along the abcissa and is numbered
from left to right. This scale requires
60 divisions to represent the minutes
in an hour but the minute gradations
can be any convenient size provided
they are large enough to permit reading the scale to the nearest minute of
time (Fig. 2).

To complete the graph, draw
straight lines from zero on the time
scale to each whole-mile graduation
on the distance scale. This family of
sloping lines represents the range of
speed in knots and each line is numbered to correspond with its point of
intersection on the distance scale.

Now here's how the thing works.
Figure 3 represents a portion of a
chart where two fixes, taken 46 minutes apart, have been plotted and
labeled as points A and B. You want
to know what speed has been made
good between these two points. The
applicable formula in this case is
$S = \dfrac{60D}{T}$. Before you can begin to

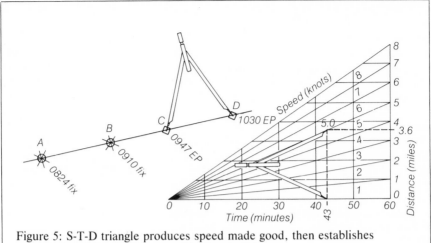

Figure 5: S-T-D triangle produces speed made good, then establishes estimated position (EP) for specific time in future

solve the problem with a calculator, however, you must determine the distance from A to B by spanning it with your dividers and transferring this measurement to the latitude scale on the chart to read the distance, which turns out to be 3.8 nautical miles. Substituting this value for D in the formula, and 46 minutes for T, gives $S = \dfrac{60 \times 3.8}{46}$.

The calculator solves this in a split second — but 10 individual keyboard entries were required to set up the problem.

To solve the same problem on the S-T-D triangle, you span the distance from A to B as before and, without changing the setting, transfer the dividers directly to the graph, positioning them at 46 minutes in the time scale, and read the answer, 5.0 knots, on the speed scale. Since the distance scale on the graph corresponds to the distance scale on the chart, there is no need to determine the actual numerical value of the distance from A to B in order to solve the problem. When you consider that transferring the dividers from the navigational plot to the graph or

the latitude scale are equivalent, it is apparent that the S-T-D triangle gives you the answer before the problem is even entered in the calculator.

Having determined your average speed over the ground, you can now compute the estimated time of arrival at any point down-course from the last fix. Now that you know where you were at point B at 0910, you can estimate when you will arrive at point C (Fig. 4). You accomplish this simply by spreading the dividers to span the distance from point B to C, then positioning them on the graph so that the upper point lies on the five-knot speed line. The time required to travel from B to C (37 minutes) is indicated where the lower point of the dividers touches the time scale. As before, it is not necessary to obtain the number of miles from B to C.

Finally, there is a chance that you need to know where you will be at some future time. This situation might come up if you want to arrange a rendezvous with another boat at some specific time; it could be 1030, or 43 minutes after his arrival at point

C. The distance he will travel in this interval is found by setting the dividers to equal the vertical distance from the 43-minute mark on the time scale of the graph to the five-knot speed line (Fig. 5). Although this turns out to be 3.6 miles, you don't really need to know this. The big point is that your dividers now are set to this value and can be used directly to prick off this distance from point C, and thereby project the location of the rendezvous at point D.

These examples show how the S-T-D triangle can be used to provide an accurate and rapid solution to any variation of the speed-time-distance problem. It is good for providing a near-real-time update of fix information, yielding fast answers to such questions as: Where am I now? When will I arrive at point X? And where will I be at time Y? It also can be used to project dead (or estimated) reckoning plots or to solve current triangles. Its best application, however, is for coping with the short-term future. In short, it is really a good way to help you keep up with your ship.

Selecting Visual Aids to Navigation

By John Ellsworth

Whenever you are sailing in coastal waters, the margin for error is very limited. This simply means you always must know your position. You probably have sailed safely in familiar waters without ever plotting a fix. You know where you are by visual references to known marks. But when you venture into strange waters, plotted fixes are essential if you are going to know your position.

The easiest and quickest visual fix is a set of cross bearings on two or more aids to navigation; three are recommended. You can also use a combination of a visual bearing and a range, three ranges, or a range and bearing (Fig. 1).

A visual bearing is obtained by a pelorus and plotted on the chart. A range can be determined visually either by a sextant or a stadimeter. Either instrument measures the vertical angle subtended by an object of known height. You then can refer to Table 9 in Bowditch (H.O. 9, *American Practical Navigator*) with the observed angle and the object's height and get the range, or distance.

When you enter unfamiliar waters, adhere to the seafaring proverb, "Too strong never breaks." If you take and plot your fixes with utmost accuracy and proficiency, you'll never be unsure about where you are.

Before you start taking sights on any aids to navigation, you should

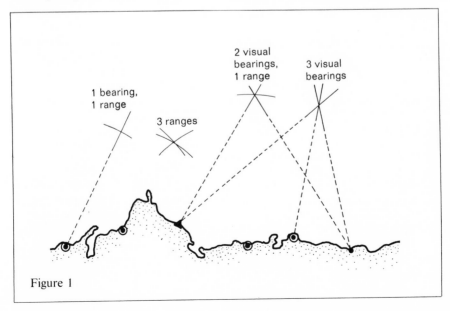

Figure 1

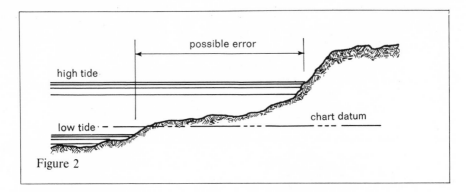

possible error

high tide

low tide · –

chart datum

Figure 2

select the ones you will use. Your choice may well influence your degree of accuracy.

The selection process can be broken down into three steps. The first step is to decide which objects you will observe as you move along your charted course. This is called the overall selection, and the marks can be labelled A, B, C, D, E, F, etc. Always do this in advance. Appraise every detail of the respective charts and review the sailing directions, light lists and tide tables.

Next, familiarize yourself with the sailing area, determine your courses and select the aids to navigation you will use to sight your visual fixes. Always try to use lighthouses, spires, cupolas, etc., for all have well-defined observation points. A bold headland is good only for sight-ing a tangent bearing.

If possible, avoid using large buildings and most mountains, for there is usually some doubt about the exact point you should use for the observation. Buoys are not recom-mended for bearing marks for they are secured by an anchor and swing in an arc. Because they are not fixed, buoys may be shifted off station by ships, storms, or tides. And occa-sionally, they are deliberately moved. Unless you keep your charts up to date with the *Notice to Mari-ners*, you may well be in error.

Try not to sight tangents off is-lands or low points of land. You will have an error if the shore is shelving and the tide is above the chart datum. And what may appear as a long point at low water may dis-appear altogether at high tide. If

Time	Bearing/Range	Bearing/Range	Bearing/Range	Remarks
1307	Howlett Lt. 330	Cupola 245	Swinford Lt. 3.2 mi.	Howlett Lt. 18 ft.
1315	Church 320	020		Swinford Lt. 68 ft.
1320	000	Edgar Spire	070/2.1 mi.	Cupola
1325	020	267	Amy Pt. Lt.	Edgar Spire
1330	100	300	050	Church
1335	Radio Twr 270/1.7 mi.	310	Suzanne's Bluff 050	Radio Twr 54 ft.
1340	278/1.5 mi.		060	Amy Pt. Lt. Suzanne's Bluff

Figure 3

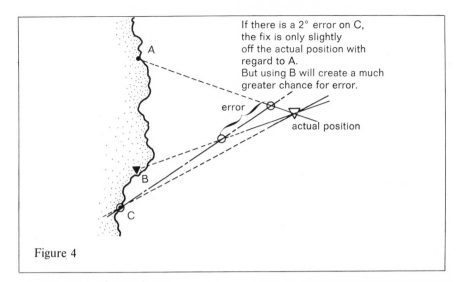

If there is a 2° error on C, the fix is only slightly off the actual position with regard to A.
But using B will create a much greater chance for error.

A

error

actual position

B

C

Figure 4

there is great tidal range, you could have substantial error (Fig. 2).

When you've determined all your potential aids to navigation as well as backups (in case those picked can't be recognized with absolute sureness), list them in a visual bearing notebook. Record tower and lighthouse heights: they'll be handy when you are determining ranges.

When you are moving along your charted course, visualize where you might expect to sight the objects and what they'll look like. When you get in the area, scan the horizon for the first sighting. If you locate and identify a distant object with binoculars, observe the cloud formation above it; it will make it easier to locate and sight the bearing. When you take your bearing, record the time, the object, and the bearing in degrees in the notebook (Fig. 3).

Once you have several of your selected aids to navigation in view, you should be aware that certain combinations produce greater accuracy than others. For example, when the angle between two objects is decreasing, a small error in either bearing will throw the fix off by an increasing amount (Fig. 4).

When you are getting a fix with cross bearings, the best fix is obtained when at least two bearing lines cross each other at 90°. You might sight one object dead ahead and another abeam. If this is not possible, always try to select objects with no less than 30° nor more than 150° between each pair.

Always consider the distance an object is away from you. The closer the better because the linear error resulting from an angular error always increases with distance (Fig. 5). For example, an angular error of 2° represents a linear error of 200 feet if the object is one mile away; at ten miles, the same 2° error represents 2,000 feet!

When you're determining range with a sextant or stadimeter, the distance, height and location are the key elements that must be considered. The closer and the higher the object, the greater is the measured angle and the more reliable is the range reading.

Remember that the stated height of a lighthouse, in the light list, is always listed above high water. Its height must be corrected for tide.

When you are "shooting" your

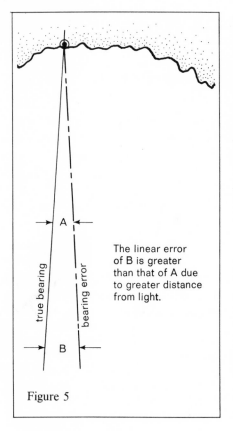

true bearing

bearing error

A

The linear error
of B is greater
than that of A due
to greater distance
from light.

B

Figure 5

bearings, the sighting sequence will affect your accuracy. Always sight first the object whose bearing is changing most slowly. This will probably be one either dead ahead or dead astern. In considering objects with rapidly changing bearings, the ones nearest the beam should be sighted last. The time of the last sighting should be the time of your plotted fix. If you combine ranges with bearings, observe the vertical angles first, since observation is quicker with a pelorus. This means you won't lose any plotting time after a sextant or stadimeter reading; and the pelorus bearings will be the most up-to-date.

When you are selecting your "targets" for bearings, keep in mind that the angles between them should be as close as possible to 90°, and that nearby objects are preferable to distant ones. And always shoot the objects having slowly changing bearings first. If you are getting ranges with vertical angles, remember that high objects near the shoreline will yield the best results.

Keep these points in mind and you should avoid the confusion that results from not knowing where you are the next time you sail into strange waters.

How Far Can You See?

By Ed Bergin

Assume you're sailing along the coast of Georgia on a hazy night. According to your dead reckoning, which you feel is quite accurate, you should be seeing the Savannah, Georgia, Light, but for over half an hour you've squinted in the dark looking for it, without success. Your chart gives the range of Savannah Light as 25 miles. The chart also tells you the light is 85 feet above water, and you know your own height-of-eye on your 35-foot sailboat is 15 feet. A recent VHF weather broadcast for the coast of Georgia has told you that visibility is 5 miles in haze.

How do you use all this information to predict when you should spot the light?

First, you must know how a navigator predicts the distance a light will be visible from his boat on a clear night. Clear visibility means you can sight a distance of 10 miles or more; reduced visibility means that distance is less than 10 miles. Once you know how to calculate clear weather conditions, you can determine the distance of a light under reduced visibility.

Distance on a clear night. Because light rays travel in a straight line and the earth's surface is curved, the distance from which you can see a light

height in feet	nautical miles	statute miles	height in feet	nautical miles	statute miles
1	1.1	1.3	40	7.2	8.3
2	1.6	1.9	41	7.3	8.4
3	2.0	2.3	42	7.4	3.5
4	2.3	2.6	43	7.5	8.6
5	2.6	2.9	44	7.6	8.7
6	2.8	3.2	45	7.7	8.8
7	3.0	3.5	46	7.8	8.9
8	3.2	3.7	47	7.8	9.0
9	3.4	4.0	48	7.9	9.1
10	3.6	4.2	49	8.0	9.2
11	3.8	4.4	50	8.1	9.3
12	4.0	4.6	55	8.5	9.8
13	4.1	4.7	60	8.9	10.2
14	4.3	4.9	65	9.2	10.6
15	4.4	5.1	70	9.6	11.0
16	4.6	5.3	75	9.9	11.4
17	4.7	5.4	80	10.2	11.8
18	4.9	5.6	85	10.5	12.1

Figure 1: Computations of horizon distance are based on a simple formula and use of height-of-eye as basis for observation. Table similar to that shown here is found in *Bowditch* as Table 8

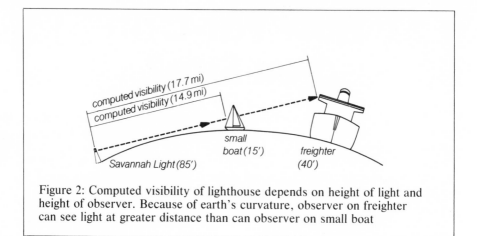

Figure 2: Computed visibility of lighthouse depends on height of light and height of observer. Because of earth's curvature, observer on freighter can see light at greater distance than can observer on small boat

on a clear night depends on two things, the height of the light and your own height-of-eye.

This height-of-light/height-of-eye relationship determines the computed visibility of a light and is tabulated in *Bowditch* as Table 8. There also are any number of calculator programs that give the same results. (The formula is $D = 1.144 \sqrt{h}$, where D is the distance in nautical miles and h is your height-of-eye in feet.) In *Bowditch*'s Table 8 (Fig. 1), you first find your own height-of-eye above the water in the height/feet column, which in this example is 15 feet. Then you find the height of the light, which we have said is 85 feet. From the nautical miles column you take 4.4 miles for your height and add that to the 10.5 miles for the light and get a total of 14.9 feet. This means the computed visibility of Savannah Light from your boat is 14.9 nautical miles.

You should now understand that since the computed visibility of a light varies according to your height-of-eye, obviously Savannah Light is going to be visible from farther away when seen from a freighter's deck having a height-of-eye of 40 feet than it is from a sailboat with a height-of-eye of 15 feet (Fig. 2).

Once you determine the computed visibility of a light you must compare that distance with the chart, or *Light List* range. This range, sometimes called the *nominal range*, has nothing to do with your height-of-eye, the height of the light, or the curvature of the earth. This range is simply the straight line distance the light's rays will travel on a clear night.

This means the *computed visibility* and the chart/*Light List* range must be compared to see which is smaller. If a light is very powerful, or strong, the chart/*Light List* range may exceed the computed visibility. If so, the computed visibility will be the distance you could expect to see the light on a clear night.

If the light is a weak light, the chart/*Light List* range may be less than the computed visibility. If so, the chart or *Light List* range is the maximum distance the light can be seen.

In Figure 3 we see that the Hatteras Inlet Light is a weak light because its chart/*Light List* range on a clear night extends only 13 miles as opposed to *Bowditch*'s tabulated Table 8, where the computed visibility of this 88-foot-high light from our 15-foot height-of-eye is 15.1 miles. Because the light rays don't reach

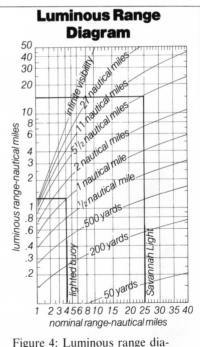

Figure 3: Very often computed visibility of light is substantially different from charted distance. In such cases always use the smaller of two distances

this far, you cannot see Hatteras Inlet Light until you reach the chart/*Light List* range of 13 miles.

On the other hand Savannah Light is a strong light that casts its beacon 25 miles on a clear night. Obviously, if the computed visibility of this light is 14.9 miles you could not physically see the light 25 miles out for, as Figure 3 suggests, your boat must travel to a point 14.9 miles from the light before you can see it. Thus on a clear night you must remember to compare the computed visibility with the chart/*Light List* range. The smaller of the two distances is the one where the light should become visible.

Distance in reduced visibility. Spotting lights in less than clear weather is another problem entirely. Let's assume you are looking for Savannah Light on a hazy night where visibility is reduced to about 5 miles. To calculate the distance you can see this light under reduced visibility conditions you use the chart/*Light List* range to find a luminous range, or distance in nautical miles the light will be visible under the prevailing conditions. You do this with a luminous range diagram like the one shown in Figure 4. These diagrams are included in the front of every chart/*Light List*.

You want to know how far Savannah Light, with a charted (or *nominal*) range of 25 miles, can be seen if visibility conditions are restricted to around 5 miles. Along the bottom of

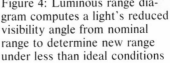

Figure 4: Luminous range diagram computes a light's reduced visibility angle from nominal range to determine new range under less than ideal conditions

Figure 4 you find vertical lines representing the *nominal,* or chart/*Light List* range of light. Along the left margin, you see horizontal lines representing the luminous (or reduced visibility) range of a light. Throughout the diagram curved lines represent different visibility distances.

In this case you enter the diagram from the bottom with the 25-mile chart/*Light List* range of Savannah Light. Move up the column until you intersect the curved line representing the present reduced visibility condition. (The 5 1/2-mile curve is used since it is closest to 5 miles.)

Use your parallel rules to go from this intersection to the left side of the diagram where you get the luminous range, or reduced visibility distance, of 16 miles. You now know that haze has reduced the distance Savannah Light's powerful beacon can travel from 25 to 16 miles.

There is one final step. This calculation still does not mean you can see Savannah Light at 16 miles. Even under reduced visibility a powerful light still can exceed your boat's computed visibility. So, as a final step, always compare the reduced visibility with the computed visibility. As we have seen, the distance from which you can see a light is the smaller of the two distances. In this case, the computed visibility of 14.9 miles *still* is *less* than the reduced visibility range of 16 miles so you should, therefore, still expect to see Savannah Light at a distance of 14.9 miles.

None of these calculations are particularly complicated, but you should always check to be sure about all distances. If you do, you know which distance you are actually going to be dealing with. Going through the steps is an informative exercise and is a procedure every careful navigator will always undertake.

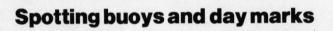

Spotting buoys and day marks

When you add some common sense, the techniques for predicting when you should see a major lighthouse also can be used for smaller aids to navigation such as buoys or day marks. The *Light Lists* also give the nominal range and height above water for many (but not all) minor lights.

For example, a *Light List* may tell you a channel light has a nominal or chart/*Light List* range of 4 miles and is 16 feet above water. Using Table 8 of *Bowditch* and assuming your height-of-eye is 15 feet, you calculate the computed visibility of the light to be 9 miles. So, in clear weather, you still would look for this buoy at a distance of about 4 miles. *Remember that in most cases the computed visibility of minor lights exceeds their nominal range.*

But if visibility is reduced to 1 mile, for example, you can use the luminous range diagram to compute the reduced visibility distance of the buoy, which in this example is about 1.3 miles. Because the computed visibility does exceed the reduced visibility, you should look for the buoy at a distance of around 1.3 miles (Fig. 4).

If a buoy's nominal range and height-of-eye above water is not given in the *Light List* you could assume a nominal range of 3-5 miles and a height-of-eye of 10-16 feet and come up with a range of estimated distances that is fairly close. However use estimates like these with a lot more caution than the estimates you derive from an actual *Light List* figure or that you derive from chart information.

—Ed Bergin

Running Fixes and Night Approaches

By Mike Saunders

Making a running fix always reminds me of that mythical bird that flies around in ever-decreasing circles until it vanishes up its own tail. With a running fix you keep sailing "around" a landmark until you know where you are. Suppose you take a compass bearing of the conspicuous monument shown in Figure 1. You lay the line on the chart, and because there is nothing else to take a bearing from, you mark an arrow pointing each way; this simply tells you that you do not know *where* you are on the line. At the same time as you shoot the bearing, you note your log reading, the time, and the course.

Continue on your way holding a steady course, and when the bearing on the monument has changed enough, repeat the same procedure. A change of 90 degrees is ideal, but you seldom get it; in Figure 2 it is only 55 degrees.

Now, starting *anywhere* on your first line of bearing, lay off the course you have steered and the log distance you have traveled between the two sights. Then also estimate the distance and the direction that the current has taken you and add that on. At the point where you end up, draw a second line that is *parallel* to your first bearing line. You can put double arrows on it (Fig. 3). This does not mean that you are now

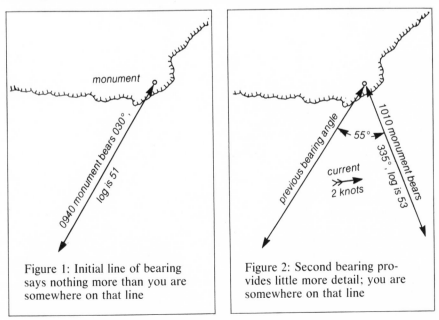

Figure 1: Initial line of bearing says nothing more than you are somewhere on that line

Figure 2: Second bearing provides little more detail; you are somewhere on that line

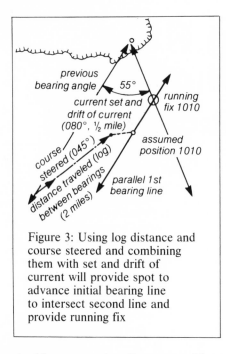

previous
bearing angle
55°

current set and
drift of current
(080°, ½ mile)

course
steered (045°)

distance traveled (log)
between bearings
(2 miles)

running
fix 1010

assumed
position 1010

parallel 1st
bearing line

Figure 3: Using log distance and
course steered and combining
them with set and drift of
current will provide spot to
advance initial bearing line
to intersect second line and
provide running fix

line cuts the second bearing line is
your exact position at the time you
took your second bearing. You will
see from Figure 3 that your true position is not the spot where you would
have ended up using your steered
course and added current.

In practice, when you round a
point of land like this, you take a
series of running fixes right away so
that you get some idea of your position early in the maneuver. Then you
can keep a check as you go on. The
classic case of doubling the angle on
the bow is merely a special example
of a running fix, but personally I
shun it because getting those bearings to double is often very difficult
to do.

The running fix is a handy trick but
not very precise for it depends entirely on the accuracy of your course
and distance estimates. And if there
are any currents flowing, some
guesswork is unavoidable. If you are
ever in doubt, you are better off to
underestimate your distance sailed
because overestimating the distance

doubly uncertain of your position
(though that may well be the case)
but merely that the new line is a
transferred position line.

Where the transferred position

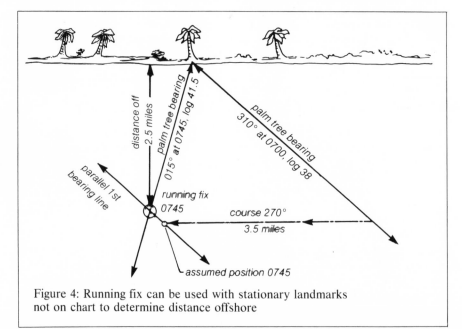

distance off
2.5 miles

palm tree bearing
015° at 0745, log 41.5

palm tree bearing
310° at 0700, log 38

parallel 1st
bearing line

running fix
0745

course 270°
3.5 miles

assumed position 0745

Figure 4: Running fix can be used with stationary landmarks
not on chart to determine distance offshore

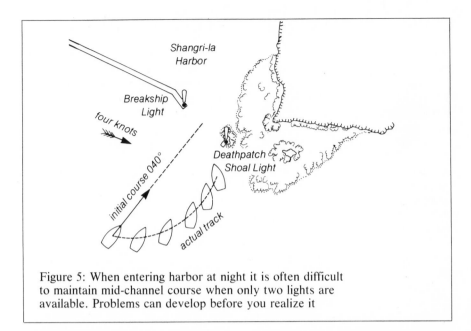

Figure 5: When entering harbor at night it is often difficult to maintain mid-channel course when only two lights are available. Problems can develop before you realize it

will lead you to think you are farther offshore than you really are. However, if you don't have two or more navigation marks to use for bearings or it is at night when you have a single light and no accurate way to judge distance offshore, the running fix is extremely useful in spite of its weaknesses.

But what do you do if you have no landmarks that can be identified on the chart? This can happen with low, featureless, sandy shore. If the shoreline is reasonably straight, then all is not lost. Pick out a rock, tree, or some other feature (preferably not a grazing horse) and take your running fix on that. The result won't be a fix as such, but it will give you a good indication of your distance offshore (Fig. 4).

What do you do if there is a landmark but you can't see it? In fact, you may hardly see your own light at the top of the mast because of fog. Do not reach for your distress kit for there may be a radio beacon nearby that can give you the same kind of running fix. In case you think this situation is farfetched, I have had to resort to this method twice in the last year. The technique you use is exactly the same as it is for compass bearings, except that you use a radio direction finder instead.

If everything else fails, yell your head off, and under the right conditions you will get some sort of answer. The method is as old as the hills, which is where you get the echo to bounce back. Ideally, you should be sailing in deep water that is bounded by cliffs; Scottish lochs, Norwegian fjords and the coast of British Columbia are supposed to be suitable areas. With a stopwatch in one hand and a belaying pin or hammer in the other, rap out a sharp sound on some hard object and listen for the echo. Assuming the echo is not drowned by booming surf, you then time it. The formula is elegantly simple. A 10-second interval is one mile; five seconds, one-half mile; one second, 200 yards; and so on.

Entrances and exits. So far, I have been talking about assessing distance off the shore, but it frequently happens that you must sail between landmarks to keep to the mid-channel of a harbor entrance, a bay exit, or a passage between islands. To steer for the middle is often all that is required. But sometimes that simply won't do. Suppose, for example, you are approaching the outer harbor entrance, shown in Figure 5, at night. The end of the breakwater and the extremity of the shoal to starboard are well marked with light-houses. You can see the lights quite clearly but it is a dark and windy night, and there is a strong cross current. You cannot judge by eye whether you are holding the approach course that will take you through the mid-channel passage.

If you simply set a course to go between the two lights, your track in Figure 5 shows what will happen to you. You will unknowingly be set toward the shoal and you will probably not grasp the situation until it has become fairly critical.

The correct method here is to open out the two light bearings *equally* on either side of your approach course (Fig. 6). At point A you have taken a fix and you know roughly where you are. You have found that the approach course is 040°, and with this figure fixed in your mind you really don't need to look at the chart again. You simply sail your boat so that the bearing of Breakship Light, to port, is as much below 040° as the bearing of Deathpatch Shoal light is above 040°. Your first bearing might be, say, 025° and 055°, respectively. In other words the two bearings are 15° above and 15° below. The second bearings should be 021° and 059°, or 19° above and 19° below. And the procedure should continue in a similar vein with each consecutive bearing. If the established difference between the bearing of one light and your 040° base course becomes smaller, head away from that light. If it is larger, head toward it. In this way you will sail your boat down the mid-channel course, regardless of where your bow is pointing.

Ad hoc transits. Approaching your

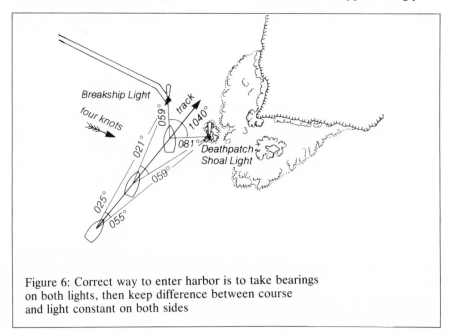

Figure 6: Correct way to enter harbor is to take bearings on both lights, then keep difference between course and light constant on both sides

mythical harbor of Figures 5 and 6 in daylight will be much easier because you are far better able to judge perspectives and distances. You can still use the *equal opening* method, but if the land behind the lighthouses is visible, there is an easier trick you can pull.

Get yourself into position A as before and then find a pair of easily seen landmarks that line up. They don't even need to be on the chart: anything will do. In our idyllic harbor example there will be a graceful stand of trees on the beach below a serene monastery on the hill behind the harbor. In actual practice, office blocks on the foreshore and concrete water tanks on the skyline are far more common. In either case, though, you simply sail in, keeping the two marks lined up (Fig. 7). You no longer need to use the ship's compass if you use this method.

Using such ad hoc transits is one of the handiest props you can find to use with inshore navigation. Transits are good, not only when you enter a harbor but also sailing anywhere in close waters where you suspect a current or wind might be pushing you off course. The marks don't need to be ad hoc either; they can be buoys, charted landmarks or whatever. Whenever they are lined up, they give you an extremely accurate position line. And a "moving" transit like a hill behind a foreshore, or a headland that lies beyond a headland, can give you a good idea of how well and in what direction you are

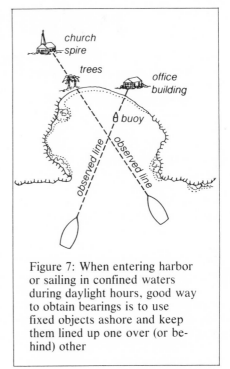

Figure 7: When entering harbor or sailing in confined waters during daylight hours, good way to obtain bearings is to use fixed objects ashore and keep them lined up one over (or behind) other

moving. In fact, you don't even need to be sailing. Using a pair of transits is a fast way to check whether your anchor is holding. Of course taking a round of compass bearings is far more precise but it does take a lot more time.

Transits are the invisible paths along which a seaman can sail his coastal route. They pre-date the compass and, along with the other suggestions I have made in this article, should be standard methods a navigator can draw upon when the occasion arises. Make sure you have all of them in your bag of skills.

Halving Your Trouble by Doubling the Angle

By Charles Mason

When you are night cruising up a coastline that comes out at you as a headland and then recedes back into a bay or inlet, you had better know where you are all the time. It is amazing how easy it is to be set into one of the bays by some tide. It can also happen if the helmsman isn't paying attention and "thinks" he may be getting a bit offshore because the land seems to be falling away from him.

One of the simplest and most prac-

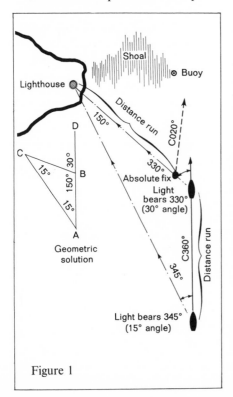

Figure 1

tical ways of determining your exact position relative to an approaching promontory is to dust off a concept that was pounded into you in high school geometry, namely that two sides of an isoceles triangle are always equal. They may come in all shapes and sizes but they have one thing in common: *isosceles triangles have two equal sides and two equal angles.*

This simple property of an isosceles triangle gives rise to the popular navigator's trick of "doubling the angle" to find out one's distance off, or position from, a known point.

Here's how it works.

Let's assume you are running due north along a coast that has an irregular shoreline. You've set a course that will take you well outside an unlit bellbuoy marking the outer end of a shoal that extends out from a headland with a lighthouse on it.

First, check your log, or your DR, for the better you can determine distance run the more accurate your solution will be.

Take an accurate compass bearing on the light. Let's assume it bears 345°. This puts it at a relative angle 15° left of the 360° course you are steering. Write down the distance logged, or your DR, and continue steering 360°.

The bearing on the light will gradually increase. Keep watching it until your original relative bearing (15°) has doubled to 30°, when the light will be bearing 330°.

Write down the log again, and subtract the first reading from it. The difference is the distance you've run between the two bearings.

If you are using DR, estimate your speed and note the times of the two bearings. Divide this elapsed time into one hour, and divide that into the speed you feel you are making. This will give you the approximate distance you have come, though it's nowhere near as accurate as a log.

Now draw a line from the light on the reciprocal bearing from your last observation: yours was 330° so the reciprocal is 150°. Take your dividers, and adjust them on the chart to the distance you have run between your two bearings. That is also the distance you are from the light, along the 150° radial. Place one end on the light, and the spot where the other end intersects the 150° line is an absolute fix. From that absolute fix you can adjust your course to take you clear of that unlighted buoy.

Remember, always run the reciprocal bearing from the lighthouse and plot the distance. You may have to change course as in Figure 1 where the new course is 020°.

Geometrically, here's why it works: We know that $\angle CBD$ is 30°. Therefore $\angle ABC$ is 150° ($\angle ABD$ is $180° - \angle CBD\ 30° = 150°$). We also know $\angle CAB$ is 15°. Therefore $\angle ACB$ must also be 15°. An isosceles triangle exists and sides AB and CB must be of equal distance.

Boat Speed and the Current

By James B. Kane

How many times have shipmates asked you, "What speed are we making?" And how many times have you wished you knew the answer, not only for those who asked, but also to help determine what time you should arrive at your destination? This article shows how to figure your boat speed without any expensive instruments, and it also tells how to allow for a current's set and drift correctly (*set* is the direction *toward* which a current flows, *drift* is the velocity) to make good a desired course.

Let's begin by finding your speed without instruments. Go to your boat and mark a distance of 16'8" on a section of the gunwale that parallels the keel. To determine your speed, throw anything that will float

— an empty bottle is fine — overboard at the marking nearest the bow. Note in seconds the time it takes the bottle to travel the 16'8".

Divide this time into ten and you have your boat speed in knots. For example, if it takes two seconds for the bottle to float to the after marking, you are doing five knots. (Of course, you should make a line fast to the bottle so you can retrieve it.)

Compensating for the *effect* of current is a bit harder. The best way, of course, is to line up an object you are heading for with something behind it ashore, use the two objects as a natural range, and steer whatever course is necessary to keep the two objects in line. There are many times, however, when there is nothing in sight to steer for, and when this happens you'll need to allow for the

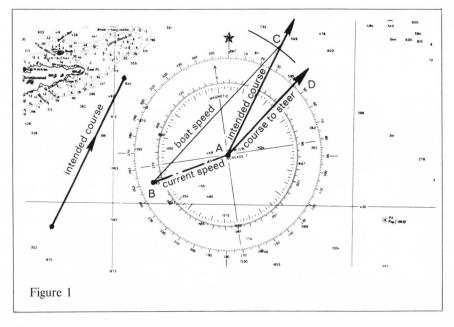

Figure 1

Inclination of set to course to be made good	.05	.10	.15	.20	.25	.30	.35	.40	.45	.50	.55	.60	.65	.70
10° or 170°	0.5	1.0	1.5	2.0	2.5	3.0	3.5	4.0	4.5	5.0	5.5	6.0	6.5	7.0
20° or 160°	1.0	2.0	3.0	3.9	4.9	5.9	6.9	7.9	8.9	9.9	10.9	11.9	12.9	13.9
30° or 150°	1.4	2.9	4.3	5.8	7.2	8.6	10.1	11.5	13.0	14.5	16.0	17.5	19.0	20.5
40° or 140°	1.9	3.7	5.5	7.4	9.3	11.1	13.0	14.9	16.8	18.8	21.2	22.7	24.7	26.8
50° or 130°	2.2	4.4	6.6	8.8	11.1	13.3	15.5	17.8	20.2	22.5	24.9	27.4	29.9	32.4
60° or 120°	2.5	5.0	7.5	10.0	12.5	15.1	17.6	20.2	22.9	25.7	28.5	31.3	34.3	37.3
70° or 110°	2.7	5.4	8.1	10.8	13.6	16.4	19.2	22.1	25.0	28.2	31.1	34.3	37.6	41.8
80° or 100°	2.8	5.7	8.5	11.4	14.3	17.2	20.2	23.2	26.3	29.5	32.8	36.3	39.8	43.9
90°	2.9	5.8	8.6	11.6	14.5	17.5	20.5	23.6	26.8	30.0	33.4	36.9	40.6	44.6

Figure 2

current mathematically when determining a proper course.

First, mark the course you want to make good on your chart and, with parallel rulers, walk it to the center of the compass rose (Fig. 1.). Extend this line an indefinite length through the course heading.

Next, plot the direction the current *is flowing* through the same compass rose and let one nautical mile represent one knot (use the latitude or the distance scale on the chart to measure). Scale off the correct current velocity (line Á-B).

From point B, using the same distance scale of one nautical mile, set your dividers to equal your *actual* boat speed and swing an arc from point B. Mark the point where the arc intersects your intended course line and label it point C. Draw the line B-C and, with the parallel rulers, transfer it to the center of the compass rose, extending it out to the edge of the rose (line A-D). This will be the correct course to steer to make good your intended course.

How do you find the strength and direction of the current? You can find both in the *Tidal Current Tables* from National Ocean Survey, Riverdale, Maryland 20840; there are two volumes, one for the Atlantic coast and one for the Pacific coast. These current tables give you both the velocity and the direction of the current's flow for any time of the day for thousands of locations along both coasts.

There is another way to determine a proper compensating course without drawing the vector diagram on the chart I have just described. That is with a Current Allowance Table I have developed which uses the ratio of the current's velocity to your own speed and the inclination of the current's set to the course you want to make good. This Allowance Table gives you the number of degrees you must allow for the current's set and drift (Fig. 2.).

To use the table, first divide the speed of the current by your own boat speed to find the correct ratio to use when entering the top of the table. Let us assume that the current velocity is two knots and your own boat speed is eight knots. Dividing

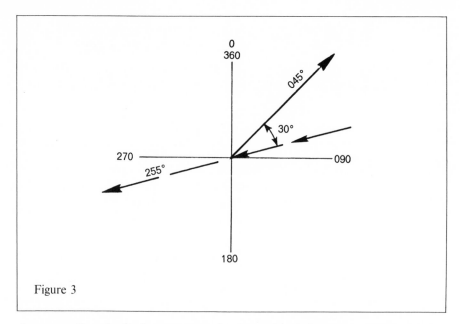

Figure 3

the current's velocity by your speed (2 ÷ 8) gives you a ratio of .25.

Now let's also assume the course you want to make good is 045° (T), and the current at the time you are to make the passage will be flowing on a course of 255° (T). The difference between the two courses is 30° (Fig. 3.).

Go down the vertical scale on the left of the Current Allowance Table until you reach the column showing 30°-150° and move to the right until you reach the .25 column where you find 7.2. Take this to the nearest degree (drop the .2) and apply the correction towards the current. Take the base course of 45° (T), add the correction 7° to get 52° (T). Once you

have this, it is an easy matter to correct it to magnetic.

The faster you go the less effect the current will have on your boat. But if you are using a vector diagram on the chart for a solution, you may be unable to fit your speed line (B-C) on the chart for it will be too long. If this happens, use either the Current Allowance Table or reduce *both* speed and current vector lines by one half or more. Make sure you reduce them both by the same factor, however.

Both ways of allowing for set and drift will give the same results. So practice them both and use the one that best suits your needs.

Understanding Apparent Current

By Robert H. Gulmon

The science of navigation is defined in Bowditch's *American Practical Navigator* as the process of directing the movements of a craft from one point to another. This might be taken to mean that the departure from point A and the subsequent arrival at point B are the main concerns of the navigator — a case of the end justifying the means. Fortunately, Bowditch dispels this notion by adding, "To do this safely is an *art*."

The last statement suggests that navigation involves something more than merely getting from here to there — and so it does. It involves selection of the optimum route from point A to point B and the techniques *for staying on it.*

The chosen route for sailing from point A to B is called the *intended track,* and there are a number of factors which might influence its selection. If there were no other considerations, a simple rhumb line might be chosen, or a great circle if the distance saved proved significant. In the case of sailing craft, it is more likely that wind, weather, and current would be controlling factors, often dictating a circuitous route to take advantage of favorable environmental conditions. Overriding all of these are safety considerations. Although navigational hazards are least expected in mid-ocean, nonetheless there are traps to snare the unwary and inept — solitary rocks, reefs, and shoals do exist beyond the sight of land. The prudent navigator plans his route to pass well clear, and preferably to leeward and down-current, of these hazards.

It is apparent, then, that having selected a track, there are good and often compelling reasons for staying on it. The ability to make good an intended track distinguishes the navigators from the guess-work artists. Unfortunately, the many "how-to" books and "quickie" courses from which most amateur navigators learn their trade tend to emphasize position finding and offer little instruction in the fine art of dead reckoning and current sailing. A fix can only tell you where you *were.* It is more important to know where you *are* — and *being where you intend to be* is the ultimate achievement.

The problem with making a sailboat go where you want it to is that it seldom goes where you point it. This capricious behavior is virtually assured by the contrary actions of wind, waves, current, and a peculiar characteristic of the sailboat itself — it must move sideways in order to advance.

Before you can figure out where to point your boat so that it will make good the intended track, you must first sort out and quantitatively evaluate these offsetting influences. For analysis purposes, the factors that cause your boat to sail in a different direction from where it is pointed can be reduced to two: *current* and *leeway.*

True current is simply the horizontal movement of a mass of water. Because of their relatively slow speeds, sailing craft are particularly sensitive to the effect of current. A one-knot current setting at right angles to the course of a boat making five knots will cause the boat's direction of travel to deviate from course by almost 12°, and the boat will be laterally displaced 10 miles for each 50 miles sailed. In the context that we will use the term, however, current will comprise more than just the horizontal movement of the water. The boat is also being offset by such factors as the force of waves on the hull, helmsman's steering error, and, if not corrected for, the errors of the compass and the mechanical log. Since we have no practical way to measure the individual effects of these factors, they are normally lumped in with true current and the result is referred to as *apparent current.*

Leeway is the leeward motion of a vessel due to wind. True leeway, as it pertains to sailboats, is expressed as an angle and is the difference between the direction the boat is pointed and the direction it actually travels *through the water,* or the angle at which the keel is offset from the apparent direction of water flow past the hull. This angular offset, or leeway angle, results from the necessity of the hull to assume an angle of incidence relative to the direction of water flow so that its underwater portion, acting as a vertical hydrofoil, will generate the hydrodynamic force needed to balance the total aerodynamic force of the sails (Fig. 1).

The magnitude of this leeway angle reflects the aerodynamic and hydrodynamic efficiencies of the sails and underwater hull and varies with different types and classes of boats as well as with sail trim, point of sailing, and wind force. A skillfully handled ocean racer might sail at leeway angles of less than five de-

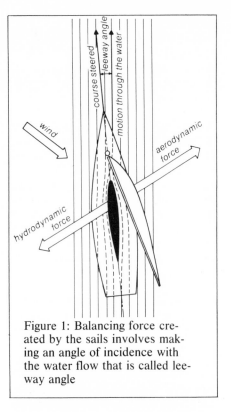

Figure 1: Balancing force created by the sails involves making an angle of incidence with the water flow that is called leeway angle

grees, modern ocean cruisers at five to seven degrees, and round or flat-bottomed, shallow-keeled craft from seven to 12 or more. Leeway angles can best be determined by actual measurements taken while under sail, and this can be done simply by streaming a weighted fishing line well astern to be clear of wake turbulence and measuring its angle with respect to the boat's fore and aft centerline.

Current and leeway, then, are both formidable factors, and acting in concert, they can deflect your boat from its course as much as 20 degrees or more. Acting in opposition to each other, the result might be little or no deflection. Whichever way they act, you cannot expect to make good a preselected track from point A to point B without considering current and leeway and determining the course to steer that compensates for the effects of both.

If you look for guidance on how to deal with current and leeway in the many books on "simplified" navigation for yachtsmen, you are not likely to find it. Such books are mainly devoted to the mechanics of position finding — how to find out where you *went* rather than how to get where you want to *go*. Even the so-called professional texts are of little help. Bowditch's *American Practical Navigator* and Dutton's *Navigation and Piloting* are written principally for navigators of large powered vessels and the special problems of navigating small wind-driven craft are largely ignored.

In these texts, the leeway of a powered vessel, which is caused merely by wind acting on the hull, is considered a relatively minor factor to be treated as just another component of apparent current. Obviously, this won't work for sailboats for which both current and leeway are significant factors of comparable magnitude. Furthermore, current tends to be directionally stable over large ocean areas while the effect of leeway is always at right angles to whatever course is being steered. Thus the two seldom act in the same direction.

When leeway is treated as part of current, as recommended by Bowditch et al., the dead reckoning (DR) position corresponding to a given fix is established by laying off on a chart the distance by log, from the previous fix, that the boat has sailed along the true course (or courses) *steered* during the elapsed time between the two fixes. The displacement of the second fix from its respective DR position is considered to be the boat's additional movement over the ground due to apparent current, which, in this case, includes the

effect of leeway. The direction in which the fix is displaced is the *set* of the current, and the distance displaced, divided by the elapsed time between the fixes, is its *drift,* or velocity. When this method is used aboard a typical sailboat to compute current, some weird and wonderful results are obtained.

Consider the case (Fig. 2a) of a sailboat on a course of true north, logging an average speed of five knots. The *true* current is setting west at a drift of 1.0 knots and the wind is from the northwest. Being on

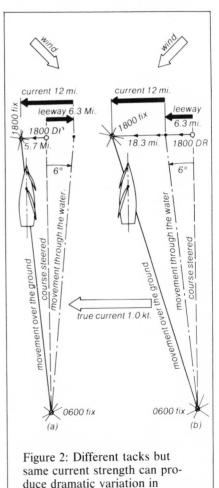

Figure 2: Different tacks but same current strength can produce dramatic variation in assumed and actual position

45

the port tack, the boat is making leeway to starboard which is determined to be six degrees. Fixes were obtained at 0600 and 1800. For the elapsed time of 12 hours between fixes, the boat's 1800 DR position is established 60 miles due north of the 0600 fix. During the period from 0600 to 1800 the *true* current would tend to push the boat 12 miles to the west while the starboard leeway angle of six degrees, acting in opposition, would tend to displace it 6.3 miles to the east. As the result, the boat would end up 5.7 miles to the west of its 1800 DR position. Dividing this resultant displacement by 12 hours yields an *apparent* current setting westerly at about 0.5 knots, or at half the drift of the true current.

Now let us see what happens if the wind hauls to the northeast and puts the boat on a starboard tack so that the leeway is six degrees to port instead of starboard. In this case (Fig. 2b), the true current would push the boat 12 miles to the west as before, but the 6.3-mile displacement due to leeway is in the same direction as that of current, and the boat would end up a whopping 18.3 miles west of the 1800 DR position. This yields a drift of 1.5 knots for apparent current — 50 percent greater than that of true current.

These examples show that apparent current obtained by the recommended method is not a reliable indication of true current and cannot safely be used as the basis for determining a compensatory course if a change of tack is contemplated.

Fortunately Bowditch, in telling steamship navigators how *not* to handle leeway, reveals the solution for wind sailors in the following description of old Nathaniel's method:

In sailing ship days it was common practice to consider leeway in terms of its effect upon the course only, and to apply it as a correction in the same manner that variation and deviation (of the compass) are applied.

But then Bowditch adds disparagingly, ". . . this method . . . is generally considered inferior to that of considering leeway as part of current."

Inferior for whom? The navigator of the *QE 2,* or the rag tender on a 30-foot sloop? For the latter, these are still sailing-ship days, and many practices of that era are as applicable to the sailing of modern yachts as they were to driving the windjammers of a century ago. These were lessons learned the hard way by professional seamen of an earlier age and should not be taken lightly by those who face similar problems today. This should be reason enough to check out Bowditch's "inferior" method to see how it might work in actual practice for sailors of modern windjammers.

When leeway is treated separately, the actual direction of the boat's travel *through the water,* instead of the course steered, is used to plot the DR position. This direction is obtained by correcting the course for leeway angle. For example, a boat on the port tack, steering 075°T, makes 5° leeway to starboard. Its direction through the water is therefore 080°T. By using 080°T instead of 075°T for plotting the DR position, the effect of leeway is accounted for, and the displacement of the fix from DR position reflects only the remaining factors that constitute apparent current — of which true current is the dominant factor.

Current sailing involves two basic steps: solving for the set and drift of the apparent current; and applying this information to determine what course to steer in order to make good the intended track.

First, let us use the method of applying leeway as a course correction to solve for the apparent current in the situation depicted by Figure 2a. The boat is on course 000°T, logging five knots on a port tack. Leeway is 6° to starboard so the boat's direction of motion through the water is 006°T. For an average log speed of five knots, the boat sails 60 miles during the elapsed time between fixes of 12 hours. The 1800 DR position is therefore established by laying off a distance of 60 miles in the direction of 006°T from the 0600 fix

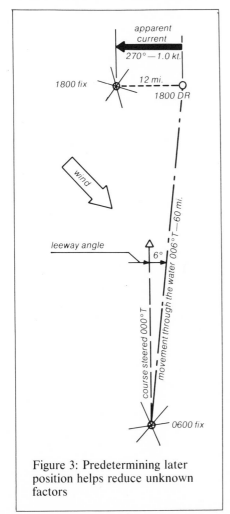

apparent
current
270° — 1.0 kt.

1800 fix   12 mi.
                1800 DR

wind

leeway angle
6°

course steered 000°T

movement through the water 006°T — 60 mi.

0600 fix

Figure 3: Predetermining later position helps reduce unknown factors

(Fig. 3). Since the 1800 DR position so obtained indicates the boat's movement through the water during the period since 0600, the displacement of the 1800 fix from the 1800 DR position is primarily due to the movement of the water itself (other factors being negligible) and results in the fix being displaced 12 miles to the west of the 1800 DR position. Dividing this distance by 12 hours will, of course, yield a drift of 1.0 knots — exactly the same as that of the true current. In practice, indeterminant steering, compass and log errors, as well as the force of waves on the hull and a probable position-fixing error will usually cause a modest discrepancy between true current and the computed value of apparent current. This, however, will normally be small and the apparent current, determined by this method, should conform more closely to true current than if obtained by the so-called standard method.

Now, let us use this current information to determine the course to steer in order to make good a given track — but let us assume, as in Figure 2b, that the wind has shifted to place the boat on the starboard tack while other conditions remain the same. Suppose the navigator desires to make good a track of 000°T, what course should he steer?

A graphic solution of this problem will require construction of a current triangle in which the lengths of sides are proportional to speeds (Fig. 4).

The navigator starts by drawing a north-south line to represent the desired track of 000°T. From any point near the top of this line he draws another line to represent the direction and velocity of the current. This current line, however, is laid off in the *opposite* direction of the set, or to the east. The length of the current line, corresponding to a drift of 1.0

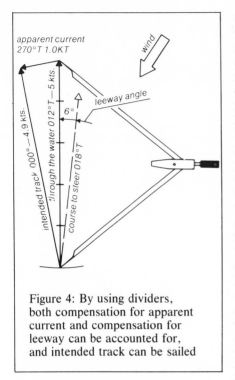

apparent current
270°T 1.0KT

wind

leeway angle

intended track 000° — 4.9 kts.

through the water 012°T — 5 kts.

6°

course to steer 018°T

Figure 4: By using dividers,
both compensation for apparent
current and compensation for
leeway can be accounted for,
and intended track can be sailed

dividers to span a length of five units, which represents the boat's average speed of five knots, and strikes an arc from the end of the current line to intersect the track line. The direction of a line drawn from this point of intersection to the end of the current line is 012°T, the direction that the boat must make *through the water* to make good a track of 000°T. For a port leeway angle of 6°, the boat's course must be 6° to the right of 012°T, or 018°T, to make 012°T through the water. The boat's speed over the ground along the track is found by measuring the length of the track line, which is 4.9 units — indicating a speed made good of 4.9 knots.

If you agree that it makes sense to deal with an apparent current whose values of set and drift don't change every time you alter course, and which reasonably reflect those of prevailing ocean currents, don't take the modern Bowditch too seriously — the "inferior" method practiced by old Nathaniel's contemporaries in sail worked for them, and it will work for you too.

knots, is 1.0 units. Any convenient unit of length can be used — inches, centimeters, or whatever. The navigator then spreads his compass or

Fighting the Currents

By James B. Kane

Most sailors have, at some point, come up against a foul current and have muttered to themselves, "I wish I could do something about this." Unfortunately, you can't do much about the flow, but you can make your predicament less severe by maximizing your chances to be in a more favorable position relative to the current.

Many currents, including both ocean currents and tidal currents, have a countercurrent that flows adjacent to, and sets opposite to, the main current. One of the best known of all the currents, the Gulf Stream, has a countercurrent between its western edge and the coast of Florida. This countercurrent runs far enough away from the shore for even large ships to take advantage of it when they are headed south.

And on the eastern limit of the Gulf Stream, boats in the Bermuda Race have been within sight of each other, but each one has been carried in opposite directions by different parts of the same current.

Before we go any further, let's define what is a *tide* and what is *current*. Tide is the *vertical* movement of water caused by celestial bodies, mainly the moon and the sun. Tidal current is the *horizontal* movement of water caused by the tide. A flood current generally sets toward a land mass or up a tidal stream; an ebb runs opposite to flood. High tide, contrary to popular belief, seldom marks the beginning of the ebb current. Quite often high tide and the beginning of slack ebb will occur as much as a few hours apart.

On the tidal section of the Hudson River, for example, the current changes one hour earlier on the west side than it does on the east side. Old tugboat captains towing acres of barges know this, and you'll see them always head toward the New Jersey shore if they're moving against the current.

The same thing holds true for practically all bays and rivers. The current generally runs weaker and changes earlier on one side of the bay or river than it does on the other, creating what is called a countercurrent.

But how do you find which is the side that changes first? The National Ocean Survey's *Tidal Current Tables* — from National Ocean Survey, Riverdale, Maryland 20840 — will provide you with the answer. Table 2 in the book gives you a list of current differences and other constants for most parts of the country. Go to the list of "subordinate stations" and find two stations in the area you are concerned with. Try to pick two that are near each other, but on *opposite sides* of the bay or river.

You might find a place not covered by the *Tidal Current Tables,* or you might not have a copy aboard. If so, remember two things: first, tidal current always changes earlier and runs weaker on the shoaler side of a waterway. Second, in a river, the deepest water and strongest current will be found at the outer edge of a bend in the river.

You will inevitably encounter cur-

TABLE 2.—CURRENT DIFFERENCES AND OTHER CONSTANTS

No.	PLACE	POSITION		TIME DIFFERENCES		MAXIMUM CURRENTS			
						Flood		Ebb	
		Lat.	Long.	Slack water	Maximum current	Direction (true)	Average velocity	Direction (true)	Average velocity
		° ′	° ′	h. m.	h. m.	deg.	knots	deg.	knots
	DELAWARE BAY and RIVER—Con.	**N.**	**W.**	on DELAWARE BAY ENTRANCE, p.58					
				Time meridian, 75°W.					
2895	Elbow of Cross Ledge, 0.8 mile S. of--	39 10	75 16	+1 15	+1 30	330	1.3	165	2.2
2900	False Egg Island Point, 2 miles off---	39 11	75 12	+0 25	+0 25	340	1.1	160	1.3
2905	Ben Davis Point, channel abreast of---	39 15	75 20	+2 00	+2 05	320	1.6	145	2.3
2910	Ben Davis Point, 0.8 mile SW of-------	39 17	75 18	+1 10	+1 00	310	1.2	120	0.8
2915	Cohansey River, 0.5 mile above ent----	39 21	75 22	+1 35	+1 25	75	1.2	255	1.4
2920	Bridgeton (Broad St. Bridge)----------	39 26	75 14	(³)	+2 30	0	0.2	180	0.3

Figure 1

rents that flow in directions other than simply from ahead or from a-stern. These, of course, will tend to set you sideways, and to cope with such currents, you'll again need to break out the *Current Tables*. Find the speed and direction the current is flowing at a specific time in the flood and ebb columns (Fig. 1). Then allow for this by using either the current allowance table in the volume or the vector method on your nautical chart.

There is one other type of tidal current which is known as a rotary current. You find rotary currents off the coast where the current flows comparatively unrestricted by the effects of the shore. A rotary current will flow through all points of the compass during a tidal period and never come to slack water. The current's set moves in a clockwise direction in the northern hemisphere. Table 5 in the *Tidal Current Tables* explains how to predict the velocity and direction of such rotary currents.

A strong wind can also influence a current. A strong northwesterly blowing onto North America's east coast, for example, will cause the ebb current to flow longer and stronger than it normally would. Such a wind can vary the printed predictions of high or low tide by as much as half an hour; and in some rare instances by as much as a full hour.

If a wind blows steadily from one direction for around twelve hours, it will actually create a current. It doesn't set exactly in the direction the wind is blowing, but rather will be deflected, by the earth's rotation, to the right in the northern hemisphere. Usually, the difference between the wind direction and the wind-driven current will be about 15° in coastal waters; it can run as high as 45° in the deep ocean.

There are a few other important things to remember about currents. If possible, try to avoid a windward tide. This is simply a tidal current that is setting in the opposite direction the wind is blowing. This combination can quickly build into a choppy and rough sea. A lee tide, of course, is the opposite of a windward tide. Here the wind blows with the tide, and the water surface is considerably smoother than it might otherwise be.

If you understand the currents and their potential effect, you can better predict the best time to schedule a cruise. And if you are racing, knowing just what current you will encounter on the course should give you an advantage over others who don't prepare as thoroughly.

Use the *Tidal Current Tables* together with your charts to determine just where the best place to be actually is. You will be surprised how much difference there actually is once you start looking into the problem. Knowing how to fight the tides properly can give you a head start toward getting what most people like to call "local knowledge."

Anticipating Collisions

By Ray A. Fletcher

Avoiding a collision between boats is the primary purpose of the Rules of the Road, both International and Inland. Although the rules are comprehensive, those rules for sailboats *under sail* (not the racing rules) can be reduced to six basic situations.

While they are not all-inclusive, and should *never be substituted* for a solid knowledge of the Rules of the Road, they do cover most of the conditions you will encounter in your everyday sailing situations such as getting under way, entering or leaving a harbor, and on the open sea.

The six paraphrased Rules can be stated as follows:

1. Exercise common courtesy and consideration.

2. When both boats are on the same tack, the windward boat stays clear.
3. When both boats are on opposite tacks, the port tack boat stays clear.
4. In an overtaking situation, the overtaking boat stays clear.
5. A sailboat· has the right of way over a powerboat except when overtaking, and in a restricted channel where the powerboat cannot maneuver.
6. A sailboat running free stays clear of a boat that is close hauled (Inland rules).

While the Rules of the Road are the determining guidelines, there will be certain times when experience and good judgment are the best ways to avoid a collision if one becomes imminent.

Here's an example. Two boats are on a collision course and you are the skipper of one boat and have a complete knowledge of the Rules of the Road — International, Inland, Special, ad infinitum — and are prepared to quote them verbatim. But the Rules of the Road is something the skipper of the other boat has never

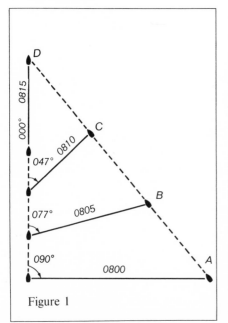

Figure 1

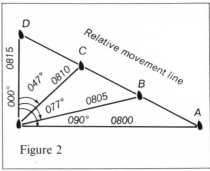

Figure 2

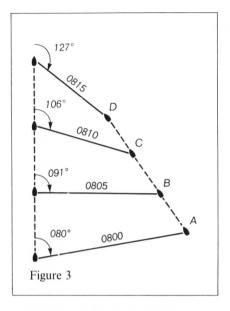

Figure 3

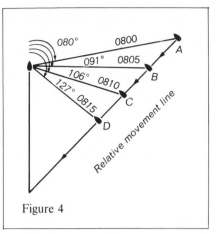

Figure 4

heard of! A collision is imminent, you know you have the right-of-way, and the skipper of the other boat is supposed to keep clear. Of course your knowledge of the Rules is going to be no help at all in preventing a collision with a totally ignorant skipper.

How do you cope with such a situation? Before I answer the question, let's first look at what makes up a collision course. Assume you now are the skipper of a sailboat standing out through a channel to sea and a powerboat is on a converging course with you. The powerboat is overtaking, but you recognize the possibility of a collision because the bearing is steady. With this knowledge you can take appropriate action ahead of time to avoid being hit.

This kind of situation can occur several times each sailing day, and it now should be obvious that just knowing the Rules of the Road and where they apply (International or Inland) is not going to be enough and is no guarantee a collision can be avoided.

The reason is that not everyone is

conversant with the Rules, and this means simply that you must improve your ability to recognize a collision situation *early* and be prepared to take action before it is too late.

What is and is not a collision situation? I've listed three categories below and you can identify each situation as it develops by taking bearings on the converging boat.

1. The converging boat will pass safely ahead of you (Figs. 1, 2).
2. The converging boat will pass safely astern of you (Figs. 3, 4).
3. The converging boat is on a collision course with you (Figs. 5, 6).

Getting a series of bearings on the other boat will give you the information you need, and there are several ways to do this.

1. Use a hand-held compass with sighting vanes, and read the magnetic bearing directly from the compass.
2. Use relative bearings taken with a pelorus or similar device. Note the boat's course each time a relative bearing is taken and combine the two readings to get a compass bearing on the other boat.

Look at Figure 1. The vertical leg of the triangle shows the cumulative track of your boat, and the hypot-

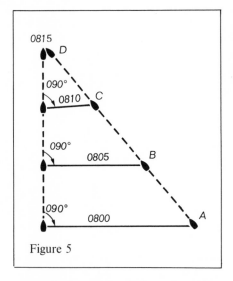

0815

D

090°

0810 C

090°

0805 B

090°

0800 A

Figure 5

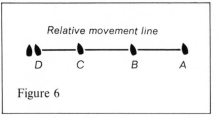

Relative movement line

D C B A

Figure 6

enuse is the track of the converging boat. The lines that extend from the vertical leg to the hypotenuse are the bearing lines taken from your boat at different times and are labelled with the angle of the bearing and the time each bearing is taken. The converging boat's positions are labelled A, B, C and D, and you can see by the bearings that the boat is drawing ahead. At point D the converging boat passes safely ahead of you (000° at 0815).

Figure 2 shows the same situation shown in Figure 1 but in a slightly different manner. In Figure 2 you are taking bearings on the converging boat but your boat is shown as being stationary. The bearing lines are labelled just as they are in Figure 1 but the hypotenuse now represents the movement of the other boat relative to the earth's surface.

The vertical line (labelled 000° 0815) corresponds to the plot in Figure 1 which shows that both diagrams come to the same conclusion which is, at 0815 the converging boat will pass directly ahead of you at a distance (assuming everything is

drawn to scale) equal to the length of the line labelled 000° 0815.

All this means that when relative bearings taken on a converging boat are moving ahead (or forward) the converging boat will pass ahead of you. Another way to say it is if compass bearings to the other boat are decreasing on your starboard side, or conversely increasing on your port side, the other boat will pass ahead of you.

The relative bearings in Figures 5 and 6 are similar to the other two sets of figures, but there is one important difference. The bearings (relative or magnetic) on the converging boat are *steady* (remain the same) and at 0815, rather than passing ahead or safely astern, there will be a collision. The conclusion: when a series of bearings on a converging boat is steady, *a collision will be the inevitable result* if neither boat changes course ahead of time.

So always watch the compass bearing, or relative bearing, of an approaching boat. If the bearing does not change appreciably there is a good chance you may have a collision and that is when you had better start using your common sense and judgment. You may be right under the Rules of the Road, but that probably won't prevent you from scraping some topside paint (at the minimum!) if the other fellow has never heard of the Rules, or if he isn't paying attention. Watch your bearings, and think ahead.

2
FOG

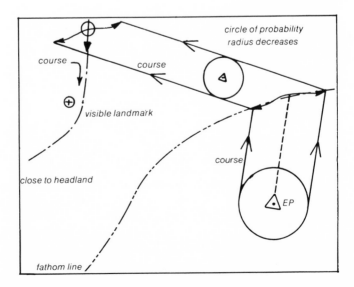

circle of probability
radius decreases

course

course

visible landmark

close to headland

course

EP

fathom line

Fighting through Fog

By Earl B. Rubell

I don't like fog. Generations of fiction writers have used its dank vapors to evoke an atmosphere of mystery. For the mariner, the dangers that lurk behind fog's curtain are all too real. Loss of visibility is accompanied by a sense of disorientation. The hazards of collision are ever-present. Unfortunately, in many cruising waters sudden, impenetrable fog is an unavoidable fact of life. Therefore, every boat that casts off should be prepared to cope with it.

First you should prepare your boat. When you cannot use your eyes, you become dependent upon your other senses and upon mechanical and electronic tools. These instruments are useful only if they are available and in working order and if you know how to use them. Make sure that the necessary equipment is aboard and operational. Practice using instruments before you have to depend on them. A basic list of equipment necessary for piloting in fog includes:

- Radar reflector
- Foghorn. The mouth-operated horns are almost failsafe but but can be tiring. Aerosol-operated horns do not require physical effort, but the cans do become empty and the valves can stick. Carrying both types is a good idea.
- Compass
- Radio directionfinder (RDF)
- Depthsounder or leadline. A good leadline of at least 10 fathoms is an excellent tool if an electronic depthsounder fails.
- Charts. Your charts should include positions and signals of radiobeacons, and AM broadcast stations. Note that you cannot rely on commercial stations that are not within sight of the shoreline for accurate bearings because radio signals become distorted when they pass over land and especially where they curve around intervening heights.
- Light list. This is the most accurate reference to the timing of foghorns, beacons, and lights that are not shown on all charts.

Radar and loran-C are wonderful tools, and though expensive, they are beginning to fit the space and budget capabilities of most small boats more and more closely.

When you are satisfied that you have prepared your boat for fog, feel free to cast off. However, setting out before your boat is thoroughly fog-ready is asking for trouble.

Fog brings with it the dual concerns of keeping track of your position and watching and maneuvering to avoid collision. This is a large double responsibility, and you should have a clear idea in advance of how to proceed.

The *International Rules of the Road* specify that in conditions of limited visibility "every vessel shall proceed at a safe speed adapted to the prevailing circumstances and conditions of restricted visibility." They go on to state that "except where it is determined that a risk of collision does not exist, every vessel

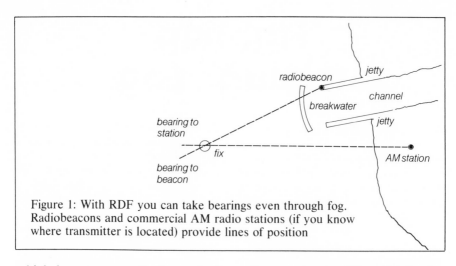

Figure 1: With RDF you can take bearings even through fog. Radiobeacons and commercial AM radio stations (if you know where transmitter is located) provide lines of position

which hears apparently forward of her beam the fog signal of another vessel . . . shall reduce her speed to the minimum at which she can be kept on her course."

Along with adopting a safe speed for the conditions, you should attempt to make yourself more "visible." This means deploying your radar reflector and signalling your presence to the eyeless world with the appropriate fog signal. In addition, keep a watch at all times. There's no guarantee that your signals or radar reflector are being picked up. It may well be up to you to maneuver to avoid a collision.

Proper signals differ slightly depending on whether you are in *inland* waters (rivers, lakes, harbors, and so on) or *international* (the open sea beginning at the mouths of rivers and harbors). In inland and international waters a vessel under power should sound one prolonged blast. Under sail in inland waters sound one blast when on starboard tack, two when on port, and three if the wind is abaft the beam. The interval between signals should not be more than a minute. If you are under sail (on either tack) in international waters signal one long and two short blasts and allow approximately two minutes

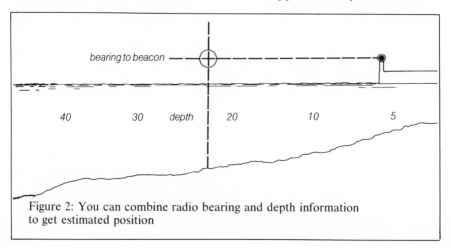

Figure 2: You can combine radio bearing and depth information to get estimated position

between each complete signal.

Be alert, as well, for danger signals. Other fog horns, the sound of engines, bow wave — any of these can tell you that another boat is near. The sound of breakers or even waves lapping against a beach or rock can tell you that hazards are close by.

It's essential to take these precautions to survive fog and to make sure that the loss of visibility doesn't produce trouble. It is nice, in addition, to know where you are and eventually to make your way home or to your intended destination. On a casual outing few of us plot courses or take fixes, but fog could ambush you as easily on a daysail as on a bluewater passage. It's a good idea, therefore, to pay attention to your position all the time. If you always know where you are, you'll never be lost. Establishing your position with RDF, depthsounder, and any other inputs (Figs. 1 and 2) is much less certain than keeping a consistent dead reckoning, either in your head or on your chart, in the first place.

Don't be too anxious to race for home. With visibility less than 50 feet it's difficult to enter any harbor safely, and unless there's reason not to, lying-to or jogging offshore until the fog lifts is the most prudent course to take. If you decide to head for port, however, there are several techniques that are applicable to any fog approach.

• Homing on a beacon can be done by tuning your RDF to a radiobeacon at the harbor entrance. Orient the RDF to the centerline of the boat, and you can steer directly down the null to the beacon. Check depths and try for other bearings to make sure that you aren't being set by wind and/or current to one side of your intended track. Determine a safe entry zone (Fig. 3) to tell which courses are safe and which aren't.

Following a depth line is easiest when there is a line of constant depth leading into the port, but even with less ideal conditions

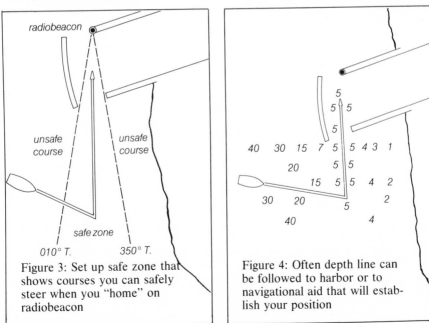

Figure 3: Set up safe zone that shows courses you can safely steer when you "home" on radiobeacon

Figure 4: Often depth line can be followed to harbor or to navigational aid that will establish your position

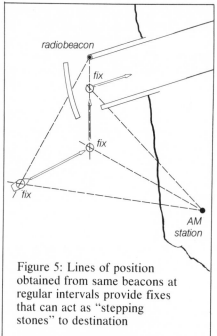

Figure 5: Lines of position obtained from same beacons at regular intervals provide fixes that can act as "stepping stones" to destination

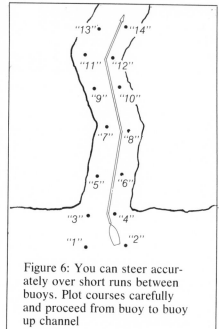

Figure 6: You can steer accurately over short runs between buoys. Plot courses carefully and proceed from buoy to buoy up channel

you can steer along a soundings curve towards your destination (Fig. 4). Remember to figure the height of the tide and the depth of your transducer below the surface of the water when comparing the soundings you receive with those listed on the chart.

- Navigating from fix to fix means using two or more beacons or lines of position to give you a fix and then using the same inputs to give you another after a brief interval. Although time-consuming, it is a good check when you are using one of the other methods, and it is a workable alternative when none of the others is available (Fig. 5).

- Following the buoys is often possible. Once you've found one of the buoys in the system marking the harbor entrance it is

usually a straightforward proposition to steer a compass course over the normally short distance to the next useful buoy, and then the next, and so on (Fig. 6).

- Following the fog horn is the least precise and most risky type of approach because determining distance and direction of sound in the fog is very difficult. Often, however, you can keep the fog horn at a relative bearing that keeps you headed on a safe course.

Fog can be disorienting and adds some danger to sailing, but if you know how to proceed, have the right equipment, and develop the calm confidence that comes with understanding collision avoidance and fog piloting techniques, you should be able to face fog when it comes and know how best to handle it safely.

When Visibility Is Reduced

By John Mellor

There are many problems a seaman has to face when he finds himself in fog. The danger of collision is a very serious matter, of course, but in this article we are going to confine ourselves to considering the problems of making a landfall. I won't be pulling any magic rabbits out of the hat such as radar, or any of the other electronic navigation devices that are available today. Instead, we are going to look at the problems of the small-boat navigator who has to rely on RDF, the Mark I Ear, the depth-sounder and, most important, dead reckoning.

RDF equipment might not seem to present much of a problem. Instead of using his eyes to take a fix, the sailor simply uses his radio, and when he approaches a lighthouse or harbor mouth having a foghorn, he listens for it to tell him where he is. Well, that is good enough if he is fully aware of the possible dangers and potential inaccuracies that are inherent in such a system.

A precise null point in an RDF signal when it is lined up on a bearing sometimes can be extremely difficult to get. The more common situation is likely to be a gradual phasing out of the signal over an arc that can go up to 10 degrees or more. The necessity for interpolating what the actual bearing is automatically produces an

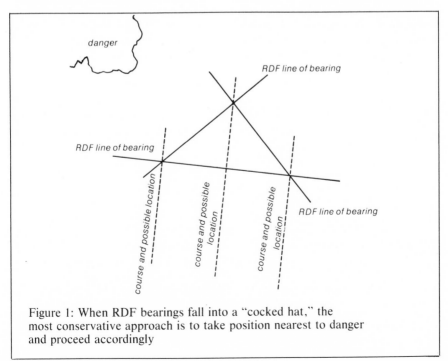

Figure 1: When RDF bearings fall into a "cocked hat," the most conservative approach is to take position nearest to danger and proceed accordingly

approximation — and the possibility of error.

If you are taking a fix that will give you a good cut from three stations these errors in approximation will show up in the form of a cocked hat, thus making you immediately aware of them.

You should then take the corner of the cocked hat *nearest* to danger as your position and steer accordingly, and with caution (Fig. 1). And with a single bearing, two bearings, or even three, if they come in at shallow angles, you also have to be very wary indeed (Fig. 2).

Two final points on the problems that might occur with RDF: Bearings taken from beyond a station's quoted range or those taken very close to a station also may be inaccurate. And RDF bearings that cross the coast at a narrow angle can be refracted in much the same way a wind is.

All this leads me to the conclusion that if you take due care over estimating null points and are careful when reading handbearing RDF compasses you can get a perfectly good RDF fix offshore within the quoted ranges of the stations. But close inshore and when making a landfall in fog for instance, I always

treat them with considerable caution. In my opinion, the care should be so great that you ought to place equal or greater reliance on your DR plot. But before we do that, let us take a look at fog signals, or I should say "listen" to them.

There are times when you can listen all day and not hear anything. For some reason, fog tends to create silent zones around a foghorn in which nothing can be heard. Sometimes these zones are very close to the sound signal, and sometimes they are far away. They always seem to be on various impossible-to-predict bearings. And when you consider the difficulty of assessing the direction of a sound signal, even if you can hear it, you do realise the total uncertainty involved in relying on them.

All this gets us down to two basic things: the DR plot and the depth-sounder. But they have some drawbacks too, as we shall see. A good DR plot requires a number of things: accurate assessment of course steered, accurate assessment of distance run, accurate assessment of tide and leeway, and *accurate plotting* of all these factors.

Assuming you have a properly swung and sited compass, the big

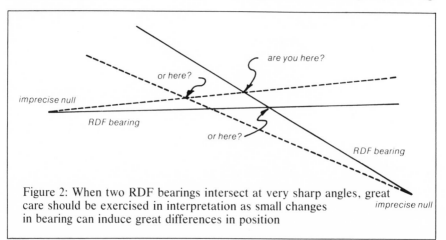

Figure 2: When two RDF bearings intersect at very sharp angles, great care should be exercised in interpretation as small changes in bearing can induce great differences in position

problem in assessing the course steered lies in convincing the helmsman of the importance of entering in the log the course he has *actually* averaged, as opposed to the one he has been asked to steer. This applies mostly to reaching conditions in the big seas when there is a tendency for the boat to broach and even the best of helmsmen are apt to finish up five degrees above the ordered course. Fortunately, in foggy conditions the wind often is not very strong so the problem is not so likely to arise. But continuing to stress the importance of keeping a reliable course should produce a pretty accurate estimate from the helmsman.

Assuming you are keeping an accurate and reliable log, the distance run should be just as accurate as the course steered. However, a wobbly course, even if it is averaged out accurately, means that the log reading is going to be slightly higher than the actual distance run because of the extra distance sailed in the wobbles. It is not a situation likely to produce large errors but it is worth keeping in mind.

Tide and leeway. These are, of course, the most likely elements that produce the greatest errors in any DR calculations because of the difficulty of assessing them accurately even with tide tables and chart information. The more experience you have with your boat, the more accurately you will be able to judge your leeway. However, as with steering, the greatest amounts of leeway usually occur in heavy weather. Fog, as we have said, tends to occur in lighter weather so the problem won't be so great as it may seem at first glance. As long as you avoid like the plague any tendency to pinch when you are close-hauled, your leeway should be virtually nil, a couple of degrees at the most.

That leaves us with the problem of tide. And this is where the flies in most of our ointments really reside. There is no way tidal strength and direction can be assessed accurately enough to make a good landfall in fog when you're relying purely on a DR. Remember that a good landfall in fog means not sighting land 15 miles away but sighting it half a mile away or less. In other words, you have to be right on.

How can you get around this last remaining obstacle? Well, an old sailor once told me that while a good DR was unlikely to be right on, it was never going to be too far out. This led me to realize that a good DR plot consists *not* of calculating a *point* at which I think I am, but constructing an *area* inside which I know I am.

In the normal course of events there is no need to bother constructing an area like this. But as I approach land in fog on my DR, I draw a circle centered on the DR position, and give it a radius equal to, or a little bit bigger than, the maximum possible error. I then can say with confidence that I am somewhere in that circle.

How do you calculate your maximum possible error and therefore the radius? It depends on a number of factors: how accurately you think you have recorded your average course and distance run; how far you have run since the last fix that you have complete faith in; and perhaps most important of all, how accurate your DR plotting normally is. If you generally find yourself five miles off after a run equal in length to the one you are pesently on, then you should construct a circle with a radius of five miles.

However, if you feel your plotting on this trip, because of fog and quiet weather, has been better than usual, then maybe you could reduce the

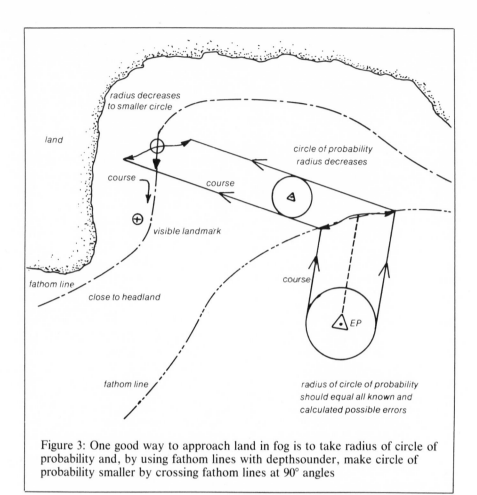

radius decreases
to smaller circle

land

course

course

visible landmark

fathom line

close to headland

fathom line

circle of probability
radius decreases

course

EP

radius of circle of probability
should equal all known and
calculated possible errors

Figure 3: One good way to approach land in fog is to take radius of circle of probability and, by using fathom lines with depthsounder, make circle of probability smaller by crossing fathom lines at 90° angles

radius to four miles. But it is very important to be pessimistic about any of this and always make the radius *bigger* than your estimated error. Otherwise the system will defeat itself. Remember that the circle must be big enough so that you *know* you are inside it. Remember too that this method is only good as a way to keep an *experienced* sailor out of trouble. It is not an idiot's guide to running about in fog.

The method requires two important things, both of which can only be gained through experience: first, the ability to plot an accurate DR and, even more important, the experience and ability to assess the

likely errors in the DR after what might be quite a long run. But if you use it properly it can get you out of all sorts of trouble. Once I made a perfect landfall after a 100-mile run in quarter-mile visibility with compass trouble by constructing a circle with an initial radius of 15 miles. Don't be optimistic about your ability to make errors. If I had made that one 10 miles I wouldn't be here now.

What do you do with this circle of position? With your depthsounder you first turn it into a line and then into a point. You do this by the simple expedient of steering so that your circle crosses a number of fathom lines that run in different directions.

Every time you cross a fathom line the circle turns into a position line. Then you steer that position line to cross another fathom line that will give you a good cut with the first. If you can find a third fathom line, that is all to the good.

The best situation to encounter is to have two fathom lines running at roughly 90 degrees to one another. If there aren't any at your destination, try to make your landfall at a spot where there are some; after that you can rockhop your way home.

What you are doing, in effect, is making a running fix with the depth-sounder. You do it by steering your circle of probability so that you are certain to cross your fathom lines on one side of a conspicuous object that lies close to the second fathom line such as a headland or conspicuous rock (Fig. 3). When you reach the second line you turn toward the object and follow the line, until it becomes visible (Fig. 4). Then you should know almost exactly where you are.

The joy of this technique is that, although is not exactly fail-safe as such, you always are in a position to know which way to turn. And finally you turn onto a fathom line that can lead close to an identifiable object. This then, gives an absolute final fix of the most reliable sort, your eyes. But remember to calculate the precise depth of water. This, of course, is the depth of the fathom line plus the height of the tide. Don't forget to check what your depth sounder reads depth from. The "observed" depth is, of course, below the surface, so corrections must always be made to get the total depth of water. And if you do find a suitable-looking area of interesting fathom lines to make your landfall in, carefully check the steepness of the bottom. If it slopes very gradually, the fathom

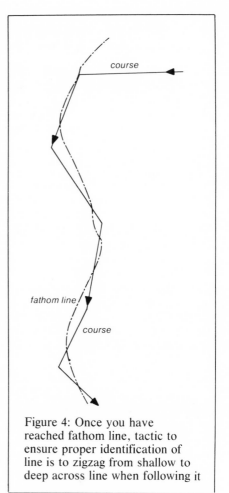

Figure 4: Once you have reached fathom line, tactic to ensure proper identification of line is to zigzag from shallow to deep across line when following it

lines might be so vague and so wide as to be useless. The steeper the gradient, the more clearly defined and therefore more accurate will be the fathom lines.

So, by all means use your RDF, but when you are making for your actual landfall, a well-plotted DR combined with the aim-off fathom line technique I have just described is, in my opinion, one of the best and safest methods around. There is an old piloting adage that says that it is better to know *precisely* where you are not, than to know *roughly* where you are. This method is the sort of thing that fits the bill very nicely.

Pre-navigation Is What Gets You Home

By Burt Sauer

The West Coast can have it at practically any time of year and so can the East Coast. I'm talking about *fog*, and for sheer annoyance and frustration, hardly anything in boating can match your realizing that, because of fog, you don't know where you are or how to get back to port. Nor does it help for someone onboard to say, "I told you two hours ago that we should head back."

What *can* help is to work out in advance the courses to home port from any and all recognizable landmarks and buoys in your part of the ocean or lake, paying particular attention to such sound emitters as bellbuoys, diaphones, whistles, and horns. Ignore any landmarks far up on shore because they won't be useful in fog. Then jot down this data in a pocket-sized notebook you can lay your hands on in a hurry.

I call this *pre-navigation*, and it is a real boon to a single-hander anytime, but it is particularly useful at

---

Typical entries might read:

Lighted bellbuoy "1" fl green 5 sec off Santa Monica anchorage area marks stone breakwater 400 yards due north.

Santa Monica Pier bearing 023M 800 yards across the intervening breakwater has foghorn on pier.

Course to Marina del Rey NW entrance is 123M (Light "3" & horn & R BN), 3.6 mi.

Course to Venice Pier 105M, 1.0 mi.

Venice Pier. Tower on end of pier well lighted. On close approach stay west of bearings 132M-312M to avoid surf line. Heavy surf at times.

Course to Marina del Rey NW entrance (Light "3" & horn & R BN) is 132M, 2¼ mi.

Marina del Rey NW entrance. Light "3" fl white 6 sec located end of west breakwater of main channel. Foghorn and R BN same location. Horn 2 blasts each 20 sec (2 sec blast, 2 sec silent, 2 sec blast, 14 sec silent). Radio beacon 289 kHz, "MR (− − · − ·)".

Light "2" fl red 5 sec marks detached breakwater stbd side of entrance.

Entrance approx 200 yards wide. Striped buoy marks center of entrance.

Steer 115M from midchannel buoy at NW entrance. Center of harbor main channel is 150 yards past NW entrance.

First leg of main channel is due north (345M).

Figure 1: Notebook entries should include specific information on aids to navigation as well as personal remarks on best way to proceed into harbor

night or in fog. List your checkpoints in some coherent order. Write down the courses and distances from checkpoints to your harbor and to at least the next two checkpoints in the homeward direction (Fig. 1). Also, list any additional information that will help you keep out of trouble. A bellbuoy may mark a reef or other obstruction below the surface, and you don't want to sail right into the obstruction while you are looking for the buoy.

This method is recommended *only for home waters* where you can thoroughly prepare data. Some of your data will come from NOS (C&GS) charts, some from the *Coast Pilot,* some from *Local Notice to Mariners,* and some you will have to develop yourself. Without the reliable local knowledge such data provides, it would be more prudent to anchor and set a watch or to keep offshore until visibility improves.

Like everything else you carry onboard, your pre-navigation notebook is only an aid — it is no substitute for cautious judgment and good seamanship. You should have your compass in the binnacle, your anchor rigged to run immediately if it is needed, and your depthsounder operating or your leadline handy for instant use.

You need a lookout forward to listen for the signals of other boats. If he or she also handles the foghorn, make certain he knows the proper fog signals and intervals. You should hoist a radar reflector as high as possible. On a sailboat, drop the jib temporarily and rehoist it with the reflector shackled to the head of the jib, unless you can send the reflector aloft on a spare halyard. An experienced hand to stand by the leadline and the anchor would also be welcome.

Even before taking these pre-cautionary measures, if you have kept your weather eye peeled, you probably will have seen the fog rolling toward you in time to ease your navigation problem quite a bit. If you're not too far offshore, you may be able to take a compass bearing on your harbor or on a prominent landmark close to it. If you don't have a handbearing compass, you can simply point the boat at your mark and read the course on the main compass. Also check the direction of wind and waves as an indication of probable drift.

If fog or distance prevents you from taking a bearing on your home port, get a bearing that will put you in the vicinity of one of the noise emitters you have logged in your notebook. Make a quick estimate of your distance from the buoy or landmark you've selected. Now, even though you get socked in, you can gauge your speed and time, and you should know approximately when you will be able to hear the bell or whistle.

If you are lucky enough to have a radio beacon located close to a foghorn or bellbuoy somewhere in your vicinity and you have a radio direction finder (RDF), you can home in on the radio beacon until you get within earshot of the sound emitter; then consult your notebook for the next course. But make sure there isn't an obstruction between you and the radio beacon.

How closely you can triangulate your position at sea with an RDF depends on the distances and directions of the beacons from one another and you, the sensitivity of the RDF, and how well you've calibrated the RDF to your boat. Masts, shrouds, and other metallic objects will cause induced currents and magnetic fields that can alter the apparent direction of the transmitters as well as cause quadrature effects that mask or blur the null. You should experiment to find the best location for your RDF and then make a 360-degree calibration chart, just as you would for a magnetic compass, if you expect to use an RDF reliably. However, quadrature effects will be minimal when the beacon transmitter is directly ahead, directly astern, or broad on either beam. Hence, you should be able to get a better null when using the RDF as a homing device than as a position finder.

After you or your lookout hear the sound of your first charted checkpoint, approach it cautiously and make a *positive* identification. Remember that you're going to use it as a point of departure through the fog to some other recognizable checkpoint. Before you sail the charted course to the next checkpoint, you want to be positive you are where you think you are.

Remember that your checkpoint either is warning of a hazard to navigation or, if it's a pier or similar structure, will itself be a hazard. So keep clear of the danger zone.

Notice I recommend that your notebook show both the course directly to the harbor and the course to the two nearest checkpoints from your present position. This means you have the choice of proceeding either to the nearest or next nearest mark, or jumping off for home port itself. What you do will depend on the relative distances you must travel through the fog to each destination and how limited the visibility is. You don't want the vagaries of wind, current, and helmsman error to put you so far off your intended track that you can't locate your next mark. It is better to lose a little time and distance to avoid getting lost.

After you depart from the initial checkpoint, hold as accurate a compass course as you can, and pay close attention to speed and elapsed time. Unknown current or inaccuracies in estimating or registering boat speed may make your arrival time differ from the predicted time, and this is one argument for choosing the shortest leg possible between checkpoints. Decide what is a reasonable margin of error; it could be 10 percent if the checkpoint is a sound emitter.

For example, assume your distance between checkpoints is 1.1 miles and your knotmeter is averaging three knots. Multiplying 1.1 by 60 and dividing by three gives an estimated time of arrival (ETA) of 22 minutes. If after 24 minutes you haven't reached your checkpoint, begin a *search pattern*.

Be careful here or you will become totally disoriented. Also, you don't want to leave any gaps. Basically, it's the same problem as trying to locate a racing mark except that, in fog, the mark you are looking for almost always will be near a danger area. Keep your eyes and ears open and be ready to alter course immediately.

Though there are several logical search patterns, my method is as follows. I sail (or power) in a *square* circle about the presumed location of the checkpoint.

You can tell from Figure 2 that the distances sailed in the search pattern are increments of the margin of error. You sail each of the first two legs for *double* the time interval you have allowed for error. Using the example, it is going to be four minutes since you will be watching (and listening) both to port and starboard. On the next three legs, add the four-minute interval to the time you previously allowed, and sail eight minutes per leg.

If the checkpoint isn't a sound

emitter, the time interval you allow for margin of error should be the time it takes you to travel the limit of visibility. Your boat travels approximately 100 feet per minute for each knot of speed, so if visibility is 100 yards and your selected search speed is three knots, this interval should be one minute. However, the legs of your square circle still should be based on *twice* this allowance for visibility, or two minutes.

As a practical matter, if you don't find the checkpoint in one complete circuit, abandon the search because the search radius of your square circle is three times the allowed margin of error, and the area searched is nine times the circle of error. It may be possible that the buoy or mark is no longer in its charted position. As Figure 2 shows, you should head back to your departure point, and start again for a different checkpoint.

In the illustrated example, running the search pattern took 36 minutes when the ETA between checkpoints was only 22 minutes. To expand the square circle into a square spiral by increasing the legs by another four-minute increment as before would use up another 68 minutes for the second sweep. Clearly it is quicker and safer to retrace your course and try again.

Whatever you do, don't try to go on from your search area, inventing a new course to some other checkpoint. You don't really know where you are, so how can you chart such a course?

If you can't find the checkpoint you departed from and you don't have a radio beacon or fixed foghorn to give you a fresh start, head cautiously in the direction of shore. When you get into shallow water you'll have the option of either anchoring until the fog clears or following the shore until you find a

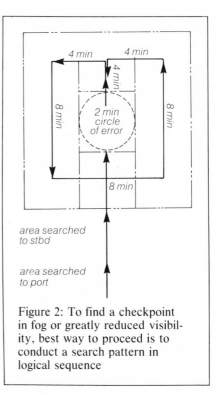

Figure 2: To find a checkpoint in fog or greatly reduced visibility, best way to proceed is to conduct a search pattern in logical sequence

buoy or other checkpoint from which to chart a new course. A depthsounder will be of great assistance in this. Before attempting to follow the shoreline, carefully check the chart to refresh your memory about all close-in hazards that may confront you in the fog. Probably some of them will serve to give you a definite position from which you can set a new course.

It is most unlikely, however, that you will miss your intended checkpoints if you can keep the distances between them to a half-hour's travel time or less. Thus, with short hops and your handy little notebook you should end up at the entrance to your own harbor with very little difficulty.

When you finally do get inside the ,harbor, you still won't be tied up to your mooring or slip. If the holding ground is good, you may choose to anchor out of the fairway until the visibility clears up. On the other hand, already being this close to home, you may want to keep going and, here again, your handy little notebook can make all the difference. The entry and exit channels of commercial harbors generally are well marked with numbered and lighted buoys. Yacht harbors, on the other hand, may not have any channel buoys or they may not be numbered or lit. Usually, their buoys aren't charted and here is where advance preparation really pays off.

On a good day make a visual check of your harbor, mentally noting hazards and checkpoints or landmarks you could expect to find in dense fog. Then, based on this initial survey, work out a plan of approach from the harbor entrance to your slip or mooring that avoids all fixed hazards by as wide a margin as possible and that utilizes the checkpoints you have found.

Inside the harbor, proceed under power even in a sailboat because you want the unrestricted visibility and the instant response. Consequently you also should be under power when you begin the next step of preparation which is to traverse the planned approach, beginning at the harbor entrance and proceeding at the minimum speed that will give your boat steerageway. Note the compass courses and elapsed times over each leg and write them in your notebook. Also note the speed indicated on your knotmeter if your boat has one. In addition to recording the checkpoints, courses, and times to be run, also note any unusual hazards to port or starboard of any leg.

Now, with your notebook in hand, run through the course once again, following the written directions and proceeding at the same dead-slow speed. Imagine that you are engulfed in dense fog and that there will be other boats nearby in that same fog. Ask yourself, Should I risk my boat and my crew in this channel in heavy fog?

If your harbor is not too complicated and your imagination is not too vivid, it may look like a piece of cake. If so, it will give you the confidence you'll need to proceed along this route when you are out in the real stuff. On the other hand, you may realize that, for you, in that particular harbor there is too much chance of grounding or collision. If so, decide in advance where to anchor once you reach home port and check out the anchorage.

The technique for travelling inside the harbor is exactly the same as it was outside. Keep a good lookout, hold a steady compass course, avoid other boats, and count off the time. Do not continue if you've missed a checkpoint. Search for it cautiously and if you can't find it, go back to your previous known position. Naturally, you should be watching the depthsounder, too, and be ready to drop anchor if the motor quits or some other emergency makes it necessary to hold your position.

Groping your way back home through the fog using this checkpoint method may be enough to make you head back at the mere hint of fog. Still, it is a simple and reliable method of finding your way home, and it *will* get you back.

Stand-off Strategy for Fog

By Burt Sauer

What should you do if you're out sailing for the afternoon and fog suddenly cuts off your view of land? This situation often strikes terror in the hearts of inexperienced small-boat sailors. In the scramble to get back to harbor, they put themselves and their boats in more danger than they would risk by staying where fog overtook them. The risks of collision and running aground increase drastically when everyone heads into shallow water and attempts to negotiate a narrow channel in dense fog.

Such accidents happen with boring regularity in my home waters of southern California where, on any foggy weekend, the harbor patrols and the Coast Guard can expect to keep busy pulling boats off the breakwaters and beaches and towing damaged vessels into harbor. All too frequently, boats are lost and lives are endangered in these accidents, so there is good reason to be apprehensive when fog rolls in.

What is the best strategy if you are caught out in fog? Naturally, no single answer fits every occasion but, first, take stock of your situation. If you have been a prudent skipper, your situation should be pretty good.

Being prudent, you have your boat equipped with life jackets, foghorn, anchor and rode, ship's bell, radar reflector, and some type of depth-sounding device. You listen to weather forecasts, watch the sky, and otherwise guard against being surprised by fog. You have a compass mounted in the cockpit. You always are reasonably sure of your position, even in fine weather, and are particularly careful to know your position if visibility is not good. And you know the approximate times of high and low tides and the probable effects of tidal currents.

Yet, despite all precautions, anyone who ventures out on the water is sure to encounter fog sooner or later. And, while foolhardiness is not a virtue, no otherwise competent sailor should stay at dockside on the mere chance that fog may develop. You can miss a lot of good sailing that way and never learn to cope with the inevitable.

Besides, unless a general fog is predicted by the National Weather Service, any sudden fog is likely to be of short duration. On the southern California coast, particularly, as well as off the New England coast, at certain times of the year, a near-perpetual fogbank sits offshore, ready to dip low and dart in quickly and to lift or recede equally quickly. With this type fog, it is a matter of waiting only a few hours at most until sufficient visibility returns for you to head safely into shallow and congested waters.

So, with your weather eye cocked, you should be able to note the approach of a fogbank and confirm your approximate position or dead reckoning position with visual sightings of landmarks before the fog shuts them off. If you are close to harbor, you may even take a compass bearing on the harbor itself so you can steer a direct course home.

If you have visibility of 100 yards

or more, you are in no real danger, and fog should not be of any concern to you, even though you can't see land. When visibility becomes less than 100 yards, the danger of running aground or colliding with other boats increases.

Your final strategy depends on *how long* you think the fog may last and how confident you are that you can bring your boat through the fog directly into the harbor. However, there are a few things you'll want to get done immediately.

When fog closes in, first have people onboard put on warm clothing (and possibly even life jackets). This is only prudent in case the worst happens. Moreover, you thus avoid being distracted later by complaints of cold or by unnecessary worries about the safety of your guests and crew.

Next, you should assign a lookout with a foghorn to go forward to keep a close watch both port and starboard. You may assign a second lookout to watch astern. The person with the foghorn should be carefully instructed as to the proper signals and the intervals they should be blown and to listen for other boats between his own signals. Also hoist the radar reflector to the top of the mast if you don't ordinarily display one at all times. Now is the time to switch on the depthsounder or get out the sounding lead. The anchor should also be prepared.

After taking steps to protect the comfort and safety of your crew and guests and to avoid collisions, you must decide whether to attempt to return to port or wait out the fog in the relative safety of deep water.

If you are over good holding ground and not in the approach lane to a harbor, your wisest course may be to anchor and set a watch, ringing your bell and making the correct sig-nals, as prescribed by the Rules of the Road, to warn other small craft. You will be in a bad spot, however, if you have to take sudden evasive action to avoid some boat charging blindly down on you and you are anchored.

If the immediate waters are too deep or the holding ground is poor or there are other dangers (shoals, reefs, traffic lanes) that prevent seeking an anchoring area or returning to harbor, you should heave-to or sail a tight pattern that keeps you in deep water out of heavy traffic until the fog lifts. Don't heave-to if a foul current will set you into danger.

Don't drop sails and begin to power if there is any wind at all. Remember, your main purpose is to keep out of trouble. The noise of the motor makes it more difficult to hear approaching boats and their signals.

Usually, fog is accompanied by a pretty good breeze. Often the wind during a fog may be so brisk that you'll need to overtrim or undertrim the sails to reduce speed. You should reduce your speed to the minimum needed for steerageway and tacking. Of course, if you are fighting a strong current, you'll want to sail fast enough to make distance away from any downstream hazards but, again, remember you're not going anywhere special — just staying out of trouble.

Basically, the idea is to aim your boat into a safe area. Since you've just traversed such an area, you can safely reverse your course unless you've just passed through a difficult channel. If sea room and safety permit, the easiest course to sail is a beam reach, going first toward open water and then returning in, say, five-minute port and starboard tacks.

If sea room is to windward, you should make one or two close-hauled

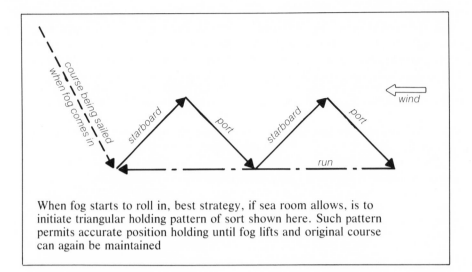

When fog starts to roll in, best strategy, if sea room allows, is to initiate triangular holding pattern of sort shown here. Such pattern permits accurate position holding until fog lifts and original course can again be maintained

tacks of equal duration port and starboard (again, five or 10 minutes should be the limit) and then run directly downwind to the initial point (see figure). Your pattern is a triangle with the sides and the hypotenuse (the upwind tacks compared to the downwind run) having the ratio 1:1.4. That is, if each tack is one mile in length, the downwind side will be 1.4 miles. To look at it another way, the downwind distance is 1.4:2 or seven-tenths the total distance sailed upwind.

Here you must make allowance for possible differences in speed when you are beating and running if you are timing your maneuver with a watch. If you make two five-minute tacks hard on the wind, one port and one starboard, and your boat speed is four knots, you will travel 1/3 mile on each tack, or 2/3 mile during the 10 minutes. You will make 1/2 mile to windward during the two tacks. If you can sail downwind at only three knots, then this leg of the triangle will take 1/2 mi:3 mi/hr or 10 minutes. If, instead you allow only seven-tenths the time sailed on the two upwind tacks, or seven minutes, for this downwind leg, you will work

yourself 300 yards farther out to sea each time. Since safety is to seaward in this case, this result is not totally bad but the whole idea is to hold your general position until a temporary or permanent lift in the fogbank permits you to make distance directly toward harbor.

If your sea room is downwind, first sail downwind a convenient time or distance, and reverse the procedure I've just described. Then, start tacking back upwind to your approximate starting position. If you're gauging the distance sailed by the elapsed time, you can adjust your close-hauled speed to nearly equal the downwind speed and thus simplify measuring the time intervals.

If visibility increases to a safe operating distance, even temporarily, you can take advantage of it to travel toward the harbor or some other location of greater safety (a good anchorage, perhaps) until at last you get a chance to run into port.

There are times when sailing a holding pattern at some distance from port is not the approach you'll want to take (for example, if you expect the fog to persist for 12 or 24 hours), but you should not feel obliged to crank up the engine and head blindly toward harbor through the fog with the mistaken idea that you have no other choice if you want to safeguard your boat and crew. Actually, it takes far more skill to negotiate harbor approaches and entrances in dense fog than it does to stand off and wait for the situation to get better.

This holding-pattern technique does not depend on electronics or shore-based aids — or even a compass. It is simple and effective, and ideal for the singlehander who does not want to leave the cockpit to study charts or play with a radio direction finder. Try it first on a clear day, starting from a buoy or other known position. You will find it surprisingly accurate.

Using the Radio Direction Finder

By Burt Sauer

If you're sailing in fog or darkness and you aren't sure of your location, a radio direction finder (RDF) can aid and comfort you. But it can do so only if you know its limitations; distance, ship's rig, and random atmospheric effects affect RDF accuracy. And although an RDF bearing is not so good as a visual bearing, it can help you find where you are or where you aren't.

Presumably, your dead reckoning puts you close enough to land so that you want to confirm your position, but with the horizon or the sky obscured, a celestial fix is out of the question. And you don't have a loran or omni set. But nearly every position within 50 miles of the US coastline is within range of one or more long-range radio beacons operated by the US Coast Guard. These and the shorter-range marker beacons, both of which are indicated on National Ocean Survey (NOS) charts, are fully described with frequencies, positions, identifying signals and nominal ranges in the *Light List* published by the Coast Guard.

To get your approximate position using these beacons, find the frequencies of the stations within your boat's possible range. Then use an RDF to find the direction of two or more beacons. The reciprocal bearings plotted from the beacons on your chart will cross your approximate position. Be particularly careful to correct the radio bearings for RDF deviation, for compass error, and for local magnetic variation.

Also, beware of physical and mental strain (particularly if you are short-handed or tired) which can cause you to commit some irredeemable navigation error. Good nulls on two beacons 50 miles away, allowing a bearing error of ± 4 degrees will define a diamond-shaped area of probable position seven miles on a side. With poor nulls, allow for a larger error margin.

But suppose you can only get one marine beacon, or maybe none? Should you tune to commercial broadcast stations, usable at considerably greater distances than most marine beacons? Maybe, but broadcast station transmitters present certain problems for radio direction finding. Few of them are marked on NOS charts because the Coast Guard believes them to be potentially inaccurate for direction finding. Recently, some of those transmitters visible from the sea have been plotted on the charts and identified, but the Coast Guard's position is still that mariners use them at their own risk.

If you are using a marine beacon or a broadcast station, avoid using a signal source whose signal path will travel over hills or lie within 15 degrees of a coastline. The shorter the signal path, the better. In the broadcast band, a station near the lower end (550 kHz) is preferable to one at the higher end (1600 kHz) if they are the same distance away. Stations or beacons near shore are better bets since there obviously can't be any intervening hills to reflect or to attenuate their signals.

Better alternatives for offshore sailors are the low-frequency aircraft beacons located near airports. Less subject to land- and sky-wave effects than broadcast stations, low-frequency aircraft beacons are still less desirable than marine beacons; radio bearings from them should be accepted with caution and due allowance should be made for error. The Coast Guard doesn't monitor their signal quality and reliability as it does the approved aids to navigation, so you take your chances. Also

the white and green rotating beacons marked on the charts with "AERO Rot W&G" are not at the same location as the low-frequency aircraft beacons, as some navigators assume. The "W&G" lights mark the mid-point of the runway, which may be four miles from the airport's radio beacon.

Incidentally, the geographic coordinates of broadcast and aircraft beacons are *not* listed in Defense Mapping Agency publication No. 117, *Radio Navigation Aids*, as reported in some articles. I am still looking for an official, authoritative, published source for this information, which currently is probably gathering dust in the files of various public agencies. I have located broadcast transmitters by telephoning local radio stations and have found aircraft beacons by borrowing a copy of the *Jeppson Airway Manual*.

When you are well offshore, you may not get any reliable cross bearing for determining your position. If you don't, try this navigation trick: recheck your radio bearing toward the long-range beacon and the line of position (LOP) from it. Plot the LOP on your chart. Study the chart carefully, making your best guess as to your present position. Then allow for reasonable error, and check whether you might run into any charted hazard in the next two hours. If you might, heave-to until visibility improves. If you can proceed and you have a choice of which way to turn, try to make some distance toward port while determining your position. To do this, turn the boat 90 degrees from the LOP and proceed for 10 miles per log or your best estimate of 10 miles based on the speed indicator and elapsed time. Now take an RDF bearing on the beacon and plot it.

Use your dividers to measure 10

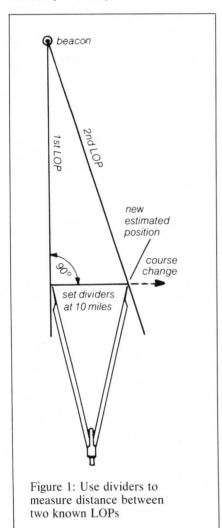

Figure 1: Use dividers to measure distance between two known LOPs

miles on the chart and, using a protractor or parallel rules, walk a 90-degree angle up and down the original LOP until the distance to the new LOP is 10 miles (Fig. 1). The point of intersection is (more or less) your present position. At a distance of 60 miles from the beacon, the 10-mile course change should alter the corrected radio bearing by about 10 degrees.

A useful variation, if you have an accurate speed or distance log, is to take RDF bearings repeatedly after making the 90-degree turn until the bearing to the beacon changes exactly 5 degrees or 10 degrees. Record the exact distance run on the new course. Divide your distance run by the sine of the change in bearing to give you your present distance from the beacon along the new LOP. The sine of 5 degrees is 0.087; the sine of 10 degrees, 0.174.

You also need cross bearings when, for some reason, you can't resolve the 180-degree ambiguity in RDF bearings by using the sense antenna. Again, you can turn at a right angle to the beacon LOP and note the change in the radio bearing as you sail the new course. The bearing will move aft on the side of the boat nearer the transmitter while it will move forward on the opposite side.

Getting an accurate compass reading can be difficult in a heavy sea. To keep the compass card from swinging wildly, stop pounding into the waves close-hauled and have your helmsman run off on the easiest heading he can find until you've gotten your null.

At 50 miles or so from a broadcast transmitter and during darkness, a sky wave commonly causes the null to shift slowly but continuously. Whenever you take RDF bearings at night, repeat the procedure at intervals of three to five minutes and see if the null has shifted. If so, continue to obtain nulls for at least 15 minutes; write them down to observe the extent of the shift. Usually, bearing angles swing back to the original value over a period of time. By adding the two extremes of one oscillation and dividing by two, you get an approximate bearing.

Naturally, with unfavorable reception, you should get bearings on as many beacons and stations as you can and evaluate each for reliability. Throw out the least reliable and plot LOPs from the others to reduce the area of probable position as much as you can.

The averaging technique will also work when you cannot get a sharp null. The mid-point between where the meter first indicates no signal and the point where a discernible signal reappears can be taken as the approximate radio bearing. Again, allow for uncertainty.

This is a good time to reflect on how closely you can fix your position with radio bearings. The idea that two intersecting LOPs determine your position has great appeal. However, we all know that three bearings rarely meet at a single point but usually form a triangle or, as the British say, a "cocked hat" (Fig. 2a). So your *exact* position is never certain. Even the best radio bearings are not so accurate as visual bearings or as LOPs taken from celestial observations.

With radio bearings, some navigators plot three LOPs, measure the longest side of the triangle, and draw a circle of probable position using this length as the radius. I know of no statistical basis for this practice, but it does help emphasize the uncertainty of your position.

My own practice is to allow a certain amount of error in each bearing,

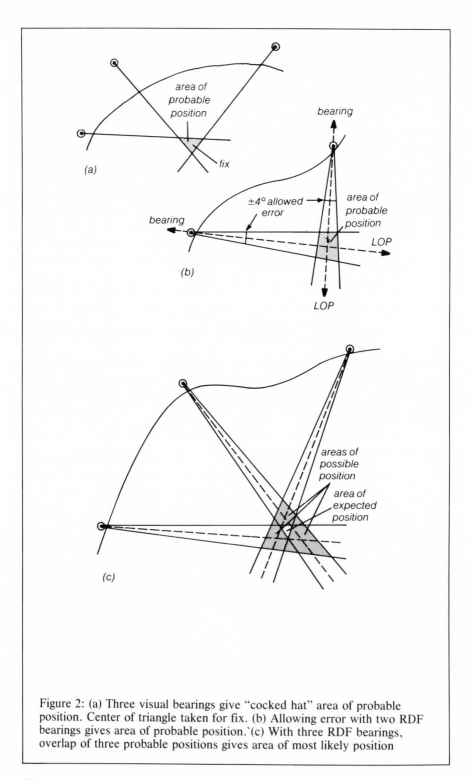

Figure 2: (a) Three visual bearings give "cocked hat" area of probable position. Center of triangle taken for fix. (b) Allowing error with two RDF bearings gives area of probable position.`(c) With three RDF bearings, overlap of three probable positions gives area of most likely position

based somewhat on intuition but guided by my knowledge of the particular RDF, the particular class of signal, and the reception conditions. Figures 2b and 2c illustrate the area of uncertainty (or, to think positively, the area of probable position) with two and three LOPs. Think of each broad LOP as a *path of position,* with the common area defined by crossing two RDF bearings corresponding to the point at which two visual bearings cross. Like the visual LOPs, this junction is a good indication of position, but with either type, you *can* be outside this point or area. Three RDF bearings should give you a smaller area common to all three. For course corrections, use the midpoint of this triangle, but remember that you don't actually have a pinpoint fix.

Your navigation problems increase many-fold when you are close inshore. Here it can be too dangerous to turn broadside to the signal path of a lone beacon and travel several miles to note the change in bearing angle. However, you have in your favor the likelihood of many more transmitters to tune on, which you can use in conjunction with other aids to navigation.

When close in, use all these sources of information. Take radio bearings frequently on all marine and aircraft beacons in range, and give the greatest credence to those that produce sharp nulls. Plot all seemingly good bearings to test their reliability further.

Reduce speed and maintain a close lookout for land, boats, and other hazards. At the same time, approach any buoys cautiously; positively identify them and consult the chart to verify their location.

When you are only two or three miles from shore and have local beacons available, you can use the

bow and beam angle and *double the bow angle* techniques of distance finding to determine how far away land is when your course roughly parallels the coast. Based on trigonometry, these techniques use angles that avoid complicated mathematics. A reasonably accurate method of determining distance traveled is essential.

In the *bow and beam* method, you hold a steady course and take RDF bearings repeatedly until you obtain the desired initial relative bearing. Note the mileage or time and continue to take bearings until the beacon bears 90 degrees. Take the mileage or time at the second bearing and calculate the elapsed distance. The distance to the beacon when the beacon is broad on the beam (point

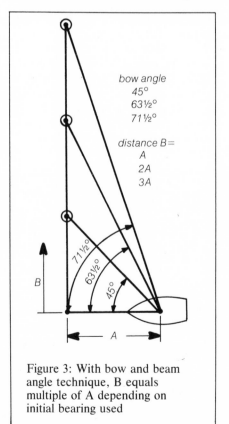

Figure 3: With bow and beam angle technique, B equals multiple of A depending on initial bearing used

of nearest approach) is a multiple of the distance made along the course between two relative bearings (Fig. 3).

Frequently you want to know at what distance you will pass a point before you come abeam of it. Two variations of the bow and beam angle method, called the *seven-tenths rule* and the *seven-eighths rule,* provide this advance information with just a little simple arithmetic (Fig. 4).

You can also find the distance to the beacon while it is still forward of the beam using *doubling the angle on the bow* technique. When the initial relative bearing has doubled, the distance to the beacon will equal the distance run between the times of the two RDF bearings (Fig. 5).

When A in Figure 5 is known, the distance (D) can always be determined (even when y is not an even multiple of x) with a slide rule, calculator, or table of trig functions. It is easiest to refer to Table 7 of Bowditch's *American Practical Navigator,* which gives you the multiplier to use with distance run between any two relative bearings to compute distance off at the second bearing. Since my volume of Bowditch is old

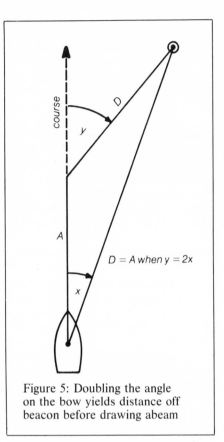

Figure 5: Doubling the angle on the bow yields distance off beacon before drawing abeam

and bulky, I keep a copy of Table 7 with my navigation gear.

These trigonometric methods will also work in reverse. That is, you can start to measure the elapsed distance when the beacon is 90 degrees relative and stop when it is 135 degrees relative, or from 135 degrees to 157½ degrees, etc.

When looking for a harbor of refuge, give preference to one marked with a light and foghorn which also has a radio beacon located with the light. (Obtain this information from the *Light List.*) Even if the area near the light doesn't offer safe shelter, it can give you a visual fix from which to chart a new course.

Shipboard sources of RDF error are usually least at the bow-on position. This permits reasonably cor-

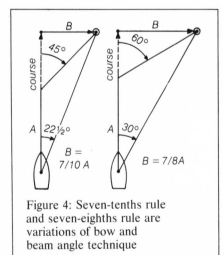

Figure 4: Seven-tenths rule and seven-eighths rule are variations of bow and beam angle technique

rect bearings with an uncalibrated RDF by simply bringing the the boat around until the null is dead ahead and by noting the compass bearing. Also, this technique sometimes gives you a sharper null when you can't get a satisfactory null at another relative bearing.

Homing is keeping the RDF null directly ahead as you proceed toward the beacon. Probably the most dependable use of the RDF, this method reduces error between the actual bearing and the RDF bearing as you get closer to the beacon. Also, because of the small or nonexistent deviation over the bow, you can home quite successfully with a borrowed RDF or on a chartered boat, even through RDF deviation hasn't been plotted for that particular unit on that particular boat. Provided you are not on the reciprocal bearing and you don't hit something first, you will eventually reach the beacon.

When homing on any radio beacon, study the chart carefully to be fully aware of possible hazards between you and the beacon. Consider the possibility that you aren't where you think you are, and check the chart for *all* hazards. Some of these may be at the site of the beacon itself, since many are mounted on rocks that suddenly appear out of the fog.

Naturally, you should employ a depthsounder, radar reflector, fog-horn, and a lookout during fog, but all these are defensive measures. A good RDF with accurate deviation can actually put you on a safe course to your destination. Take as many bearings on as many transmitters as you can and plot them. You will soon know which are good from the consistent way they plot, and you will see a progression of estimated positions (EPs) as you work along. A visual fix on a landmark or buoy helps you estimate the RDF accuracy under prevailing conditions and can improve your results with the RDF even more.

In times of good visibility, never pass up a chance to check RDF bearings against visual bearings when you happen to pass within sight of any transmitter. Writing course, visual bearing and RDF bearing into the log will help you evaluate the relative reliability of marine beacons, aircraft beacons, and broadcast stations.

An RDF is no substitute for good seamanship. The entrances to many harbors are unsafe in a heavy sea; a tricky channel is hard enough in bright sun and far too risky in fog or darkness. During fog, a prudent seaman keeps clear of areas where merchant ships converge. But knowing your location is still the name of the game, and careful navigation can keep you out of trouble.

3

CELESTIAL

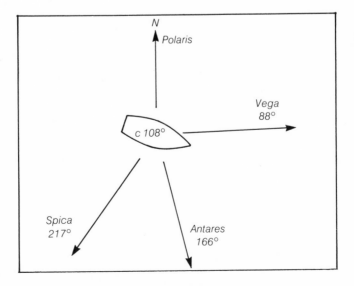

Celestial Navigation Simplified

By Bill Thomte

Celestial navigation has always had an air of mystery about it. But today anyone who is able to add and subtract with accuracy can easily navigate by celestial means.

Celestial navigation is based on two facts. They are:

1. The positions in the heavens of celestial bodies have an equivalent position on the surface of the earth.

2. We can find our own position if we know the direction and distance to this equivalent position.

The *Nautical Almanac* gives us the geographical location of the Sun, Moon, Venus, Mars, Jupiter, Saturn and 57 stars used for navigation. But these locations are described in terms different from those used for a

On Earth	Measured		In Heavens	Measured
Latitude	North or south from the Equator	=	Declination	North or south from the Equator
Longitude	East or west from Greenwich Meridian through 180°	=	Greenwich Hour Angle (GHA)	West from Greenwich Meridian through 360°

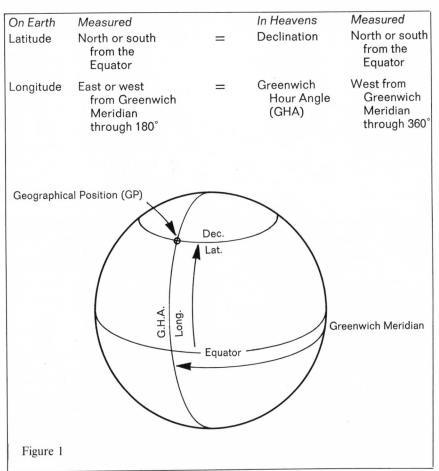

Figure 1

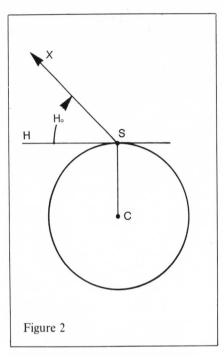

Figure 2

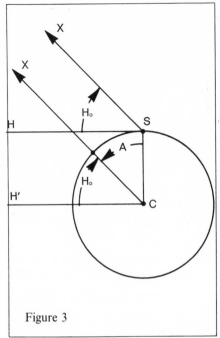

Figure 3

position on the earth's surface.

Latitude's celestial equivalent in the *Almanac* is Declination. Declination, like latitude, is measured from the Equator north or south through 90°.

Longitude, measured east or west from the Greenwich Meridian through 180°, has its equivalent in the Greenwich Hour Angle (GHA) which is only measured west from Greenwich through 360°.

The equivalent position of a celestial body on the surface of the earth is known as the Geographical Position (GP) of the body.

GP is defined as the point where a line drawn from the center of the body to the center of the earth intersects the earth's surface.

As the earth rotates relative to the body its GP will travel around the earth's surface. Consider the case of the sun whose GP continuously moves westward around the earth.

Figure 1 shows the earth and the GP of a celestial body whose position we know from the *Nautical Almanac*. To determine the distance from our own position to this GP, we must measure the angle between the horizon and the celestial body.

This measurement, known as the observed altitude (H_o) is made with the marine sextant. The H_o is shown diagramatically in Figure 2. The celestial body is represented by "X", "S" is our position on the surface of the earth, and the line SX is the line of sight to the celestial body.

Line HS represents the horizon; C represents the center of the earth. Line CS is the radius of the earth. The horizon line and the radius form a right angle and are perpendicular to each other.

Figure 3 has two additional lines. Line H'C is drawn parallel to line HS and line CX may be said to parallel line SX, for the distance from point S to X is almost infinite.

So we can therefore consider angle H_o to be equal at point S and point C. The Geographical Position

(GP) on the surface of the earth is found on line CX.

The distance to the GP from our own position S is represented by the arc on the surface between these two points or angle A.

Now if the distance to the GP is equal to angle A, and if angle H'CS is 90°, then angle A plus H_o must also equal 90°. Since we can measure H_o with the sextant, angle A will equal $90° - H_o$.

Such an angle in degrees must be converted to minutes of arc; one degree equals 60 minutes of arc and one minute of arc equals one nautical mile. $90 \times 60 = 5400$ and $5400 - H_o$ (expressed in minutes of arc) will give our distance to the GP in miles.

Now to summarize: to find the direction and distance to the GP of a celestial body do the following:

1. Find the GP of the body from the almanac.
2. Obtain the H_o and observe its direction.
3. Convert the H_o to minutes of arc.
4. Subtract the value of H_o in minutes of arc from 5400.

Every celestial observation and celestial fix is based on these simple steps and they are not mysterious at all.

Dusting off the Sextant

By John Ellsworth

Instrument error for a well-con-structed and calibrated sextant shouldn't exceed 0.1′, and this gives you theoretical accuracy within 200 yards for a line of position. Such accuracy is pointless though unless you develop good sighting skill.

There is only one sure way to increase the accuracy of your sextant sights. Practice taking sextant sights in your backyard.

Practice sights in your backyard? Yes. By using liquid as a reflecting surface, you can create your own artificial horizon. Davis Instruments makes an artificial horizon that consists of a plastic container, four sun shades, and a lid. It uses water as the reflecting surface, it folds together after use, and it is fairly compact.

If you wish, however, you can make and use your own. It's not so portable as the Davis device but it will work just as well; and it's fairly simple to make. On the day you plan to practice shooting — possibly a couple of hours before noon — fill a clean cake pan with motor oil, though any dark viscous liquid will have excellent reflecting qualities. Shelter the oil from the wind and dirt by placing a sheet of glass (a small window pane or the glass from a picture frame will do fine) over the pan and secure it with two shock-cords. Hook the two cords on one edge of the glass, run them parallel underneath the pan, and hook them on the opposite side (Fig. 1).

Now position yourself so you can see simultaneously the sun reflected in the oil and the actual sun in the sky. Take your sextant and bring the two images together so that they are tangent to each other. If you are making a sighting of the lower limb (LL), make the bottom of the *sky* sun just touch the top of the *oil* sun. For an upper-limb (UL) sighting, use the two other sides (Fig. 2). Practice this maneuver until you can bring the two objects together quickly and smoothly.

Personally, I prefer a lower-limb sighting when the lower limb is visible, simply because it's much easier to graze the lower limb on the horizon than the upper limb when you gently rock the sextant to give a pendulum effect. Rocking the sextant when you are sighting is a technique that assures your sextant is truly vertical, which it has to be to obtain a correct altitude reading (Fig. 3).

Your artificial horizon:
1 cakepan
1 qt. of motor oil
1 sheet of glass
2 shock cords

Figure 1

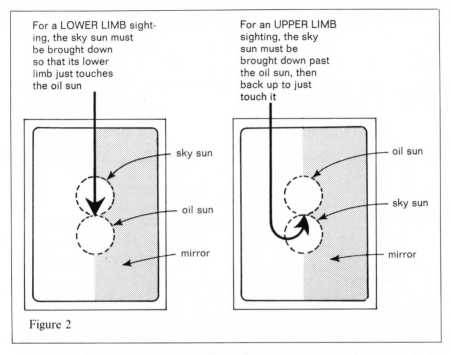

For a LOWER LIMB sighting, the sky sun must be brought down so that its lower limb just touches the oil sun

For an UPPER LIMB sighting, the sky sun must be brought down past the oil sun, then back up to just touch it

sky sun

oil sun

mirror

oil sun

sky sun

mirror

Figure 2

At sea, a fuzzy horizon, a rough sea, or your own fatigue may impair the accuracy of your sextant sight. Under such conditions it's difficult to get a single reliable shot, and it is a good idea to average multiple sightings of a single object. This can be done quickly and easily on graph paper. To prepare for this eventuality at sea, you should practice averaging 10 or more quick successive sun shots as you use the artificial horizon. Here's how.

To time your sightings, use either a stopwatch or a wrist watch with a sweep hand. You can get an exact time by telephone. You'll hear, "At the tone, the (daylight) time will be . . . (whatever time it is) . . . beep." If you use a stop watch, start it at the beep and then record the telephone time. Then when sighting the sun, just use the stopwatch time and apply it to the correct time after the sightings.

If you use a wrist watch, either set it to the correct time, which will probably take a few beeps by the phone operator, or just record the difference in time. In the latter case, simply apply the difference to your recorded times *after* you have finished your sightings.

Since you'll want speedy shots, have an assistant do the clockwork and recording. (It's very handy if the recording sheets are on a clipboard.)

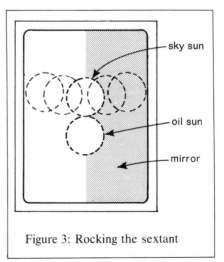

sky sun

oil sun

mirror

Figure 3: Rocking the sextant

		HS
GMT		(using artificial
h	m s	horizon)
17	54 05	59° 32'.2
	55 23	59° 28'.0
	57 04	59° 22'.8
	58 05	59° 17'.6
	58 22	59° 15'.0
	58 56	59° 13'.4
	59 37	59° 09'.8
18	00 48	59° 03'.6
	01 47	58° 58'.4
	02 10	58° 53'.8

Figure 4

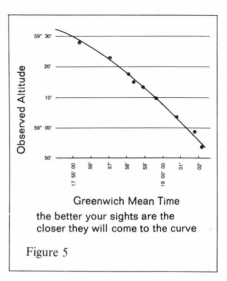

Greenwich Mean Time

the better your sights are the
closer they will come to the curve

Figure 5

To assure attention and accuracy from your helper call out *standby* while you are rocking the sextant and adjusting the micrometer drum, just on the verge of tangency. When the objects touch, call out *mark,* at which moment your assistant should record the exact time. Then tell your helper the altitude on the sextant so that he, or she, can record it next to the time.

After 10 shots, your readings, when the times are converted to Greenwich Mean Time (GMT), might appear as they do in Figure 4. Take these readings and plot the GMT versus your observations (HS) on graph paper and with a French curve, fair a curve through the points (Fig. 5). As you can see by this figure, the closer the observed body is to your local meridian, the sharper the curve is going to be.

This may be illustrated even better by Figure 6 which shows how a noon sight would appear if a curve were faired between a series of plotted local noon altitude and time readings.

The curves in both these figures represent the sun's transit, or path through the sky. If the curve is correct, you can use the time and corresponding altitude of any point on the line for your reading.

If you practice using the graph paper and the curves along with your artificial horizon, you'll see the drawn curves will get closer to the plotted points as you improve your technique.

Once you have become proficient in your sextant technique using the artificial horizon and the graph and curve method, how do you obtain a corrected altitude (HC) from your HS so that you can practice plotting your line of position?

As an example, let's start with an HS of 59°21'.0 (from the curve on Fig. 5). Now as we continue, refer to Figure 7. First, apply the index correction (IC), which of course is the

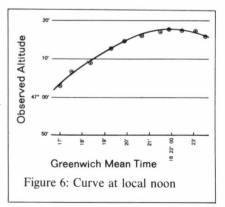

Greenwich Mean Time

Figure 6: Curve at local noon

predetermined instrument error. Then divide the resulting figure by two. You do this because you not only measured the angle at which the sun hit the oil (which is the angle of incidence) but also you measured the equal angle of reflection from the oil to your eye.

To this new figure, apply the remaining corrections, which are upper limb (UL) or lower limb (LL) correction, refraction (R), and horizontal parallax (HP), if it is applicable. Since there is no dip (D) of the horizon, you don't have to make a correction for the height of your eye.

You end up with an HC of 29°54'.1, and from here, all you have to do is to take your HC and work the solution out as you normally would. Then plot your line of position.

A good day's practice is to take a morning sun line, a noon sight for latitude, and an afternoon sun line. If you're accurate, your three lines of position should cross together very closely on your plotting sheet.

HS	59° 21.1
IC±	+ 1.4
	2)59° 22.4
	29° 41.2
LL+, or UL—	+14.6
Also called	
semi diameter (SD)	29° 55.8
R	− 1.7
HP	(NA)
HC	29° 54.1

Figure 7

You might also want to practice some star shots, but they're quite difficult to catch in a reflected image. But the moon is another story, and on some days you can be very lucky; both the sun and the moon may be in the sky at the same time.

It takes a great deal of practice to develop the finesse needed to make an accurate observation at sea. But if you start practicing ashore now, you'll be that much further ahead when you do go to sea.

The Noon Sight

By Paul Dodson

The noon sight is a good place to begin for anyone taking his first practical step into celestial navigation. But it is equally valid for every ocean sailor, whether he be a cruising man or an ocean racer.

Navigators have used the noon sight for centuries to obtain their latitude. The theory is to observe the angle of the sun just as it reaches the highest point in its movement across the sky.

This moment occurs when the sun crosses *your* meridian travelling from east to west and is called Local Apparent Noon.

Local Apparent Noon is obviously 1200 hours Local Apparent Time (LAT), and this is what the old sailing ships set their clocks by; remember Winslow Homer's famous painting "Eight Bells."

But in order to standardize time within countries and throughout the world we have adopted the standard of Mean Time which is, in effect, the time kept by the "mean sun" travelling around the earth once exactly every 24 hours. (The "real sun" varies and does not keep such regular time.)

To make things even easier, the world is further divided into time zones and zone time is the Mean Time that is standard throughout a given time zone. These zones are 15° in width, and of course there are 24 of them around the world (24 × 15° = 360°).

Local Mean Time (LMT) is of course going to be the mean time at *your* meridian; but the only time this will be the same as your zone time will be when you are right on the central meridian of your zone.

Knowing LMT means that you can easily find out the approximate time of Local Apparent Noon (LAN) if you roughly know your longitude. If you can estimate your longitude within one degree you can compute the time of LAN within four minutes.

To convert to Local Mean Time from zone time you must know how far east or west you are from your zone's central (or standard) meridian. We know that the degree of longitude equals 4 minutes of time, and if you are east of your zone's central meridian your LMT is going to be ahead of zone time.

Example: Your longitude is 74° West and you have Eastern Standard Time on your watch. At 1205 (EST) your LMT is 1209, four minutes ahead of zone time. Remember, when the sun gets to the central meridian (75°W) it has already passed your own meridian (74°W); therefore your LMT is going to be later than zone time.

The LMT of the sun's meridian passage is easily found in the almanacs. In the *Nautical Almanac* it is found in the lower right hand corner of the appropriate daily page, opposite the date. The *Air Almanac* has a table in the back section showing these times. These LMTs of meridian passage remain constant from year to year.

For example, the sun's meridian passage (LMT) is 1147 on October

11. If your longitude is 72°30′W, on that day LAN would be 1137 (2°30′ = 10 minutes) Eastern Daylight Time. Add one hour to make LAN 1237.

Take your sextant and start observing the sun about 5 minutes before LAN (10 minutes for beginners).

As the sun approaches its meridian passage it will rise more and more slowly, and in the horizon glass of your sextant you will keep bringing the lower limb of the sun down to the horizon so that it just touches it as you pivot the sextant around the line of sight in order to swing the sun like a pendulum on the horizon.

At Local Apparent Noon the sun will "hang" at constant altitude for about two to four minutes before you detect a drop in the sun's altitude. The maximum altitude reading on the sextant during this hang period is the sextant reading you must use to determine your latitude.

The sextant reading must then be accurately corrected for height of eye (dip), refraction, the sun's semi-diameter, and the index error of the sextant; and you must know the sun's declination at the time of meridian passage.

In the *Nautical Almanac* the inside front cover has a table to find the dip correction for height of eye and a table of altitude corrections for the sun which combine the refraction and semi-diameter corrections into one "main correction."

The *Air Almanac* has the dip correction on the outside back cover, the refraction correction on the inside back cover, and the sun's semi-diameter in the lower right-hand corner of the daily pages.

In both almanacs the sun's declination is found on the daily pages but it is computed by Greenwich Mean Time. Your local zone time must be corrected by the number of hours it varies from Greenwich time. Eastern Standard Time has a zone time of +5, so at 1200 Noon (EST) in New

Examples:

subt. (diff)		subt. (diff)		add (same)		add (same)		subt. (diff)	
z	65°S	z	65°N	z	30°N	z	30°S	Decl.	20°N
Decl.	20°N	Decl.	20°S	Decl.	20°N	Decl.	20°S	z	10°S
Lat.	45°S	Lat.	45°N	Lat.	50°N	Lat.	50°S	Lat.	10°N

Sample Problem:
Using Air Almanac, and height of eye of 9′:

		+	−	
LAN sextant reading:				50°47′3″
Corrections		+	−	
Index Correction			1′5″	
Dip			3′0″	
Semi-Diameter		15′8″		
Refraction			1′0″	
Totals:		+15′8″	−5′5″	
Net Correction:				+10′3″
Corrected Altitude:				50°57′6″
Zenith Distance (z):	(90° − Corrected altitude)			39°02′4″N
Declination of Sun:				8°14′2″N (same, add)
	Latitude:			47°16′6″N

York it is 1700 (GMT) in London. If the time of LAN was 1137 (EST), the sun's declination in the *Almanac* would be found opposite 1637 (GMT) on the proper date.

Knowing the corrected sextant altitude of the sun at LAN (meridian passage) and the sun's declination at that time, you are now ready to find your latitude at the time of LAN.

Zenith is a point in the celestial sphere directly over your head, and the zenith is exactly 90° above the horizon. Zenith distance (z) is an arc above your head between your zenith and the sun. Zenith distance (z) is equal to 90° minus the altitude of the sun above the horizon. For example if the sun's corrected altitude is 60°, the zenith distance (z) is going to be 30° (90° − 60°).

Zenith distance (z) is labeled either North or South. If you are north of the sun (i.e., facing south to take the Noon sight) z is North. Another way to remember this is that if your zenith is North of the sun, z is North.

The sun's declination will be labeled either North or South in the almanacs depending on whether it is north or south of the Equator.

To find your latitude: (Use whichever rule applies)

a) Add zenith distance and declination together if they are both of the same name (N or S). The sum is your latitude.

b) Subtract the smaller of the two from the larger if they are of contrary names, and the difference is your latitude. (If angle labeled N is larger, the latitude is N, and vice versa.)

These few calculations are all that's required to find your exact latitude from the Noon sight. The total equipment required is a chart with your approximate position (DR position), a watch with the approximate time, a sextant and an Almanac.

Getting Down to Sight Reduction

By James B. Kane

No matter what sight reduction method you use in celestial navigating, you're looking for one thing — a line of position (LOP). And a LOP obtained from the sun or a star does the same thing for you as does a bearing on a lighthouse. You know you're somewhere on that line. To get a fix you must simultaneously obtain at least one more LOP. Where the LOPs cross is your fix. Or, in

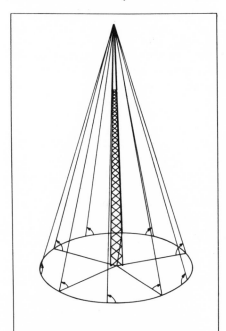

Figure 1: A television tower with guy wires extending out an equal distance creates good example of what circle of equal altitude is

cases where you only have the sun handy, you can get your position by using a running fix, the way you sometimes do when you're unable to get bearings on more than one lighthouse.

First, let's see what all the methods of sight reduction have in common. When taking a sight of the sun or a star, you're getting the height in arc (degrees and minutes) that the body is above the horizon. You call this sight, before applying corrections to it, *sextant altitude* (hs). After correcting hs you call it your *observed altitude* (H_o). More about these corrections later.

Using sight reduction tables, you compute an altitude (Hc) from an assumed position (AP) or from a dead-reckoning position (DR). the difference in Hc and Ho, subtracting the lesser from the greater, is the *intercept (a).* Sometimes you'll hear intercept called altitude difference. The reason is that it is the difference in minutes of arc from your AP (or DR) to the LOP on which you actually are located.

To understand what Hc and H_o are all about, let's say we have a TV tower with many guy wires running from its top out to 75 feet from its base (Fig. 1). Naturally each of the guys cuts an equal angle with the ground. By connecting these points, which cut an equal angle at the ground, you'll create a circle with the TV tower at its center. These points create a circle of equal altitude.

Accordingly, each distance, or radius, from the tower will create a different circle of equal altitude and an entirely different set of equal angles. Like the TV tower, the sun and stars also have circles of equal altitude. Obviously, we have no tower holding up a star. If we had such a tower, you would call the position of its base on earth the geographical position (GP) of the star. As the earth rotates, the GP of each star and the sun move west.

Naturally circles of equal altitude move west with the sun and stars. Circles of equal altitude of the sun and stars generally take in huge areas of the earth's surface. They have such a large circumference that any segment of one, such as you would plot on a chart, would seem to be a straight line. This short segment of a circle of equal altitude is an LOP.

Let's go back to our TV tower. You face the tower and you estimate you're 75 feet from it. Then you compute what your angle at the ground should be with the top of the tower at this distance. You come up with 60½ degrees. But measuring the angle accurately with a sextant, you get 62 degrees. Because you have a larger observed altitude than the one you computed with the sextant, you know you're closer to the tower than 75 feet for as you move toward the tower, the angle will increase. You know you're 1½ degrees closer to the tower than you originally judged. This same rule applies when obtaining our intercept (a).

All methods of sight reduction such as H.O. 208 Dreisonstock, H.O. 211 Ageton, H.O. 214 and H.O. 229 enable you to get a Hc. Of course, when getting your Hc, you work from a position close to where you believe yourself to be. H.O. 211

and 208 use a DR position; H.O. 214, 229 and 249 use an AP or assumed position. You choose your assumed position by taking a latitude to the nearest whole degree. Then you select an assumed longitude which enables you to have a local hour angle with a whole degree. All of the sight reduction methods I have listed above have instructions on their use in front of their tables.

Another thing common to all methods of finding your LOP is that a celestial LOP will run exactly 90 degrees from the azimuth or bearing of the body you're using. Stop and think for a moment and you'll see why this is. The azimuth you have of the sun or a star is merely a radius of the circle of equal altitude. It's a line drawn from your position to the GP of the sun or a star (Fig. 2).

Of course, you'll need your corrected altitude and to get this, you apply correction to your hs. The inside cover of the *Nautical Almanac* has the altitude correction tables. The correction for dip (D) means the correction for your height of eye above the water. Pages 258 and 259 in the *Almanac* explain how to use these tables by showing examples. The examples call hs *sextant altitude* and H_o *corrected sextant altitude*.

Crank into the reduction tables your latitude, local hour angle and declination of the sun or a star and take out your Hc and azimuth. Find the difference between H_o and Hc. The difference should be in minutes. Each minute is a nautical mile. This is your intercept or *a*.

Example: H_o 49°48.4'
Hc 49°57.4'

<u> </u>

a   9.0' away

If your H_o was greater than your Hc, your intercept would be *toward* the sun or star instead of away.

To show how you plot this on a

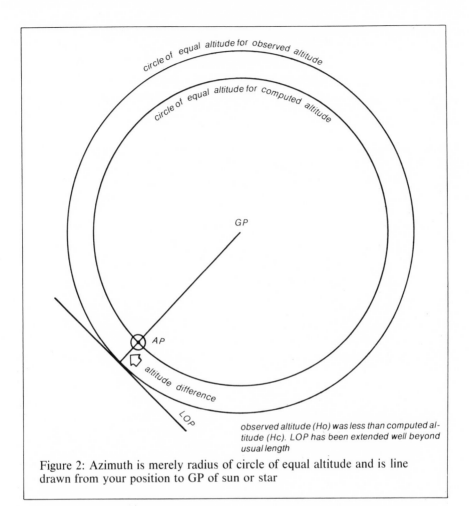

circle of equal altitude for observed altitude

circle of equal altitude for computed altitude

GP

AP

altitude difference

LOP

observed altitude (Ho) was less than computed altitude (Hc). LOP has been extended well beyond usual length

Figure 2: Azimuth is merely radius of circle of equal altitude and is line drawn from your position to GP of sun or star

chart or plotting sheet, let's say you took an azimuth of 223° and an Hc 49° 48.4' from the tables. Your AP is Latitude 25°N and your Longitude is 15° 20'W. First plot your AP (Fig. 3). This gives you a place to work from. At the compass rose, set your parallel rulers to the azimuth you got from the tables (223°). Walk this azimuth over to your AP and lightly trace it with a pencil. Measure on this line from your AP the intercept (toward or away) from the GP as the case calls for. In our case it's 9.0' away. Use the latitude scale when measuring the length of the intercept.

After marking the distance of the

intercept from your AP, place the 90-degree edge of a triangle against the parallel rulers so you can run a perpendicular through the intercept. Now you've plotted your LOP.

For the most accurate results when taking star sights, you should advance or retire all your LOPs along your course line to a common time.

Table 208, Dreisonstock, and Table 211, Ageton, are small. Using either of these tables requires considerably more work, and more chance of error, than using either 214 or 229.

On the other hand, 208 and 211 take less room on your bookshelf.

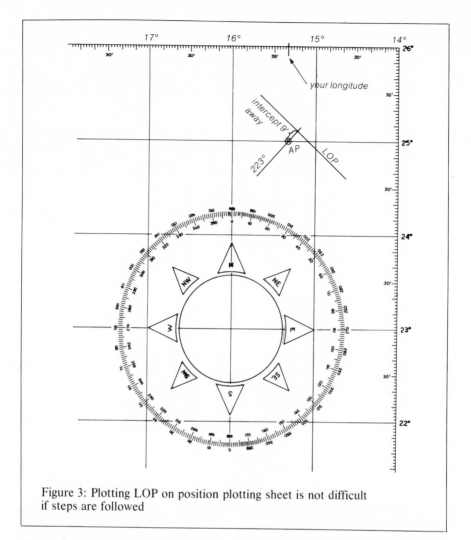

Figure 3: Plotting LOP on position plotting sheet is not difficult if steps are followed

You can easily carry either of them from one boat to another.

Publications 214 (no longer being printed) and 229 take less figuring to arrive with an LOP. But they come in nine volumes (214) and six volumes (229). Publication 249 comes in three volumes, and the Oceanographic Office calls them "Sight Reduction Tables for Air Navigation." But don't let the name fool you. With a *Nautical Almanac* you still can use these tables for marine navigation. Marine sight reduction tables give the Hc to the nearest 10th of a minute

of arc. Table 249 gives the Hc to the nearest minute of arc. This means the most you could be off with Table 249 is one half minute. A fix within a half minute of where you actually are is good. Other than at noon, how often will two people simultaneously taking a sight come within a half minute of each other on their sextants? Very seldom.

Because the *Nautical Almanac* has the corrections for a marine sextant inside the cover, you should use a *Nautical Almanac* with H.O. 249.

Volume II or H.O. 249 takes in

latitude 0° to 39°. Volume III takes in latitude 40° to 89°. You use them the same way you use 214 and 229.

Volume I isn't a permanent table. It's recomputed every five years. It consists of tables for seven selected stars. The Oceanographic Office looks toward brightness, spread of azimuth, altitude and continuity when it selects stars for the table. Volume I also acts as a starfinder.

So, in a fairly small clamshell, that's what navigating by the sun and stars is all about. Look at all the tables before you buy them. Today, few navigators use H.O. 208 and 211. If you like H.O. 214 or 229 best, remember you don't have to buy all the volumes. Buy only the volumes for the latitudes you sail. After all, few sailors go above 60° latitude.

Sunlines . . . Valuable Checks

By Paul Dodson

Taking a noon sight is a relatively simple matter. But any offshore sailor can make good use of the sun at times other than just noon to get a line of position.

Getting such a (sun) line tells the navigator any number of things about where he is. But its usefulness depends upon what time of day he takes his sight. The trick is to learn when to take a sunline so that it is most helpful.

A sunline or line of position is simply a line drawn on the chart (or plotting sheet) that is perpendicular to the sun's bearing.

The sun rises in the east, sets in the west, and its bearing, or in celestial terms *azimuth,* is continually changing during the day along with, of course, its altitude or height above the horizon.

In the Northern Hemisphere during the spring and summer the navigator has an opportunity to take a sunline when the sun's bearing is exactly due east and again when it is due west. If he can take it just at this moment he can plot a line of position from the sun that is exactly vertical (north-south) on the chart. Assuming his sight is accurate, he will then know his precise longitude at that moment.

If the weather is clear he can use the sun to determine his longitude early in the morning, his latitude at noon, and his longitude again in the late afternoon.

If you were sailing either 090° True or 270° True, these morning and afternoon sunlines of longitude would also provide an accurate check on the distance run along your dead reckoning track for you would then know accurately your average speed over the bottom.

If you were still heading due east or due west a noon sight would, in addition to giving you your latitude, tell you how far left or right of your track you were and thereby serve as a check on your course.

But more often than not your course will be something other than true East or West, and you will want to take a morning and afternoon sunline that will provide a line of position parallel and perpendicular to your course.

Let's look at some sunlines that were taken at the most advantageous moment to maximize the information they give.

Figure 1A shows what a noon sight can do to improve one's DR, and Figue 1B shows what a proper morning or evening sunline can do.

If you were approaching land and the sun were directly ahead bearing 225° True, you could find, with a sunline, your distance from the coast and could also check the distance you had run along your track since your last fix. The same information, of course, can be obtained if the sun were directly astern (Fig. 1C).

Figure 1D shows a line of position with the sun abeam and proves the obvious value of a sunline to check one's course error when approaching a landfall.

All these examples prove the value of a good sunline when its

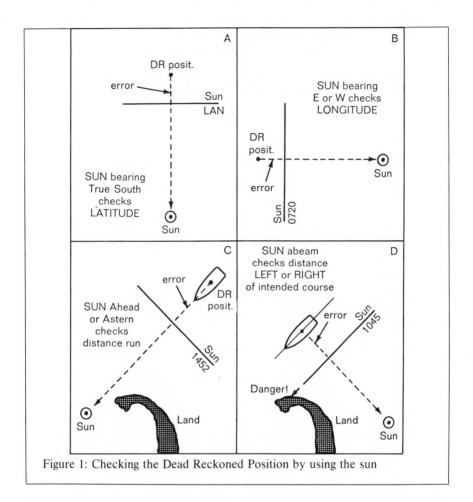

Figure 1: Checking the Dead Reckoned Position by using the sun

bearing is *where you want it*. Look again at Figure 1D. If your course in this example is 225°T, you should plan to take a sight when the sun's azimuth is 135° (225° − 90° = 135°).

To find the time when the sun's azimuth is going to be 135° requires using a table of computed altitudes and azimuths such as HO 214, 229 or 249, or the azimuth tables HO 260.

For this example we will use HO 249, *Sight Reduction Tables,* Vol. III. Originally designed for air navigation, it is commonly used by sailors because of its speed and convenience.

As with any of the tables, HO 249 is tabulated using three elements of information: (1) assumed latitude (the nearest whole degree of latitude to your DR position); (2) the declination of the body — the sun in this case; and (3) the Local Hour Angle (LHA) of the body, represented by the angle between your meridian and the celestial body's meridian measured westward around the earth.

Using these three pieces of information and HO 249 you can determine two other values: The computed altitude of the body, and its azimuth.

Go back to Figure 1D. On September 1, 1971, we are approaching land on a course of 225°T. Our approximate latitude is 42°10′N. Consulting

4° c d Z	5° Hc d Z	6° Hc d Z	7° Hc d Z	8° Hc d Z	9° Hc d Z	10° Hc d Z	11° Hc d Z	12° Hc d Z	13° Hc d Z	14° Hc d Z	LHA
00 +60 180	53 00 +60 180	54 00 +60 180	55 00 +60 180	56 00 +60 180	57 00 +60 180	58 00 +60 180	59 00 +60 180	60 00 +60 180	61 00 +60 180	62 00 +60 180	360
59 60 178	52 59 60 178	53 59 60 178	54 59 60 178	55 59 60 178	56 59 60 178	57 59 60 178	58 59 60 178	59 59 60 178	60 59 60 178	61 59 60 178	359
58 59 177	52 57 59 177	53 57 60 177	54 57 60 177	55 57 60 177	56 57 60 177	57 57 60 177	58 57 60 176	59 57 60 176	60 57 60 176	61 59 60 176	358
50 60 175	52 50 60 175	53 54 60 175	54 54 60 175	55 54 60 175	56 54 60 173	57 54 59 174	58 53 60 174	59 53 60 174	60 53 60 174	61 53 60 174	357
44 +60 172	52 44 +60 172	53 44 +60 172	54 43 +60 171	55 43 +59 171	56 42 +60 171	57 42 +60 171	58 42 +59 171	59 41 +59 170	60 41 +59 170	61 40 +59 170	355
37 60 170	52 37 59 170	53 36 60 170	54 36 59 170	55 35 59 169	56 35 59 169	57 34 60 169	58 34 59 169	59 33 59 168	60 32 59 168	61 31 60 168	354
29 60 169	52 29 60 169	53 28 59 168	54 27 60 168	55 27 58 168	56 26 59 167	57 25 59 167	58 24 59 167	59 23 59 167	60 22 59 166	61 21 59 166	353
20 59 167	52 19 59 167	53 18 59 167	54 17 59 167	55 16 59 166	56 15 59 166	57 14 59 165	58 13 59 165	59 12 59 165	60 11 58 164	61 09 60 164	352
10 60 166	52 08 59 165	53 07 59 165	54 06 59 165	55 05 59 165	56 04 58 164	57 02 59 164	58 01 58 163	58 59 59 163	59 58 58 162	60 56 58 162	351
58 +59 164	51 57 +58 164	52 55 +59 163	53 54 +58 163	54 52 +59 163	55 51 +58 162	56 49 +58 162	57 47 +59 161	58 46 +58 161	59 44 +58 160	60 42 +59 160	350
45 58 163	51 43 59 162	52 42 58 162	53 40 58 161	54 38 58 161	55 36 58 161	56 35 57 160	57 32 58 160	58 30 58 159	59 28 57 159	60 25 58 158	349
31 58 161	51 29 58 161	52 27 58 160	53 25 58 160	54 23 58 159	55 21 58 159	56 19 57 158	57 16 58 158	58 14 57 157	59 11 57 157	60 08 57 156	348
16 58 159	51 14 58 159	52 12 57 159	53 09 58 158	54 07 57 158	55 04 58 157	56 02 57 157	56 59 57 156	57 56 57 156	58 53 56 155	59 49 57 155	347
00 57 158	50 57 58 158	51 55 57 158	52 52 57 157	53 49 57 156	54 46 57 156	55 43 57 155	56 40 57 154	57 37 56 154	58 33 56 153	59 29 56 153	346
42 +57 157	50 40 +57 156	51 37 +57 156	52 34 +57 155	53 31 +56 155	54 27 +57 154	55 24 +56 153	56 20 +56 153	57 16 +56 152	58 12 +56 151	59 08 +56 151	345
24 57 155	50 21 57 155	51 18 56 154	52 14 57 154	53 11 56 153	54 07 56 152	55 03 56 152	55 59 56 151	56 55 55 150	57 50 56 150	58 46 55 149	344
06 56 154	50 01 57 153	50 58 56 153	51 54 56 153	52 50 56 151	53 46 56 151	54 42 55 150	55 37 55 150	56 32 55 149	57 27 55 148	58 22 55 147	343
44 57 152	49 41 56 152	50 37 55 151	51 32 56 150	52 28 56 150	53 24 55 149	54 19 55 149	55 14 55 148	56 09 54 147	57 03 55 146	57 58 53 146	342
23 54 151	49 19 54 150	50 15 55 150	51 10 55 149	52 05 55 148	53 00 55 148	53 55 55 147	54 50 54 146	55 44 54 146	56 38 54 145	57 32 53 144	341
01 +55 149	48 56 +56 149	49 52 +55 148	50 47 +54 148	51 41 +55 147	52 36 +54 146	53 30 +54 146	54 24 +54 145	55 18 +54 144	56 12 +53 143	57 05 +53 142	340
38 55 148	48 33 55 147	49 28 54 147	50 22 55 146	51 17 54 145	52 11 54 145	53 05 54 144	53 58 54 143	54 52 53 143	55 45 52 142	56 37 53 141	339
14 54 147	48 08 55 146	49 03 54 145	49 57 54 145	50 51 54 144	51 45 53 144	52 38 53 143	53 31 53 142	54 24 53 141	55 17 52 140	56 09 52 140	338
49 54 145	47 43 54 145	48 37 54 144	49 31 53 143	50 25 53 143	51 17 54 142	52 10 53 141	53 03 53 140	53 56 52 140	54 48 51 139	55 39 51 138	337
23 54 144	47 17 53 143	48 10 54 143	49 04 53 142	49 57 53 141	50 50 52 141	51 42 52 140	52 34 52 139	53 26 52 138	54 18 51 137	55 09 50 136	336
56 +54 143	46 50 +53 142	47 43 +53 141	48 36 +52 141	49 28 +53 140	50 21 +52 139	51 13 +52 138	52 05 +51 138	52 56 +51 137	53 47 +51 136	54 38 +50 135	335
29 53 141	46 22 53 141	47 15 52 140	48 07 52 139	48 59 52 139	49 51 52 138	50 43 51 137	51 34 51 136	52 25 51 135	53 16 50 134	54 06 49 134	334
02 52 140	45 53 52 140	46 46 52 139	47 38 51 138	48 29 52 137	49 21 51 137	50 12 51 136	51 03 50 135	51 53 50 134	52 33 49 133	53 33 49 132	333
32 51 139	45 24 52 138	46 16 51 138	47 07 52 137	47 59 51 136	48 50 51 135	49 41 50 134	50 31 50 134	51 21 49 133	52 10 50 132	53 00 48 131	332
02 52 138	44 54 51 137	45 45 52 136	46 37 50 136	47 27 51 135	48 18 50 134	49 08 50 133	49 58 50 132	50 48 49 131	51 37 48 131	52 25 49 130	331
32 +51 137	44 23 +51 136	45 14 +51 135	46 05 +50 134	46 55 +51 134	47 46 +49 133	48 35 +50 132	49 25 +49 131	50 14 +49 130	51 03 +48 129	51 51 +47 128	330
01 51 135	43 52 50 135	44 42 51 134	45 33 50 133	46 23 50 132	47 13 49 132	48 02 49 131	48 51 49 130	49 40 48 129	50 28 47 128	51 15 48 127	329
29 51 134	43 20 50 134	44 10 50 133	45 00 50 132	45 50 49 131	46 39 49 130	47 28 48 130	48 16 49 129	49 05 47 128	49 52 48 127	50 40 46 126	328
57 50 133	42 47 50 132	43 37 49 132	44 26 50 131	45 16 49 130	46 05 48 129	46 53 48 128	47 41 48 127	48 29 47 127	49 16 47 126	50 03 46 125	327
24 50 132	42 14 49 130	43 03 49 130	43 52 49 130	44 41 49 129	45 30 48 128	46 18 48 127	47 06 47 126	47 53 47 125	48 40 46 124	49 26 46 124	326
50 +50 131	41 40 +49 130	42 29 +49 129	43 18 +48 128	44 06 +48 128	44 54 +48 127	45 42 +47 126	46 29 +47 125	47 16 +47 124	48 03 +46 123	48 49 +45 122	325
19 49 130	41 05 49 129	41 54 49 128	42 43 48 127	43 31 47 127	44 18 48 126	45 06 47 125	45 53 46 124	46 39 46 123	47 25 46 122	48 11 45 121	324
49 49 128	40 31 48 128	41 19 48 127	42 07 48 126	42 55 47 126	43 42 47 125	44 29 47 124	45 15 47 123	46 02 45 122	46 47 45 121	47 32 45 120	323
08 48 128	39 55 48 127	40 43 48 126	41 31 47 125	42 18 47 125	43 05 47 124	43 52 46 123	44 38 46 122	45 24 45 121	46 09 45 120	46 54 44 119	322
31 48 127	39 19 48 126	40 07 47 125	40 54 47 124	41 41 47 123	42 28 46 123	43 14 46 122	44 00 45 121	44 45 45 120	45 30 45 119	46 15 43 118	321
55 +48 126	38 43 +47 125	39 30 +47 124	40 17 +47 123	41 04 +46 122	41 50 +46 122	42 36 +45 121	43 21 +45 120	44 06 +45 119	44 51 +44 118	45 35 +44 117	320
19 47 125	38 06 47 124	38 53 47 123	39 40 46 122	40 26 46 121	41 12 45 121	41 57 45 120	42 42 45 119	43 27 44 118	44 11 44 117	44 55 43 116	319
42 47 124	37 29 46 123	38 15 47 122	39 02 46 121	39 48 45 120	40 33 45 120	41 18 45 119	42 03 44 118	42 47 44 117	43 31 44 116	44 15 43 115	318
05 46 123	36 51 46 122	37 37 46 121	38 23 46 120	39 09 45 119	39 54 45 119	40 39 43 118	41 23 44 117	42 07 43 116	42 50 43 115	43 34 43 114	317
27 46 122	36 13 46 121	36 59 46 120	37 45 45 119	38 30 45 118	39 15 44 118	39 59 45 117	40 44 43 116	41 27 43 115	42 11 42 114	42 53 43 113	316
49 +46 121	35 35 +45 120	36 20 +46 119	37 06 +45 118	37 51 +44 118	38 35 +44 117	39 19 +44 116	40 03 +44 115	40 47 +43 114	41 30 +42 113	42 12 +42 112	315
10 46 120	34 56 45 119	35 41 45 118	36 26 45 117	37 11 44 117	37 55 44 116	38 39 44 115	39 23 43 114	40 06 43 113	40 49 42 112	41 31 42 111	314
46 45 118	34 17 45 118	35 02 45 117	35 47 44 116	36 31 44 115	37 15 44 115	37 59 43 114	38 42 43 113	39 25 42 112	40 07 42 111	40 49 42 110	313
52 45 118	33 37 45 117	34 22 44 116	35 06 44 115	35 51 43 115	36 34 44 114	37 18 43 113	38 01 42 112	38 43 42 111	39 25 42 110	40 07 41 109	312
13 44 117	32 57 45 116	33 42 44 116	34 26 44 115	35 10 43 114	35 53 44 113	36 37 42 112	37 19 43 111	38 02 42 110	38 44 41 109	39 25 41 108	311
33 +44 116	32 17 +45 115	33 02 +43 115	33 45 +44 114	34 29 +43 113	35 12 +43 112	35 56 +42 112	36 38 +42 111	37 20 +41 110	38 01 +42 109	38 43 +40 108	310
53 44 115	31 37 44 114	32 21 44 113	33 05 43 113	33 48 43 112	34 31 42 111	35 13 43 111	35 56 42 110	36 38 40 109	37 19 41 108	38 00 41 107	309
12 44 113	30 56 44 113	31 40 43 112	32 23 43 111	33 06 43 110	33 49 41 110	34 30 42 109	35 12 42 108	35 54 40 107	36 34 41 106	37 17 40 106	308
32 44 113	30 17 43 112	31 00 43 111	31 43 43 110	32 25 42 110	33 07 42 109	33 49 41 108	34 30 40 107	35 11 40 106	35 51 40 105	35 51 39 105	307
43 43 112	29 34 43 111	30 17 43 111	31 00 43 110	31 43 41 109	32 25 41 108	33 07 40 108	33 49 41 107	34 30 40 106	35 11 40 105	35 51 39 104	306
09 +44 111	28 53 +43 111	29 36 +42 110	30 18 +43 110	31 01 +42 109	31 43 +42 108	32 25 +41 107	33 06 +41 106	33 47 +41 105	34 28 +40 105	35 08 +40 104	305
28 44 110	28 11 43 110	28 54 42 110	29 36 43 109	30 19 41 108	31 00 42 107	31 42 41 106	32 23 41 106	33 04 40 105	33 44 40 104	34 24 39 103	304
46 43 110	27 29 43 109	28 12 42 109	28 54 41 108	29 35 42 107	30 17 41 106	30 58 41 105	31 39 40 104	32 19 40 104	32 59 40 103	33 39 39 102	303
04 43 109	26 47 42 108	27 29 43 108	28 12 41 107	28 53 41 106	29 34 41 105	30 15 40 104	30 55 40 104	31 35 40 103	32 15 39 102	32 54 39 101	302
22 43 109	26 05 42 108	26 47 42 107	27 29 41 106	28 10 41 105	28 51 40 104	29 31 40 103	30 11 40 103	30 51 39 102	31 30 39 101	32 09 38 101	301
40 +42 108	25 22 +42 107	26 04 +42 107	26 46 +41 106	27 27 +42 105	28 09 +40 104	28 49 +41 103	29 30 +40 102	30 10 +40 102	30 50 +40 101	31 30 +39 100	300
15 42 107	24 40 41 107	25 21 42 106	26 03 41 105	26 44 41 104	27 25 41 103	28 06 40 103	28 46 40 102	29 26 39 101	30 06 39 100	30 45 39 099	299
42 107 106	23 58 42 106	24 38 42 105	25 20 41 104	26 01 41 103	26 42 40 103	27 22 40 102	28 03 40 101	28 43 39 101	29 22 39 100	30 02 39 099	298
32 106	23 14 41 105	23 55 42 104	24 37 41 103	25 18 40 102	25 58 41 102	26 39 40 101	27 19 40 100	27 59 39 099	28 38 39 099	29 17 39 098	297
49 42 105	22 31 41 104	23 12 41 104	23 53 41 103	24 34 41 102	25 15 40 101	25 55 40 100	26 35 40 099	27 15 39 099	27 54 39 098	28 33 39 097	296

Figure 2

the *Almanac* for that day we find the sun's declination is about 8°25′N. Now all we need to know is when the sun's azimuth will be 135°.

Turn to HO 249 and enter the tables for 42°, the nearest degree of latitude. Since both latitude and the sun's declination are North, look at the column headed 8°, on the page titled: "Declination (0°-14°) *same name as latitude*." In the column labelled "Z" (for azimuth) look for 135°. We see a Z value of 135 opposite the Local Hour Angle (LHA) value of 331 (Fig. 2). We can also see that the sun's altitude will be approximately 47°27′ at this time.

All that now remains is to find out when the sun will have an LHA of 331°. To obtain this we must know our own approximate longitude, which, let's assume, is 70°W. If the sun were 331° to the west of us, it must therefore be 41° west of Greenwich (0° longitude), and have a Greenwich Hour Angle (GHA) of 41° (331° + 70° = 401° − 360° = 41°).

To find the time when the sun has a GHA of 41°, return to the *Almanac* for the proper date (in this case 9-1-71), and interpolate the given values. You will find that when the sun's GHA is 41°, Greenwich Mean Time will be 1444. However, if your watch is set, for example, to Eastern Daylight Time (four hours earlier than Greenwich time), the proper zone time for this sunline is going to be 1044 EDT.

At that moment the sun's true bearing or azimuth will be 135° and you will have the sunline you need to help tell you where you are.

Precomputed Sun Sights

By Crocker Wight

Solving a celestial sight almost at once can make the practical end of navigation much simpler. Obtaining a fast solution is even more valuable for an ocean racing navigator who must often contend with bad weather, exhaustion, and difficult working conditions.

But one system does most of the preliminary computation at home. Because this "precomputation" can be done in a more leisurely fashion than if it had been done on board, it eliminates errors that might be created by the shipboard working conditions already described.

Once these precomputations are made, all a navigator needs to do is compare his actual sight with his precomputed one in order to obtain a line of position. The sun is particularly well adapted for precomputation as both the horizon and the sun itself are visible all day long, weather permitting.

Normally, the sextant angle (Hs) of the sun is obtained and then corrected for refraction, semi-diameter, parallax, and dip. The first three are combined into one main correction, and dip is treated separately. The net result of all these corrections is a true or corrected altitude (Ho) which is then compared with the computed altitude (Hc) to determine the distance from the assumed position (towards or away from the sun) that the line of position should be constructed.

Precomputing sun sights can be accomplished using HO 249 Volume II for latitudes 0° to 39° or Volume III for latitudes 40° to 89° together with the *Nautical Almanac* for the determination of the Greenwich Hour Angle (GHA) of the sun and its declination (Dec.).

The first step is to select the days and also the hours that you plan to take your sights. (Note the Increments and Corrections section of the *Nautical Almanac* is eliminated if you take them exactly on the hour.)

The next step is to determine an assumed position for each observation. One good way to do this is to plot the fastest and the slowest speeds that you might conceivably make good along your proposed DR track. If the cruise or race is long, the same latitudes may have to be considered for successive days.

The steps involved in precomputing a solution for a sunline are illustrated in Figure 1. This particular ex-

Precomputation of the Lower Limb of the Sun for Monday, June 19, 1972 at 1200 GMT (0800 EDT)

```
LAT = 35°
GHA = 359° 40.5'
DEC =  23° 26.0'
AZ  =  82°

ASSUMED LONG = 66° 40.5'
LHA = GHA - ASSUMED LONG
    = 359° 40.5'
    -  66° 40.5'
LHA = 293° 00.0'

DEC = 23° 26.0'
          d = +28
            = 12.0' (FROM TABLE)
Hc  = 31° 15.0'
    +     12.0'
Hc  = 31° 27.0'
          MAIN CORRECTION = +14.4'
           DIP CORRECTION = - 2.7
           NET CORRECTION = +11.7'
Hp = Hc + NET CORRECTION REVERSED
   = 31° 27.0'
   + (-11.7)
Hp = 31° 15.3'
```

Figure 1

ample comes from precomputations prepared for the Bermuda Race for Monday, June 19, 1972, at 1200 GMT (0800 EDT), latitude 35°N.

First get the Greenwich Hour Angle of the sun (359°40.5') and its declination (23°26.0') from the *Nautical Almanac* for the selected day and hour. Next select, on 35°N, an assumed longitude which, when subtracted from the GHA of the sun, will give the result, the Local Hour Angle (LHA) in a round number. You will need this for entry into the tables.

In this case we therefore adopt an assumed longitude of 66°40.5'. It is near the rhumb line but it has the same number of minutes as the GHA. Subtracting the two results gives an LHA of exactly 293°.

Then using the three arguments, Latitude 35°, LHA 293°, and the even degrees of declination of 23°, enter HO 249, Volume II, page 213, and read Hc 31°15', d of +28, and an azimuth of 82°. Although you entered with the declination of 23°, the actual declination was 23°26.0'. The d correction of +28 must therefore be applied to the extra 26' of declination. Table 4 at the back of HO 249 gives this correction to altitude of 12'. Add this to the 31°15' to get the Hc of 31°27'.

You must now apply the main correction and the correction for dip to your Hc. Both are normally applied

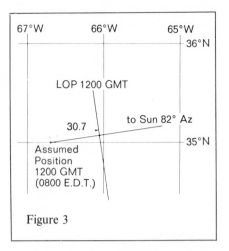

Figure 3

to the sextant angle (Hs) which in precomputation you will not determine until the planned time for observation.

The same result can be obtained, however, if you use the Hc (31°27') and reverse the signs on both corrections. Take 31°27' and go to the inside front cover of the *Nautical Almanac*. Read off the main correction of +14.4' (using the lower limb of the sun) and −2.7' for dip. We'll assume your height of eye will be 8 feet above sea level when taking sights. The net correction is +11.7'. But you now *reverse* the sign and *subtract* 11.7' from the Hc of 31°27.0' to get a precomputed altitude (Hp) for June 19 at 1200 GMT of 31°15.3'.

With a series of such precomputations you can make a sheet of precomputed altitudes for an entire day and even an entire race (Fig. 2)!

All you need to do now is to compare this precomputed altitude directly with the actual sextant altitude when it is taken, and the line of position (LOP) can be drawn with great speed and accuracy.

On the appropriate day (June 19, 1972) at exactly 1200 GMT (0800 EDT), go on deck and take your sight of the lower limb of the sun. Let's

EDT	DR Long.	Hp	Az
8 a.m.	66°40.5'	31°15.3'	82°
10 a.m.	66°40.2'	55°43.4'	100°
12 Noon	66°40.0'	76°42.0'	151°
2 p.m.	66°39.7'	66°42.2'	245°
4 p.m.	66°39.4'	42°40.7'	270°

Figure 2

assume you have no sextant error and you read 31°46′ directly from the sextant. All you have to do now is subtract the precomputed Hp of 31°15.3′ from the sextant reading of 31°46′ to get 30.7′. This means that your line of position (LOP) can then be constructed in the normal manner at right angles to the azimuth line of 82°. It will be located 30.7 miles from your assumed position *towards* the sun (Fig. 3).

If the sextant angle were smaller than the precomputed angle, the line of position would still be drawn at right angles to the azimuth but in the opposite direction, i.e., away from the sun.

Perhaps the sun is temporarily obscured at the planned observation time. You can still use the precomputed altitude method. If you take a later sight, move the assumed position one full degree to the west for each four minutes after the scheduled time for observation. For larger or smaller times, the distance west is proportionally larger or smaller. The change in azimuth for short time delays will not create any serious errors in plotting the line of position.

Let's assume the clouds clear away and the sun, which has been rising, is observed at a higher altitude of 32°35′ (Hs) exactly 4 minutes after the hour you had originally selected. Move the assumed position 1° to the west to 67°40.5′. Subtract the original precomputed altitude for 0800 EDT (31°15.3′) for the new sextant reading and you will get a difference of 1°19.7′ or 79.7′. The line of position is then constructed just as before but from the *new* assumed position, and this LOP will be 79.7 miles *towards* the sun because the actual sextant altitude is greater than the precomputed altitude.

The biggest advantages of this method are the speed with which a line of position can be determined and the fact that the preparatory work can be done in advance slowly, accurately, and without pressure or distraction. For an ocean racing navigator, lines of position can be drawn easily every hour or even more often if desired. A minimum series of daily sights could be at 8 a.m., 12 Noon, and 4 in the afternoon.

And for the cruising man, the "too much like work" atmosphere is supplanted by the pleasure and ease of taking the results of a sextant observation and using it with a precomputed altitude. It may be the technique you've been looking for!

Precomputed Star Sights

By Robert Silverman

Many cruising and racing sailors shy away from star sights. During the past four years while we have been cruising, I have kept a casual running survey in my conversations with other boat people and found this to be the case. In most instances, people lacked confidence in bringing down the correct star. Difficulty in dealing with a fading horizon was the next common complaint, and finally, some people did not want to bother with what they felt was an excessive amount of computation.

Hundreds of small boats do make long, difficult passages year after year, arriving at their destinations by using morning, noon, and afternoon sun observations, and advancing each line of position (LOP) in a system of running fixes. In most cases this will suffice. However, the accuracy of this procedure is only as good as the navigator's estimate of his speed and course made good — judgments that can be greatly influenced by a cranky windvane or fatigue in a short-handed crew. But, if you can get a good star fix, you know, without doubt, that the vessel's position was such-and-such.

By precomputing star sights, a navigator can find the desired stars in the sextant's telescope before they are visible to the naked eye. Thus the best possible horizon is available, and you don't waste time searching and fumbling for the cor-

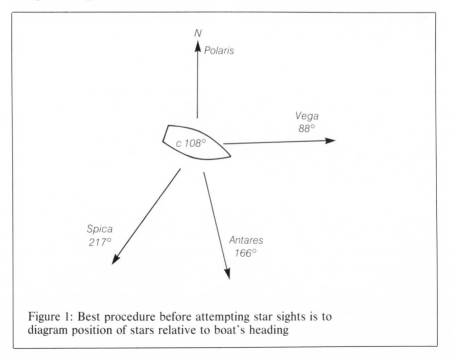

Figure 1: Best procedure before attempting star sights is to diagram position of stars relative to boat's heading

Precomputation for Sextant Setting and Bearing of Antares

Local time	19h 42m
Add zone description	2h
GMT	21h 42m
Greenwich Hour Angle Aries, June 30, 1978 (from Nautical Almanac)	244° 05.9'
SHA (Sidereal Hour Angle) Antares added	112° 58.4'
Greenwich Hour Angle Antares, 21 42m GMT	357° 04.3'
Assumed Longitude 32° West, subtracted	32° 04.3'
	325
Subtract from 360	360
	325
Local Hour Angle Antares	35°
Enter H.O. 229 with arguments LHA 35°, Latitude 39 North, and declination of Antares, South 26° 23.0'	
Computed altitude	16° 55'
Set sextant	16° 55'
True bearing of Antares at 21h 42m GMT	147.3°
Add westerly variation	18°
Magnetic bearing Antares at 21h 42m GMT	165.3°

rect celestial body. Precomputation does involve some extra steps, but they are simple and take little extra time. With good preparation and good weather, you can observe a round of stars in a matter of minutes and even in poor weather, the navigator has the advantage of being prepared *in advance* to snap a star sight if the star suddenly appears in a break of overcast conditions.

I am assuming that you understand the principles of celestial navigation and can plot a star sight. If you can't, there are many thorough texts on the subject that will describe the method and procedure to you.

To begin any precomputation, first compute the actual local time of sunset for your position. Then, select a time between sunset and civil twilight, and this time will be the starting point for your observations. You must convert it to Greenwich Mean Time (GMT), and you must compute the Local Hour Angle of each selected star for that time.

Then, with the Local Hour Angle, the latitude, and the star's declination, you can enter H.O. 229 and take out the computed altitude and the true bearing. Set your sextant to the altitude and convert the true bearing to magnetic.

At the selected time, position yourself toward the known bearing of the star. As you sweep the sextant in slow, horizontal arcs to scan the field of view, the star should appear in the field. If time passes and the star does not appear, adjust the setting of the sextant. The altitude of the star is always changing — 15 minutes of arc for the passage of every minute of time. The altitudes of stars in the east will be increasing while those in the west will be decreasing.

Once the star does appear in the field of view, you can refine the sight and time it in the usual way. Then continue around the horizon, taking as many stars as possible, always remembering to note the time and to adjust the sextant settings accordingly. It is not necessary to worry about a bearing for the change is very small.

Then calculate the difference in time between the actual time of the sight and the time that you pre-selected for starting. Next, turn to the increment and correction tables in the *Nautical Almanac* and convert this time to arc. Add this number to the precomputed Greenwich Hour Angle (GHA) of the star, correcting it to the actual time of the sight which you then finish and plot in the usual way.

You will encounter certain problems before you become thoroughly acquainted with this procedure. Like most other aspects of sailing, practice and experience are the best teachers. However, the following thoughts should be helpful.

• For someone unfamiliar with star sights, begin by observing the major constellations at night, picking out the various navigational stars and noting their movements with time.

• When you should start taking observations is something that cannot be stated with certainty, for the weather always affects the state of clarity. But because bright stars such as *Vega* appear early in the duration between sunset and civil twilight, common sense dictates that you take the brightest stars first. Take stars to the east earlier than stars in the west for the easterly horizon will fade first. In tropical latitudes, you must start earlier and work more quickly for the period of twilight is shorter than it is in the higher latitudes.

• To minimize confusion when you are beginning to take a round of stars, have a diagram of the boat's heading with the direction of each selected star indicated by an arrow. Calculate the true direction of each selected star from H.O. 229 *Sight*

Precomputation using H.O. 249, Vol. 1

GHA Aries, 21h 42m GMT	244° 05.9'
Subtract assumed longitude	32° 05.9' West
LHA Aries	212°
Enter 39° North Latitude page for stars with LHA Aries	212°
Set sextant to precomputed altitude of Antares	16° 55'
True bearing 148° Convert to magnetic	166°

Computation of Antares

Antares observed	21h 50m 53s GMT
Time difference between actual sight and precomputation	8m 53s
Convert to arc in increments and minute correction table	2° 13.6'
Add to precomputed GHA Antares	357° 04.1'
GHA Antares at time of sight	359° 17.7'
Assumed Longitude, subtract	32° 17.7' West
	327
Subtract from 360	360
	327
Local Hour Angle Antares at time of sight	33°
H.O. 229 entered again	
Computed altitude	17° 42.7'
Observed altitude	17° 51.6'
Intercept Toward	8.9'
Zn	149°

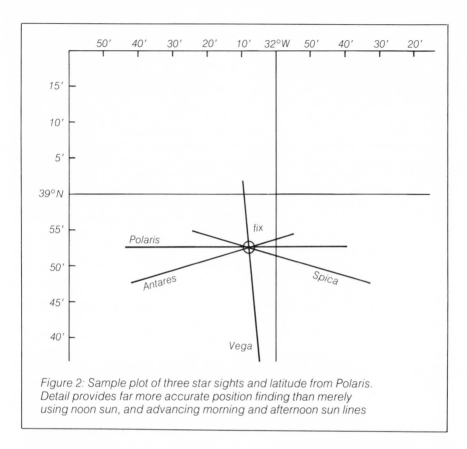

Figure 2: Sample plot of three star sights and latitude from Polaris.
Detail provides far more accurate position finding than merely
using noon sun, and advancing morning and afternoon sun lines

Reduction Tables for Marine Navigation or take it from H.O. 249 *Sight Reduction Tables for Air Navigation*. Then correct it to magnetic and orient it to the boat's course (Fig. 1). For further reference, make, in advance, a table showing each star's altitude and its change with time, for no one I know can keep track of so many numbers in his head.

• Choose a sextant that has a telescope with a wide field of view and good light-gathering characteristics. This is very important. The older sextant with a long brass scope that looks so nautical may not be the best choice for star work. Its field of view could be so limited that you would have a hard time finding the desired star.

• Finally, you can simplify the entire procedure by using Vol. 1 of H.O. 249. This volume has as its argument the *Local Hour Angle of Aries* in the left-hand column. You compute this from your longitude, turn to the correct latitude page, and find a group of stars presented.

These stars have been preselected for their availability, with precomputed altitudes and true bearings for each degree of change in the *Local Hour Angle of Aries*. Sometimes stars that you have used before are not listed, for their altitudes may be considered too high or too low. But if you are used to picking out a particular star (and familiarity is the best guide), you can precompute any of the navigational stars not offered in H.O. 249 from H.O. 229.

Here is an example, from start to finish, for the star *Antares,* taken at sea between Bermuda and the Azores (39°N, 32°W).

Calculation, Local Time of Sunset. Time of sunset from *Nautical Almanac,* June 30, 1978, for Latitude North 35°

19h 18m

Correction for Assumed Latitude North 39° from table p. xxxii. To be added

06m

19h 24m

Subtract zone description for Longitude 32° West for local time

2h

17h 24m

Convert assumed longitude 32° West to arc from time table and add

2h 08m

19h 32m

By inspecting the *Nautical Almanac* for the duration between sunset and civil twilight, you find a period of 29 minutes. Personally, I would allow 10 minutes to pass for sufficient darkness for then you can see in the sextant's telescope bright stars such as *Vega* or *Antares,* although they are not yet visible to the naked eye.

So, in this example, you would add 10 minutes to the local time of sunset (19h 32m) so the local time 19h 42m is when you should begin observing.

Following the same method, you observe *Vega* and *Spica.* Finally, you set the sextant to your assumed latitude (39 degrees) and make a timed observation of *Polaris.* Figure 2 describes the resulting plot.

Under practical conditions, three stars well spaced around the horizon are sufficient for a fix. But I urge those of you who want to perfect your technique to take advantage of those beautiful clear twilights you often experience at sea and to take as many star sights as possible. Remember always to try to have them well spaced around the horizon. The expertise you gain might one day provide you with that slim margin between a safe passage and an uncertain position.

Latitude by Polaris and Mintaka

By William V. Kielhorn

Polaris is really a rather poor navigational star. To begin with, it is a little less bright than second magnitude (Mag. 2.1), and therefore it cannot be seen unless the sky is quite clear when the horizon is still faintly visible. Furthermore, because the southern parts of the north-latitude oceans are generally a little cloudy or hazy, you might well forget this star when you are at 10°N or less. Nevertheless, Polaris does have some redeeming properties: the best one of course is that it is very near the north celestial pole.

This was not always the case. Only 2000 years ago Polaris was about 18° from the North Pole. How would you like to assume this was the "Pole Star" and end up with a maximum error more than 1000 miles from your true latitude? That could ruin your landfall, for sure. But you may rest easily; for now, and for the rest of your lifetime, this star will remain very close (within 1°, or 60 nautical miles) to the North Pole.

Some night this winter, when the sky is sparkling clear, point your camera towards the North Pole, and leave the shutter open for the whole night. You will find the concentric trail of Polaris and all the circumpolar stars etched beautifully on your film. Polaris will describe the smallest circle on the exposure.

The navigators of Europe and the Mediterranean countries knew much about Polaris as a "pole star" in the eleventh century A.D. and devised intricate methods for correcting its position for use in determining latitude. Remember, Polaris was still quite far from the North Pole then, and corrections were very important. Most of the systems were based on the relative angular position of "The Guards," which were comprised of the outer two stars of the "Little Dipper" (Ursa minor), Kochab and Gamma-Ursae minoris.

In one system the North Pole was represented to be at the heart of a

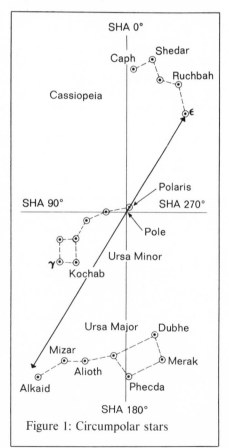

Figure 1: Circumpolar stars

man standing upright on the northern horizon, his arms extended east and west. Various rules were applied for corrections as "The Guards" approached the imaginary figure's arms, feet, or head. It was all very romantic, and some of the rules appeared in poetry of the times. Even Columbus used these methods, although he could use meridian altitudes of the sun, as well. It is certain, however, that Columbus used Polaris not only for latitude, but also for direction. In fact, his log is the earliest written record of a navigator that shows the variation of magnetic north from true north as determined by observations of Polaris.

Figure 1 illustrates the primary circumpolar stars contained in the three prominent constellations of Ursa major, Ursa minor, and Cassiopeia. Strangely, one of the stars of greatest importance in this discussion doesn't even have a name listed in the Almanacs. This is the northernmost of the five stars forming the "W" (or the "M") of Cassiopeia and is designated as ϵ (epsilon) Cassiopeia. This weak star has almost the same sidereal hour angle (SHA) as Polaris, and therefore Polaris is in line with it and the North Pole. The same line extended past the Pole just clears the last star of the "Big Dipper" (Alkaid).

In 1974, Polaris had a SHA of 328°08′ and a declination of 89°9.0′; it therefore was 51′ from the North Pole. It is apparent that when ϵ-Cassiopeia is *at the same altitude* as Polaris, then the true altitude of Polaris is equal to your own latitude; when ϵ-Cassiopeia is *directly above* Polaris you must subtract 51′ from the true altitude of Polaris to obtain your latitude. And when ϵ-Cassiopeia is *directly below* Polaris,

51′ must be added to the true altitude to get your latitude.

If you have a small six-inch slide rule aboard, and you should have, it is easy enough to estimate the angle of ϵ-Cassiopeia to the right or left of Polaris and multiply 51′ by the cosine of that angle to find the correction, *subtracting* when Cassiopeia is *above* Polaris, and *adding* when Cassiopeia is below Polaris.

For example, let's assume that ϵ-Cassiopeia is 45° to the right (or left) of Polaris, and above it. What is the correction?

$$51' \times \cos 45° = 51' \times .71 = 36'$$

If your corrected sextant readings are:

H_o 41°21′
Corr.   (−) 36′
              40°45′N latitude (answer)

If ϵ-Cassiopeia is not in view, use Alkaid and *reverse* the sign of the correction.

Some major navigational textbooks, such as Dutton's, have a simple table for Polaris corrections. The following table is one updated for the star's present declination:

ϵ-Cassiopeia

Angle from vertical	Correction
0°	51′
10°	50′
20°	48′
30°	44′
40°	39′
50°	33′
60°	26′
70°	17′
80°	9′
90°	0′

How could you do all this if you had no *Almanac* and thus couldn't convert sextant altitude to true altitude? It is done easily enough. On the average cruising yacht, your height of eye is about 10 feet. Also the chances are you won't be cruising in the Arctic, and you won't see Polaris when you are near the equator anyway. So, assume you are somewhere between 25°N and 50°N. The correction for refraction is constant to about a mile (one minute of arc) for this whole range. Apply the total correction to the sextant reading (assuming no additional instrumental errors) as follows:

Corr. for H.E. 10 feet = $-3.1'$
Corr. for refraction   = $-1.5'$

Total = $\overline{-4.6'}$

If you are working to the nearest minute of arc (which is adequate for Polaris sights) just subtract 5 feet from your sextant reading.

Let's take a whole example and see how it works. You are cruising the North Pacific one evening and sight Polaris. Epsilon Cassiopeia appears below Polaris at an angle of about 25° to the westward of the vertical (Fig. 2). Assume the sextant has no significant instrument error, and reads 30°15′, what is your latitude?

$30°15'$ H_s
$-5'$ Corr.

$30°10'$ H_o
$+46'$ $51' \times \cos 25°$, or table

$30°56'$ N. Latitude

Don't be too fussy with Polaris. Because of its weak magnitude the horizon will be pretty dark when it appears, and you will be doing well to get your latitude accurate to a few miles. As I said, Polaris is not a very good navigational star, but it does have some very convenient attributes.

Latitude and Azimuth by Mintaka.
You may have never heard of the star Mintaka; it isn't listed as such

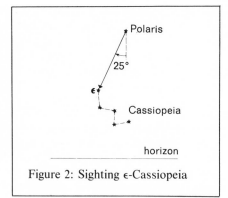

Figure 2: Sighting ε-Cassiopeia

among the stars in the *Nautical Almanac*. Another name for it is Δ-Orionis (delta-Orionis), and it appears as the northernmost star in the "belt" of Orion at a declination of about 0°19′S. Because it is so close to the celestial equator it, like Polaris, may be used for determining latitude without using your tables or having to memorize very much. This beautiful winter constellation is shown in Figure 3.

On a clear moonlit evening the horizon may stand out in the path of the moon while Mintaka rises to its highest as it crosses your meridian. When it does so, just add 19′ to your corrected sextant altitude. If you are in the northern oceans subtract this angle from 90°00′, and there it is — your latitude. Of course, you can do a "meridian altitude" with any celestial body, but who can always remember all those declinations?

Mintaka is superb as a directional star. As long as you are not in latitudes higher than 60° (and who wants to be?), no matter what the time of year, Mintaka will faithfully rise almost exactly true east and set true west. But a word of caution here. You can see a star well before it rises and well after it sets because of the refraction of light in the earth's atmosphere. The rule is this: for the stars, sun, or planets, observe rising

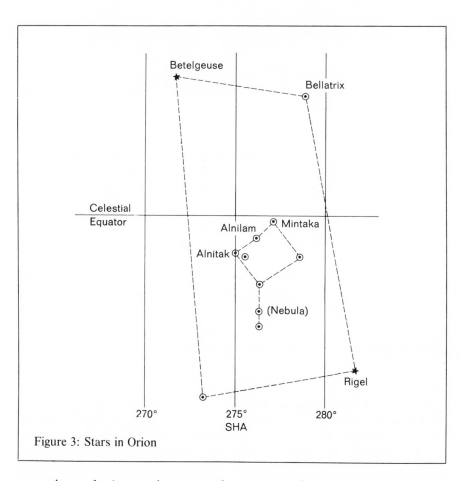

Figure 3: Stars in Orion

or setting at the *instant* the center of the body is about one sun diameter (actually about 35′) *above* the horizon. With a little practice you can get pretty good at this.

The one exception is the moon. It is so close to us that the horizontal parallax is significant. So *its* rising and setting moment is calculated when the *upper* edge (upper limb) just touches the horizon.

So you can see that latitude by Polaris or Mintaka is not a big prob-lem when the sky is really clear. You don't really need an Almanac, Sight Reduction Tables, or even a very good memory. Just remember that Polaris is 51′ from the pole in the direction of ε-Cassiopeia, and Minta-ka is 19′S of the equator. With this information, you can find your lati-tude and direction easily without tables, much more accurately than the ancients. And look how well *they* did!

Set Your Sights on Celestial

Every now and then you read of yet another shipwrecked sailboat and are reminded that not all ocean voyages become fully realized escapes to a South Seas utopia. More passages than you think terminate with the loss of the boat and a threat to the lives of the crew.

While the story of a foundering sailboat brings to mind the image of a raging gale and mountainous seas, often these wrecks occur in conditions quite unlike those presented in Hollywood dramas. Most shipwreck victims have little chance to use their life raft or bluewater survival skills. What they do use are heavy boots and thick clothing to prevent abrasion as they make their way ashore over a tide-swept reef.

The uncharted reef seldom is responsible for the loss of a cruising boat. Most of the time the fault rests with the crew rather than with the Hydrographic Office. Being where you *think* you are and knowing what navigational trick to use next are requirements that are at the heart of every safe passage. Dead reckoning can be deadly, and speed and direction estimates should never be the primary factors in offshore navigation. Current set and leeway effects can become significant over successive days of an offshore passage, so it is imperative that you are able to fix your own position.

Obviously when you are in sight of recognizable land features, your handbearing compass becomes a vital instrument. In the pelagic realm, the sextant and chronometer become the basic tools of the trade. Though modern electronic equipment has facilitated position determination, making an offshore passage without a capable celestial navigator aboard is simply poor seamanship.

What are the differences between "textbook" navigation and the reality of getting a celestial offshore position aboard a small boat? Cruising shorthanded for four years with my wife and two young children across three great oceans, I became very conscious of the problems involved with achieving navigational accuracy. By the time we sailed from California to French Polynesia we had heard a half-dozen tales of cruising tragedy. Five of them occurred because the boat was thirty miles or more away from its estimated position. Reliance upon dead reckoning (DR) and an occasional noon sight seemed to be the most prevalant navigational technique for those boats. But as I mentioned earlier, current can drastically affect the accuracy of every speed and direction that is based on estimates. Getting latitude and longitude from a single noon sight can add inaccuracies, for even though the arithmetic is simple, errors can crop up from the near-zenith position of a tropical sun during a good portion of the year. Timing the exact meridian passage is difficult; the end result is that anyone who navigates solely by noon sights and DR is not using celestial navigation to its maximum accuracy.

What you need is a multifaceted approach, and all your DR records should be updated daily by celestial fixes. In comparing the two positions, your DR position and the fix position, you can then see the effect of current and leeway on your progress. Current charts, accurate speed and distance measuring instruments, and a careful recording of all course information increase your accuracy. Even so, a DR-dominated method of offshore navigation can lead to trouble.

My own celestial techniques vary with the area. If I am in open ocean well away from hungry reefs, I follow a simple process of sun sight observations. I take two sights, one in mid-morning and the other in early afternoon. I choose times to give me approximately a 90-degree intersection of the line of positions (LOPs), I advance the first LOP to the second LOP; the intersection gives me a double fix. Of course, errors can come in from the data I use to advance the first observation to the second. Fortunately, the near midday sun in tropical regions changes its azimuth quickly, and the time involved between the two sights is going to be only a matter of two to four hours. When the time span is this short, your speed/distance position indicators are more reliable, and the potential for error when advancing an LOP should be minimal.

As I near my landfall, or I come to a reef-strewn passage such as the Lau Islands of Fiji, I supplement my sun with star, planet, and moon observations. Dusk and dawn rounds of these celestial sights give the most precise fix, for all the errors involved in advancing an earlier LOP are eliminated.

Choosing the right time for a star sight is critical, for good horizon contrast and the celestial body brightness are indirectly correlated. I like a good horizon contrast and so take my sights early in the evening twilight period. The *Nautical Almanac* has daily time calculations you can use to figure the optimum time for a dusk or dawn round of observations. If there is a full moon, I try to take sights throughout the night. And by choosing stars that have LOPs approaching a right angle, I minimize the effects of horizon parallax. Being able to use whatever celestial body is available is a very important skill that you must have if you are sailing offshore.

Sailing from Tonga to Fiji, we were confronted by nearly continuous overcast. On the second day out, during partial breaks in the dense cumulus overcast, I did get a hazy sun shot late in the afternoon. Later that evening another break in the clouds gave me a chance to measure the altitude of the moon, and after I advanced the LOP of the sun sight to the later moon sight I had a reliable fix. I found a current had moved us twenty-five miles north over the forty-eight-hour period!

Though lack of visibility can be a problem for any offshore navigator who relies on celestial techniques, fortunately the tropical regions of the world experience clear conditions more often than any other region; conditions on my way to Fiji were the exception rather than the rule. This is why the trade-wind belts of the Pacific, Atlantic, and Indian oceans are well suited to celestial navigation.

At first, I used *H. O. 249* for my sight reductions. *Volume 1* of the series is especially good for fast star computations. Certain stars are preselected and partially computed, and they are usually visible. When they are obscured, the planets can be worthwhile targets; Venus and Jupiter both are considerably brighter than first magnitude stars. Occasionally, the difference in luminescence between stars and planets may be enough to get you a celestial observation.

During our Indian Ocean and Atlantic Ocean passages, I used a programmed calculator for my sight reductions. It proved to be a reliable, versatile time saver, for it eliminated all the long-hand calculation as well as the plotting of an LOP. Final calculator readouts are given in latitude and longitude. Most programmed calculators can store and compare sights, and the chance of an arithmetical error is greatly reduced. Calculators are good navigational aids as long as you know what to do in the event of electronic failure. A pencil, paper, and reduction table system must also be completely familiar to you.

A few sextant tricks have proved helpful to me. Most important is the old *twist of the wrist* rule. When measuring the altitude of a celestial body, I rotate my sextant-holding hand from side to side. The image of the body I am looking at scribes an arc tangent to the horizon, and I adjust the micrometer drum so the lower limb of the sun or the point image of a star touches at the bottom the arc. This means the object now is perpendicular to the horizon, which is vital for an accurate fix.

I have removed the four-power telescope from my sextant and find it improves my sight taking as well as my accuracy. Under most conditions, a sailboat under 60 feet isn't stable enough to benefit from the magnification of a sextant telescope. The increased image size may be a slight advantage, but the increased apparent motion and decrease in the field of view are a noticeable deterrent to accurate sight taking. However, a two-power scope might be helpful in light to moderate sea conditions.

My wife records the time (Coordinated Universal Time) from the chronometer during each sight. When I have the celestial image situated on the horizon, I call, "Mark." She records the seconds, minutes, hours, and date, in that order. I use 10 and 15 mHz WWV broadcasts to determine any chronometer error. Rather than resetting the timepiece to compensate for variations from the Coordinated Universal Time, I log the deviation and compute a rate. If for some reason the radio time signals can't be received, I use this rate to compensate for the timepiece error.

Be sure you select a timepiece with an easy-to-read minute scale. You can have an accurate watch, but it is no help to you if you can't read the minute hands. A few seconds of error can be a problem, but a whole minute can lead to real trouble. Select a chronometer with an easily read dial or one with a digital readout.

Being well organized is another important key to success in navigation. The location of things in a navigation area and the work process itself should be standardized, for following a familiar format always seems to improve the overall result. I find that during the first few days of a passage the boat's motion and the return to offshore living makes me prone to navigational errors. But if I use a well-practiced routine the transition is simplified. On a passage that begins with a hazardous leg, I always spend additional time on my celestial work. If reefs are nearby, but haven't been sighted, I advance several sun LOPs during the day, and I also shoot a round of stars at dawn and dusk. I

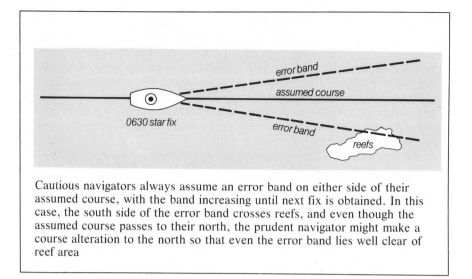

Cautious navigators always assume an error band on either side of their assumed course, with the band increasing until next fix is obtained. In this case, the south side of the error band crosses reefs, and even though the assumed course passes to their north, the prudent navigator might make a course alteration to the north so that even the error band lies well clear of reef area

check my chronometer daily using the WWV broadcasts.

Long-distance sailing veterans also develop their own limits of navigational accuracy, which basically are estimates of how far off course they *could* be under existing conditions. They can then plot a course line as a *stripe* whose width depends on the accuracy and frequency of the navigational input. When gale conditions exist, boat motion and overcast affect the accuracy of celestial sights and the error band widens. When the sea is calm and the sky clear, the potential for accurate celestial navigation is high, and under these conditions, the width of the error band is narrow. The amount of time between sights should also be reflected in the error band. As the time from the last fix increases, your error band width should also increase (see figure).

Plotting an error band rather than a single course line drives home an important navigational concept. A navigator who is wrong about his "pinpoint location" is in more serious trouble than his counterpart who uses the error band concept.

Discovering how far off your celestial pencil line you might be is another part of being a good navigator. The best way to learn how good your celestial accuracy is, is to practice with landmarks you can use for reference backed up, if possible, by electronics. Understanding how far you could be away from your celestial fix, because of your own capabilities, is almost as important as getting the fix itself.

Start by plotting the band on both sides of the course line and let the band gradually expand as the time from the last fix increases. The next fix that you establish with a landmark or electronic aids should fall within the error band. The closer you are to your assumed position, the better. If your error band always seems to be too wide, the accuracy of your celestial sights is good. But remember that error always varies with sea conditions and the quality of your celestial observations. Once you know your own potential for inaccuracy you can be ready for potential chart hazards that lie within your error tolerance zone. My point is that thinking of your boat as a pinpoint on a chart will work only for those with a satellite navigation system aboard or those using a small scale chart of the entire solar system.

The South Pacific is filled with testimonies to navigational inaccuracy. These coral reef monuments come in wood, fiberglass, ferrocement, and steel. Insurance companies attach a one out of every ten statistic to their listings of world cruising casualties. And a vast majority of those who do come to grief are very surprised to discover where they actually are when they hit. The answer is that celestial navigation, when it is properly used, can get you there and back, safely.

4

RACING

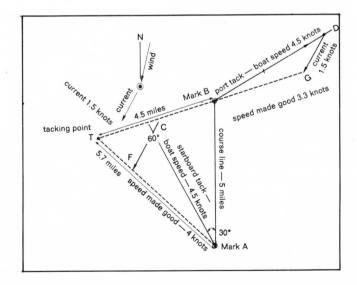

Good Navigation Begins at Home

By Richard T. du Moulin

You are about to make a Bermuda landfall without visibility in a storm, and you discover you can't find the correct chart. Your quick sextant shot of the sun through a break in the clouds is useless because your *Nautical Almanac* is out of date. Your only log impeller has just been knocked off, and the cook is taking bets on how far off your next position will be. It would be unfortunate indeed if any of these things happened on your next ocean voyage or race, but the probability is fairly high that you will leave several key navigation items ashore or that some of your instruments will either be inoperative or uncalibrated.

To be ready for sea, an ocean racing or cruising boat must not only be well designed and well built, she must also be prepared in all possible ways. Tuning, sail inventory, crew training, helmsman experience, fuel/food/water supplies, and safety and repair equipment and procedures are some of the more important areas. But detailed preparations must also be made and completed for your navigation station. Usually the state of the nav station is the responsibility of the navigator, and for some cruises and races this preparation— the ordering of charts and gathering of information—can take several months. The following steps outline the preparations you, as a navigator, must make:

• Inventory, inspect, and test all navigation instruments, charts, publications, and gear aboard your boat.

• List all necessary instruments, charts, publications, and gear needed for the cruise, the race(s), and return passage. This listing alone often requires considerable research and thinking.

• Compare this list with the actual inventory list to determine what additional items must be ordered and what gear needs repairs.

• Gather all the information concerning strategy: weather patterns and broadcasts, currents, past races, and special race instructions. You as a navigator are always a key source of information and strategy during a cruise or race.

• Test and calibrate all your instruments at least several days before the race.

• Stow all listed gear aboard the boat.

• Take a final inventory of all gear the day before the race or cruise starts.

A checklist makes your navigator's job much easier and more thorough. My own checklist is included here, but each navigator or skipper may want to customize it to suit his own boat and tastes. The critical thing is to *have* and to *use* a list of some kind. Otherwise, it is going to be almost inevitable that some day you will be in a situation that requires a certain chart or piece of gear, and you will not have that essential piece of information that will allow you to make the right decision.

NAVIGATOR'S CHECKLIST

Instruments

1. Main compass(es)
   recent deviation card
   light working?
   spare bulbs?
2. Spare compass(es)
   recent deviation card
   satisfactory mounting
3. VHF or SSB radios
   radiocheck all frequencies
   all stations marked?
   correct frequencies (crystals are
      hard to get)
   spare antenna tested?
   call sign posted?
4. Radio direction finder(s)
   checked on a nearby beacon
   best position on boat
   spare batteries?
5. Depthfinder(s)
   tested against leadline?
   necessary correction posted?
   spare batteries?

6. Speedometer/log
   each thru-hull unit on calibrated
      carefully measured runs?
   correction factors posted?
   spare batteries?
   spare thru-hull units (impellers
      or wands)?
7. Chronometer
   safe storage
   calibrated over a period of at least
      one week?
   correction factor taped on case
   spare battery
8. Barometer (barograph)
   calibrated against local weather
      station?
   (extra paper, ink, key for baro-
      graph?)
9. Sextant(s)
   safe storage
   index correction
   filters attached
   general condition
   light functioning
   spare battery?

10. Loran, omega, etc.
    antenna working?
    all available stations tested?
    necessary charts
11. Omnirange
    antenna okay?
    nearby station tested?
    IFR supplement (listing stations)
12. Radio receivers
    antenna okay?
    key frequencies (time signals,
       weather) checked?
13. Miscellaneous
    instruction manuals for all instru-
       ments
    spare fuses and parts
    wiring diagram of yacht
    running lights functional
    battery generator/alternator
       functional

Charts and publications

1. *Charts*: folded, labeled, updated, preplotted courses, and notes all required charts: _____ spares of: _____
   charts of harbors of refuge along the course: _____
   Pilot Chart(s) of months: _____
   current charts: _____
   loran charts: _____
   chart catalog
2. U.S. Coast Guard Light Lists: _____
3. Radio aids to navigation (appropriate sections)
4. Radio weather aids (appropriate sections)
5. Sailing directions (appropriate sections)
6. Coastal pilots: _____
7. IFR supplement (Omni stations) for months: _____
8. Aeronautical charts: _____
9. International Rules of the Road
10. Nautical Almanac (correct year)
11. Air Almanac (correct quarter)
12. Celestial tables: HO 249, Vol. I, II, III
13. Celestial tables: HO 229, Volumes _____
14. Sight reduction forms
15. Starfinder
16. Dutton's navigation text
17. Bowditch text
18. USYRU Racing Rules
19. Circulars (2) of the race
20. Special race instructions
21. Calculator (if allowed), spare battery, and converter

Implements

1. Large parallel rules (18")
2. Small parallel rules (12")
3. Rolling parallel rules
4. Dividers (2 pairs)
5. Compass (circle-drawing type)
6. Triangles [45°-45°-90° (2); 30°-60°-90° (1)]
7. Pencils (12)
8. Pens (6)
9. Pencil sharpener
10. Magic markers
11. Cellophane tape
12. Pads (3)
13. Small notebooks (2)
14. Racing logs (2), bound and printed
15. Weather log
16. Speed-time-distance slide rule
17. Downwind tacking tables

This list covers a wide range of materials and instrumentation that you can add to or subtract from, depending on your own sailing situation

Keeping on Top of the Situation

By Michel G. Emmanuel

Today's electronic instruments, which are available at reasonable prices, allow even those offshore racers that are campaigned on a modest budget to be well equipped in this department. Electronic instruments measuring boat speed, relative wind angle and apparent wind speed, when properly installed and accurately calibrated, are basic to maintaining consistently high performance. But what's the best way to record the information gleaned from them? By keeping proper logs.

What form a log should take is a question that each owner or navigator must answer in accordance with personal preference, for a log is a personal thing. Many experienced offshore sailors use relatively simple forms while others prefer to record a greater variety of information.

I would like to suggest that, ideally, an offshore racing log should be kept in two parts: a *deck log* and a *navigation log*. While the navigator may supervise the keeping of the deck log, it should be the primary responsibility of the watch captains to make the entries. The navigation log, on the other hand, is *solely* the navigator's responsibility. The two should supplement each other so that, when read together, they give the complete picture.

The Deck Log. A clipboard holding sheets of paper ruled into appropriate columns makes a satisfactory deck log. Although it is primarily a performance record, the deck log can serve an important secondary function as a check list for the watch on deck. Each skipper will have his own opinion about the layout and data to be collected but such a log can, and should, take in everything from the date, time, tack, compass heading, wind, sea conditions, halyard and backstay tensions to trim, heel, and sails in use.

All entries should be made in the deck log at half-hour intervals on a routine watch, more often if conditions change. The helmsman and watch captain always should agree on the average compass heading steered during each half-hour segment and enter that course in the log. As minor changes in wind direction and velocity occur, trim adjustments also should be made and logged. Major changes in wind and sea conditions will require sail changes and other gear adjustments. While the deck log can carry *true* wind direction and velocity (as well as *apparent* wind) I would like to suggest that this entry is more properly placed within the navigator's operational area and should be put in the navigation log.

Painted reference marks and numbers help the crew to record the positions of jib leads as well as traveler and centerboard positions. Tension on the jib halyard can be measured by marking the wire halyard and noting the position of the mark or marks relative to a scale of numbers painted or glued to the side of the mast. Allowance should be made for stretch, however, and always remember that there is no substitute for properly eyeballing a sail. There are too many variables involved to permit a sail to be trimmed just by the numbers.

Backstay tension is easy to measure if the adjuster is a hydraulic one and incorporates a gauge; if the backstay adjuster is a turnbuckle, numbered marks should be painted on it. Angle of heel is taken from the athwartships inclinometer, and trim angle can be measured from a more sensitive fore- and aft-mounted spirit level.

The *remarks* column in the deck log can be used to record observations about how the boat feels, sail shape and draft, how much helm is being carried, cunningham adjustment, reefs taken, navigational aids in sight, indications of current from buoys and lobster pots, relative positions of other boats, weather phenomena and other pertinent data.

As each page of the deck log is completed, it should be sent to the navigator for information and safekeeping until it can be used for postrace analysis. As a library of information is accumulated over a period of time, the data can be organized and plotted either in graph form or as data for polar diagrams.

The object of any exercise in statistics is to collect and arrange for handy onboard reference all available facts regarding a boat's performance. This will permit quick determination of:

- Optimum speed under given wind and sea conditions and point of sail
- When to make sail changes to keep the boat at optimum speed
- Optimum sailing angles when tacking upwind, downwind or crosswind
- Best angle of heel and fore-and-aft trim under given wind and sea conditions to maintain optimum speed
- Proper sail shape and trim for best speed under given wind and sea conditions

I'm not suggesting that you need a five-foot shelf over the navigator's berth to hold all this performance data. A ring binder should be sufficient to contain the graphs and polar diagrams. Additional information, such as a list of sheet leads for each sail, or backstay pressures for various conditions, can be posted in a convenient spot.

A deck log file should start with a boat's earliest sail drills, and it can continue throughout its entire racing career — this is particularly helpful when crew personnel are constantly changing. In addition to its on-deck use as a check list and as a storehouse of information, the deck log provides a continuous flow of navigational information during the navigator's off-watch periods.

The Navigation Log. While the watch crew on deck are absorbed in their work, the navigator is faced with a different set of problems. Chief among them is keeping the boat on the fastest course to the next mark. This involves the exercise of many skills, not the least being a good working knowledge of meteorology. Because many navigators keep a separate weather log and prepare rough weather maps from radio information, the navigation log frequently makes no provision for weather data. This is the case in the example shown in Figure 1.

The navigation log should contain as much detail as the navigator feels is needed and no more. In fact veteran navigators often work from logs that are quite simple but cover all the salient points. Coupled with their charts and plotting sheets, all the necessary information is, in fact, meticulously recorded.

In an offshore race of any distance, the basic form of the naviga-

Navigation Log

date / time	tack	true wind	true wind speed	app wind speed	app wind dir	course mag	leeway	current	heading	boat speed	log	dist traveled	water temp	sails in use / last fix / remarks
Race S.O.R.C. OCEAN TRIANGLE										Date	2/14/77			
0920	P	290	6	185	4	075			075	5	0	0	78°	STARTED WITH 3/4 OZ. SPINNAKER. SET STAYSAIL
0945	P	310	6	70	5	075	3°	5°	080	5.5	1.9	2.1	79°	3L3-3699 HOLDING / 3L5-1660 COURSE
1000	P	310	6	70	5	075	3°	10°	085	5.5	3.6	1.7	80°	3L3-3701 COMING INTO / 3L5-1669 THE STREAM
1300	P	040	14	40	17	075	4°	20°	110	6.5	16.2	3.1	82°	3L3-3710 ON COURSE / 3L5-11789
1330	P	045	16	45	19	075	4°	20°	110	6.6	19.4	8.2	82°	3L3-3712 SEAS / 3L5-1760 BUILDING
1400	P	075	16	35	21	075	4°	20°	180	6.6	226	3.1	82°	3L3-3713 HEADED / 3L5-1790 TACKED AT 1402
1410	S	075	16	33	20	075	4°		030	6.7				SEAS EASIER ON THIS TACK

Figure 1: Navigation log contains specific information data available in deck log. Action of true wind is maintained by navigator in this log

tion log shown in Figure 1 should suffice. You will note that it places the responsibility for keeping track of the speed and direction of the *true* wind on the navigator. This permits him quickly to compute and predict in advance the direction and speed of the apparent wind on a new heading so he can anticipate which sails can be carried and relay this to the skipper and watch captains. An accurate record of the true wind is also desirable for purposes of constructing the polar diagrams I have already referred to. The actual use of the diagrams during a race should be based on true wind for more precise results.

Note that all courses and headings in Figure 1 are recorded as magnetic. Most navigators determine and plot their courses directly from the inner, or magnetic, compass rose printed on the chart. Doing this eliminates the possibility of error in adjusting a true course for variation, provided the compass rose on the chart that is nearest the boat's present position is used. All magnetic courses should be adjusted for leeway and current set before arriving at the magnetic heading the helmsman is given to steer. The average heading actually steered during a particular period should be taken from the deck log or deduced from the navigator's observation of the compass at the chart table.

The more frequently readings are taken and entries are made in the navigation log, the more accurate a boat's dead reckoning position is likely to be: entries should be made at least every half hour. Inasmuch as most of the input is taken from the deck log, this should be no problem, even when the navigator is off watch.

One reading that should never be overlooked, however, is the odometer log which should be read regularly *without fail*. The usual location of the odometer log is at the chart table so when the navigator turns in he must instruct the watch captain to read the mileage every half hour and enter the reading in the appropriate column of the navigation log.

On races that cross the Gulf Stream, or any similar current, water temperature readings should be read and logged every half hour as well.

In some situations the navigation log may be tailored to a particular race. For example, events such as the Southern Ocean Racing Conference Ocean Triangle or Lipton Cup races, each of which features a double crossing of the Gulf Stream, force navigators to depend heavily on loran navigation. Frequent loran readings are taken to establish the set of the current and continually to correct the heading required to stay on course. It is convenient in such cases to determine, in advance, what available loran rates will give the best lines of position and a column should be included in the log for each individual rate. This makes it easy to record readings from two or more rates side by side in the log and then plot them directly either on a loran chart or on other charts by using the appropriate loran tables.

A more serious side of any log is its legal implication. In the event of an accident resulting in injury to a crewmember, damage to another boat or loss of a man overboard, it behooves the careful navigator to write an accurate narrative description of the happening. The resulting log entry may become an important link in the chain of evidence which will define the legal liabilities of the persons involved. For this reason the facts should be carefully determined and the entry well thought out before it is made. Similarly, in protest situations the committee hearing the charges often will give considerable weight to a detailed description of the event that has been properly recorded in the log.

As any offshore racing yacht nears the finish line, the conscientious navigator corrects his watch time to exact local zone time, notes the time of finish in hours, minutes and seconds, and records it in the log. It is an entry that is often forgotten in the excitement of the finish. But it shouldn't be, for there have been many races with no committee boat on the finish to take official times. If the navigator doesn't keep track of the finish time in his own log, he neither can check the time given him by the race committee, nor can he substantiate his own finish if he hasn't written it down. It's an entry that belongs at the end of any proper racing log.

The Racing Navigator

By Richard T. du Moulin

In the modern sense, a navigator, particularly a racing navigator, is no longer the man who keeps you off the bottom. He also is the fellow who should help keep you *out* of the bottom — of the race results, that is. Here is an outline of what a contemporary navigator's tasks should cover.

In addition to being responsible for the position and navigational safety of the boat (the traditional Prince Henry chores), the navigator is fast becoming the prime source of miscellaneous but relevant information. His factual input to tactical decisions can make or break a race.

With watch captains busy on deck and the skipper distracted by anything and everything, one person must be given the responsibility for "loose ends." The navigator, when he is not piloting the boat through dangerous waters, can be this "glue" man. He can gather all extraneous information and put it together for presentation to everyone concerned before and during the race. It is a good idea for the entire crew to meet before each start to discuss everything from the course, expected weather, current, and log entries, to safety and man overboard procedures. Mistakes are still made, but they come less frequently.

The navigator can be a valuable asset for both day and distance racing. On a small boat, one man can be the navigator/tactician, while on a larger boat there might be one or even two full-time navigators and a separate tactician. However, my main point is that at least one man must be assigned the tasks related to navigation.

For day racing, a navigator's tasks can be divided into pre-race tasks and in-race responsibilities.

Pre-Race Tasks

1. Check all instruments, charts, publications and gear. Make sure all necessary navigation equipment is on board and is functioning properly. Test the speedometer and log, wind instruments, depth finders, and radio receivers. Make sure all the correct charts, current tables and charts, pencils, dividers, parallel rules, etc., are on board.

2. Study the weather situation. Cut out the local newspaper weather map and call the airport weather bureau. Listen and copy the VHF, Federal Aviation Longwave, and Coast Guard broadcasts. Make an educated guess of what might be expected from local and national conditions.

3. Study the current situation. Determine current changes and velocities from the Tables; use local current charts if available. Look at the current picture and spend a good bit of time thinking about how it will affect strategy.

4. Read the Race Circular. Check the starting time and signals, recall and postponement procedures, radio frequencies to monitor for recalls, etc. Do not skim over *anything* and underline *all* key items.

5. Plot the course. As soon as the course is known, plot all the legs of the race. Note the marks and the direction of rounding. Write down all compass courses, and distances. Have either the skipper or someone else doublecheck all your work, including the names of the marks. One person can easily misread a signal flag or a race circular.

6. Calculate the time allowances. If a scratch sheet with time allowances has not been issued by the race committee, calculate the time you will have to give your close competition. This information is vital to the tactician or skipper if it becomes necessary to decide who to cover, or who split from whom during the race.

All these items should be attended to *before* the start of the race for they provide many basic facts which the afterguard must consider *during* the race. To get maximum benefit, this information also must be posted in the cockpit for quick and easy reference. A plastic covered form (Fig. 1) is one convenient way. Specific information for each race can be written with a grease pencil, and in this way the navigator's "epistle" can be read and committed to memory by everyone.

After the tactical and strategic issues have been discussed, and a "game plan" formulated, the navigator should turn his attention to getting the best possible start. On many boats it is the navigator's job to call the time and listen for any recalls, either visual or those made on the radio.

After the start, the navigator begins the second part of his task.

Procedures During a Race

1. Record all wind changes. Either the navigator or the tactician

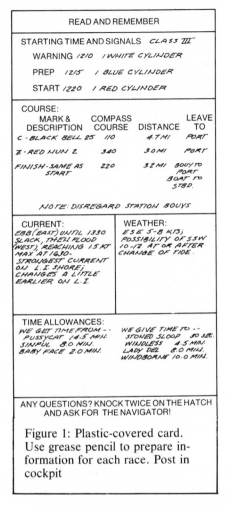

Figure 1: Plastic-covered card. Use grease pencil to prepare information for each race. Post in cockpit

should record compass headings on each close hauled tack so the boat can be kept "in phase" with shifts. Taking readings up to an hour before the start will give you a much healthier feel for what's happening.

2. Keep track of laylines. If the boat is on a windward leg, keep the tactician posted on the distance to the layline. It will keep him from overstanding the mark or reaching the layline too soon.

3. The navigator must keep track of the current and constantly recompute the course allowance neces-

sary to counter the effects of currents.

4. Compute the apparent wind angle and speed for the next leg. By drawing wind vectors, the navigator can tell the tactician what the apparent wind direction and velocity will be on the next leg. Once these two factors are known, the proper sail can be selected and made ready. If you are on a reach or run, knowing this information is essential if you are to select the correct spinnaker.

5. Keep track of the weather by noting both local signs (smokestacks, clouds, etc.) and checking the weather broadcasts.

6. Advise the tactician about tacking downwind. It is tremendously helpful if the navigator can calculate the speed vs. course considerations involved in tacking downwind. This is very important in any close race.

7. Keep the tactician aware of all relevant facts, and make any reminders in plenty of time to be of benefit. Such things as, "You have to leave that government buoy to starboard," should be made well in advance of the actual arrival time.

8. Be ready for fog or a squall. If it appears that visibility may become reduced, always maintain a good fix and be prepared to pilot the boat to the finish line.

Assigning all these tasks to one man, the navigator, before and during a race allows the skipper or tactician to have the maximum information he needs to make a decision. While the navigator should not make the decision, his work should improve any decisions that are made.

It pays to have a navigator of some sort, even on a small boat. If he is needed to help gybe, tack, douse, or change sails, he can lend a hand. But the rest of the time, he should stay on top of his *primary* job: being a navigator.

The Navigator's Worksheets

By Richard T. du Moulin

The traditional tasks of an ocean racing navigator have not changed nearly so much as have some of the new equipment and information now available to him. The capability of obtaining accurate fixes at most any time in most ocean races has made it possible to navigate *continuously* throughout a race, not just with "morning and evening stars with a few sun lines thrown in."

In fact, very accurate distance recording logs when used in conjunction with electronic navigation now permit a navigator to estimate current set and drift hourly and half-hourly.

Weather satellites have greatly enhanced the quality and timeliness of offshore weather forecasts. This, combined with the availability of compact, high-quality radio receivers, provides the navigator with even more information.

Even on a race that does not allow electronic navigation, the large entry lists, weather information (often maps), and daily position reports do make this kind of racing very competitive, and the navigator's job becomes even more demanding.

Some ocean racing boats have gone to a two-navigator system to allow continuous monitoring of weather and other reports. Continuous navigation can go on indefinitely yet each man can get some sleep. Two men also tend to notice each other's errors. Don't forget, the worst thing to have is a sleep-starved navigator who can neither focus his eyes nor make a correct tactical decision.

In a boat too small to carry two navigators, a crewman on each watch with some piloting or navigating experience should be delegated the responsibility of recording weather broadcasts and maintaining a DR plot (charting the boat's position using the average course steered and the recorded distance).

To ensure that these two crew members fully understand their duties, a small notebook or possibly a plastic card marked with a grease pencil can make good reminders. Before he turns in, the navigator should write down all key information — scheduled weather broadcasts, radio monitoring period, expected navigational sightings, strategic considerations, and what time or situation he should be awakened. *Navigator's Notes* (Fig. 1) is a sample page. All navies have similar devices; in the US Navy it's called the *Captain's Night Order Book*.

Because such information is the basis of the navigator's work (and the afterguard's strategy decisions) it is important to maintain complete and accurate logs. Failure to do this is as sloppy as not putting cotter pins in your rigging. While every skipper and navigator can make up his own format, I recommend heavy paper, printed professionally, and bound with plastic spirals. This type of paper is more resistant to water damage and can be saved and studied for later races.

Vital log entries include: *exact* time (to nearest minute), log reading

NAVIGATOR'S NOTES

DATE _18 -19 JUNE_

WEATHER BROADCASTS — (Local Time)

BERMUDA WEATHER @ 2000, 0300, 0700
STATION ZBM - 1340 KC
2670 KC USCG/NY @ 2315, 0515

RADIO TELEPHONE MONITORING —

2400 -0015 ON 2182 KC, JUST LISTEN

NAVIGATIONAL CONCERNS —

MAY SEE LOOM OF BERMULA TO SOUTH
BUT DOUBTFUL

STRATEGIC REMINDERS —

IF SEA TEMP CHANGES MORE THAN TWO
DEGREES OR WIND LEADS/LIFTS
MORE THAN 10 DEGREES - WAKE
NAVIGATOR. WIND MAY HEAD AND
INCREASE AS HURRICANE NEARS;
LOOK OUT FOR WIND SQUALLS.

WAKE UP NAVIGATOR AT _0500_ OR
IF THERE ARE ANY MAJOR CHANGES

Figure 1

My favorite log format is shown in Figure 2.

The log should be shown to the entire crew before the race, and log entries should be explained. The skipper must hold each watch captain responsible for having his watch make proper and timely entries. A good practice is to have each man make his own entry when he gets off the helm.

Entries should be made at least hourly and after every major course alteration (tacks, gybes, major shifts). Furthermore, I believe it is better to have the entries made by the crew rather than by the navigator for they are the ones on deck, and they have a better feel for average course, speed, wind velocity/ strength, clouds, sea condition, etc.

After reading the data in the log, the navigator then can begin to interpret everything else to determine what was, what is, and what soon may be happening. If you look at the sample (but real) Bermuda Race excerpt in Figure 2, you will see that several major things happened:

(1) The wind headed 5° at about 0530

(taken at the exact minute of entry), average course steered, average speed, wind direction and velocity (relative and/or true), barometric pressure. In the Bermuda Race and SORC, water temperature also is a key entry. One large space should be free for remarks about: sail combinations, heel, other boats sighted, course and distance to next mark.

DATE _19 JUNE_   RACE _BERMUDA_

TIME	LOG READING	COURSE		AVERAGE		WIND				BAROM	MISC. (water temp, sea state, etc.)	SAILS
		AVG STEERED	DESIRED RHUMB	SPEED	HEEL	RELATIVE		TRUE				
						Direction	Velocity	Direction	Velocity			
0430	74.03	173	182	8.0	26°	40	35	125	30	30.56	76°/10-15 SEAS	
0521	81.18	175	182	8.1	28	40	35	125	30	30.56	SAME	
0556	85.63	180	182	8.0	28	38	35	130	30	30.58	SLIGHT VEER	
0630	90.07	175	177	8.0	30	38	40	130	35	30.56	STRONGER / 15' SEAS	#3 DOUBLE REEF
0702	94.15	175	177	7.6	30	38	40	130	35	30.55	BDA REPORTS 25' SEAS !	
0747	00.20	165	169	7.0	30	33	40 r	130	35 r	30.52	ALLOWING MORE FOR LEEWAY & SET	
0905	10.08	158	169	8.0	30	35	40 r	130	35 r	30.51	147 MILES TO K. SHOALS	
			(Note navigator's markings such as circles for emphasis, and changes of desired rhumb.)									

Figure 2

(2) The wind velocity increased steadily from 30 to over 35 kts.

(3) The barometer began dropping steadily at 0556

(4) Bermuda radio reported 25′ seas, 10′ larger than at the present location.

Further clarification of what is happening can be achieved by graphing the barometric pressure, wind direction, and wind velocity (Fig. 3).

All the entries, graphs, and weather forecasts help in the making of key tactical decisions. In this case, the decision was made to harden up (from 180° to 158° mag.) and gain maximum distance to weather before heavier seas increased leeway and wind-driven currents near Bermuda forced the boat to leeward of layline.

Such a decision might not have been made soon enough if accurate and complete information *in readable form* had not been available.

It is often helpful for a navigator to plot data on graph paper. Not only can barometric pressure, wind direc-

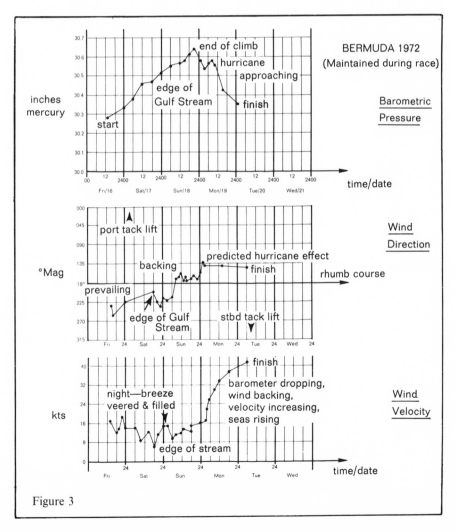

Figure 3

DATE/TIME	FREQUENCY	STATION LOCATION	WEATHER INFO.		
			BAR.	WIND	MISC.

Figure 4

tion, and velocity be plotted against time, but many other relations can be explored.

Graphs highlight trends and changes, many of which can have a direct effect on strategy. They are particularly useful when conditions are abnormal, or when you are sailing in unfamiliar waters where *everything* is abnormal!

A separate weather log should be maintained in addition to a navigation log. It can be either a spiral binder or a professionally printed log. A sample format is shown in Figure 4. This type of log makes the regular navigation log neater because it allows weather entries to be sloppy, an unavoidable occurrence when one is copying voice transmissions.

Before the race, the navigator(s) should find out the time and frequency of *all* available weather broadcasts and list them in the weather log. This does require a considerable amount of research, and it is tempting to rely on race committee handouts and old schedules. Many times you will find these are either incomplete, or other sources are not mentioned.

The culmination of the navigator's work comes when he discusses strategy with the rest of the afterguard. His best thinking about the race course must be transformed into winning strategy. The skipper should get his watch captains, navigator(s), and other heads together whenever necessary, and in any case before the start, at major turning marks, immediately after unexpected developments, and after receiving new and relevant information. At all these meetings, the navigator should:

(1) lay out the big chart, indicating the boat's position, those of key competitors, and the bulk of the fleet

(2) summarize the weather and the current and be very frank about all uncertainties

(3) show and describe all graphs and other analyses he has done in order to highlight trends

(4) bring up any other relevant facts (special race instructions, etc.).

The general discussion that follows such a presentation should stimulate the concrete observations and gut feelings of everyone present. This is the only kind of discussion that will produce an intelligent, winning strategy. But it is the navigator who must set the stage.

The Best Course to Windward

By Alan J. Alder

Most sailors have wrestled more than once with the question of what heading is best for their boat on a beat to windward. Picture yourself in a race faced with these alternatives.

Apparent Wind Angle	Boat Speed
20°	4.4 knots
22°	5.2 knots
24°	5.8 knots
26°	6.4 knots
28°	6.7 knots
30°	7.0 knots
32°	7.3 knots
34°	7.6 knots

Assuming the next mark is dead to windward, what apparent wind angle would you choose? Obviously the farther "off the wind" you sail, the greater the boat speed, but the "bigger" and slower course is closer to the mark. Before you read further, write down your own estimate of the optimum angle and we will see later how close you came.

It is well known that the *apparent* wind (the wind perceived on-board the moving yacht) differs in both angle and velocity from the *true* wind (the wind perceived from a stationary reference point). The amount of

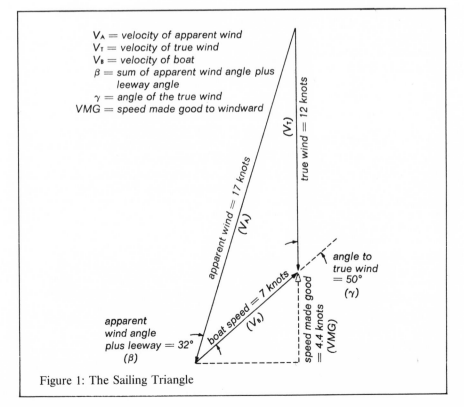

V_A = velocity of apparent wind
V_T = velocity of true wind
V_B = velocity of boat
β = sum of apparent wind angle plus leeway angle
γ = angle of the true wind
VMG = speed made good to windward

true wind = 12 knots (V_T)

apparent wind = 17 knots (V_A)

boat speed = 7 knots (V_B)

angle to true wind = 50° (γ)

apparent wind angle plus leeway = 32° (β)

speed made good = 4.4 knots (VMG)

Figure 1: The Sailing Triangle

difference increases with the speed of the yacht.

Figure 1 illustrates the standard graphical representation of these factors, and this diagram is sometimes called "The Sailing Triangle." A number of books and articles suggest methods (usually graphical) of solving for actual speed made good to windward when given the three factors measurable on the moving boat (apparent wind angle, apparent wind velocity and boat speed).

If you are interested in the mathematical solution, here are the equations:

(Figure 1 contains the symbols)

$$V_T = \sqrt{V_A{}^2 = V_B{}^2 - 2V_A V_B \cos\beta}$$

$$\gamma = \arctan\left(\frac{\sin\beta}{\cos\beta - V_B/V_A}\right)$$

$$VMG = \cos_\gamma V_B$$

(Usually VMG is considered as a ratio of V_T) $VMG/V_T = \cos_\gamma V_B/V_T$

Obviously, when you are racing to windward it is highly desirable to know what apparent wind angle yields the highest speed made good to windward (VMG).

Both the graphical solution (drawing of a true-to-scale sailing triangle) and the mathematical solution are cumbersome and time consuming. Several manufacturers of sailboat instruments recently have begun offering VMG computers that connect to their apparent wind and boat speed instruments, but few of us are equipped with these devices.

By programming an electronic digital computer to solve the equations for the sailing triangle and plotting the results, I have developed the "computer" shown in Figure 2.

It provides you with a rapid solution of *relative* VMG in order to determine the optimum apparent wind angle. The word relative is emphasized because *true* VMG is affected by the boat's leeway angle, and at present, few boats are instrumented for this measurement.

Happily, when using this "computer" we can ignore the boat's leeway angle without affecting the determination of the optimum apparent wind angle.

This "computer" is not necessarily intended for use during a race, but rather to calibrate the boat during practice (in order to determine the optimum apparent wind angles for racing).

To use the computer, begin at the minimum apparent angle at which your boat can sail to windward, and take a series of readings at intervals of 2 degrees. At each point, hold the boat at a constant apparent wind angle, and trim your sails for best boat speed. Then record the following:

A. Apparent Wind Angle (to the nearest whole degree)

B. Boat Speed (estimate to the nearest tenth of a knot)

C. Apparent Wind Speed

Try to work quickly for these comparative readings are more valid if the true wind velocity is constant. (Do not attempt to calibrate your boat on a gusty day.)

After a series of readings (perhaps ranging from 20 degrees to 34 degrees) your work sheet might look like this:

Apparent Wind

Angle	Velocity	Boat Speed
20°	15.9 knots	4.4 knots
22°	16.5	5.2
24°	16.9	5.8
26°	17.1	6.4
28°	17.3	6.7
30°	17.4	7.0
32°	17.4	7.3
34°	17.3	7.6

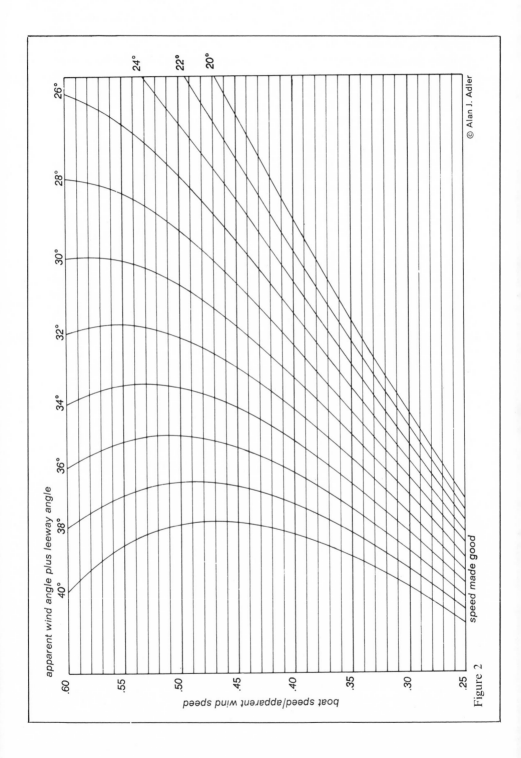

Figure 2

Now, for each reading, divide the boat speed by the apparent wind speed (a small slide rule or calculator is handy for this).

Now your chart might look like this:

Angle	Apparent Wind Velocity (knots)	Boat Speed (knots)	Boat Speed Apparent Wind Vel.
20°	15.9	4.4	.277
22°	16.5	5.2	.315
24°	16.9	5.8	.343
26°	17.1	6.4	.374
28°	17.3	6.7	.387
30°	17.4	7.0	.402
32°	17.4	7.3	.420
34°	17.3	7.6	.439

Next plot a mark on the computer for each wind angle and its corresponding boat speed/apparent wind velocity.

The series of marks on the chart will form a peaked curve, and the right-hand peak on the curve is your optimum heading for sailing to windward.

In the example shown in Figure 3, the optimum angle is 26 degrees.

If you chose that angle for the example at the beginning of the article you win the cigar.

You should also note that the consequences of sailing 4 degrees too tight are a bit worse than sailing 4 degrees too free.

Because of transient variations of the wind and boat speed, it may help to take several sets of readings on each heading and average them. It also may be necessary to draw an average curve (through the set of points) in order to smooth the data and find the proper peak.

Keep in mind that your optimum heading can vary with wind and sea conditions. In light winds the best

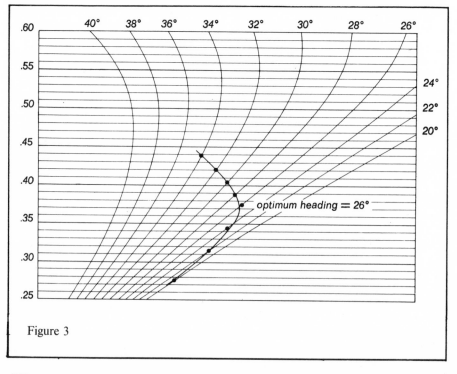

Figure 3

heading may be one or two degrees closer to the wind than it might be in heavier air.

You will find that plots made in lighter winds will appear farther to the right on the computer chart. This is because the computer "thinks" in terms of speed-made-good as a *percentage* of true wind speed. In light winds, a yacht sails at speeds that are a higher percentage of wind speed.

If you are a serious racer you should calibrate your boat in various wind conditions and with various sails. Having this information saves you the trauma of experimenting during the actual race.

And remember that in *ocean* sailing you must continually vary the boat's heading in order to maintain a constant apparent wind angle. Going up a wave, the boat will slow down and can be pointed up closer to the wind while still maintaining the same apparent wind angle. Coming down a wave, boat speed will increase and you should bear off in order to hold the same apparent wind angle.

Anticipating possible protests over my ignoring leeway angle, I invite you to try the following test yourself.

1. Using the data in the example, try adding to each heading any reasonable assumed leeway angle you wish. For most sailboats, 4 degrees is a good estimate. In light winds the leeway will be slightly lower and in heavy winds, particularly if the boat is overcanvassed, the leeway will be several degrees greater. Also, the leeway increases as the boat is pinched closer to the wind.

A typical table of leeway angles might be as follows:

Apparent Wind Angle	Leeway Angle (Wind)		
	(Light)	(Medium)	(Heavy)
20°	4°	5°	6°
27°	3°	4°	5°
35°	2°	3°	4°

2. Use the "computer" as I have already described but plot the points of intersection between V_B/V_A and the *sum* of apparent wind angle plus leeway angle.

You will find you have created a new curve somewhat to the left of the example curve plotted with zero leeway.

3. Find the point on the curve that is farthest to the right and note the corresponding sum of apparent wind angle plus leeway angle.

4. Subtract the assumed leeway angle leaving the apparent wind angle.

This should be the same optimum apparent wind angle as the earlier example.

Finally, if you still are in doubt, calculate VMG from the equations given. The VMG will vary with assumed leeway angle but the apparent wind angle which gives the highest VMG will remain the same.

Happy computing! If you can win the weather leg usually you've got the race half won.

Beating to Windward

By William R. Knowlton

Beating to windward with limited visibility presents its own set of problems. The least complicated situation occurs when the next mark lies directly to windward, no currents are involved, and there are no obstructions or tactical considerations. In these rather rare (and delightful) circumstances, an easy tactic is to make a series of equally timed tacks away from and toward the course (or rhumb) line.

Although the possible combinations are infinite, about 70% of the distance between marks can be covered in two tacks, each one equal to about half the length of the rhumb line (Fig. 1). If these are followed by a series of short tacks, calculated to keep within sight range of the course line, eventually the mark should materialize.

For example, suppose the next buoy lies four miles directly upwind and you can make four knots to windward. This means that if you were able to head directly for the mark, you could make it in one hour. Therefore, when you are beating you might stay on the first leg for half an hour and then tack back toward the course line for another half hour. At this point you should be back on the rhumb line (direct distance between

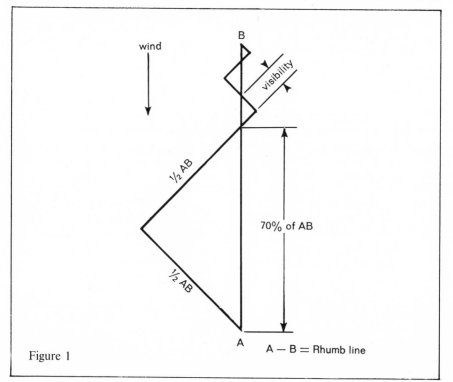

wind

B

visibility

½ AB

½ AB

70% of AB

A

A — B = Rhumb line

Figure 1

the two buoys) and have covered about 70% of its length.

Because it took 60 minutes to cover 70% of the length, it should take about $\frac{3}{7}$ of 60 minutes or 25.7 minutes to cover the remaining 30%, about 13 minutes on each tack.

However, now let's assume that the last mark was only faintly visible six minutes after you rounded it. You decide to play it safe and continue on the first tack for five more minutes (maybe the fog has come in), then tack back five minutes to the course line. This is followed by another pair of five-minute tacks. You now would have used up 10 of the 13 minutes allotted to each tack,

so a pair of threes should bring us right to the mark.

If it fails to appear, because you have been in "sight" range of the rhumb line for some time, it is reasonable to assume that it is still ahead. You might have misjudged your speed, have made more leeway than expected, or the helmsman might have sagged off a bit. Therefore, the logical move is to continue for a few more short tacks before taking another action.

Let's still assume currents are not a factor but now assume that Mark B is not directly to windward of Mark A; but still it can't be fetched on either tack. You can determine the

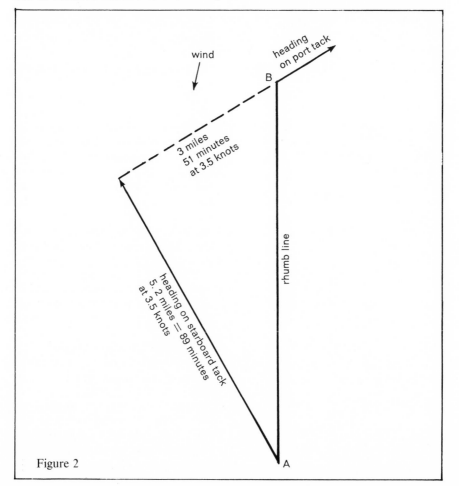

wind

heading on port tack

B

3 miles
51 minutes
at 3.5 knots

rhumb line

heading on starboard tack
5.2 miles = 89 minutes
at 3.5 knots

Figure 2

A

length of the required long and short tacks to windward by extending a line that represents the heading on one tack (correcting for leeway) from Mark A and a similar line representing the *reverse* of the heading on the other tack from Mark B (Fig. 2). The junction of these two lines on the chart shows the point where the boat should tack if it follows the diagram plan.

When the length of these lines is measured, the time to spend on each tack can be determined from the formula:

$$\text{time (in minutes)} = \frac{\text{distance (in miles)}}{\text{speed (in knots)}} \times 60.$$

Therefore, if it turns out that the two legs were 5.2 and 3 miles respectively and boat speed was 3.5 knots, the long leg would be 5.2/3.5 × 60 or 89.1 minutes, and the short leg: 3.0/3.5 × 60 or 51.4 minutes.

Theoretically, it makes no difference in what order the tacks are taken or how many shorter tacks they are split into. As long as about 89 minutes are spent going in the direction of the long leg, and 51 minutes in the direction of the short leg, there will be no real difference. However, if a boat were abnormally slow in stays, or made an unusual number of tacks, some allowance would have to be made for the time lost. But normally this is insignificant.

You must be extremely careful to note the time when passing a mark and when coming about. My usual practice, if my plan shows I should spend 89 minutes on the starboard tack and 51 minutes on port, is to write the figures on the deck or on a piece of Plexiglas, along with the time I round the mark. If I spend 22 minutes on starboard for the first leg, I note when I tacked and then subtract the 22 minutes from the starboard (89 minutes) total, and write in the remaining 67 minutes. I do the

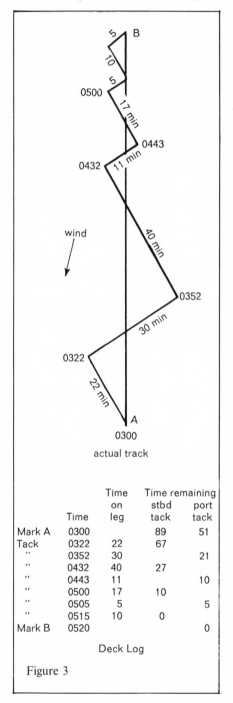

	Time	Time on leg	Time remaining stbd tack	port tack
Mark A	0300		89	51
Tack	0322	22	67	
"	0352	30		21
"	0432	40	27	
"	0443	11		10
"	0500	17	10	
"	0505	5		5
"	0515	10	0	
Mark B	0520			0

Deck Log

Figure 3

144

same for each succeeding tack (Figs. 2 & 3).

When tactics permit I plan to arrive at a point I am certain is both short of the mark and contains an equal number of minutes to be completed on each tack: 10 minutes, for example. At this point, I should be directly downwind from the mark and, although not on the rhumb line, I should be near it.

By running short equal tacks, not greater in length than my visibility, I can, in effect, run a rather preliminary and automatic search procedure, covering quite a lot of ground at small cost in time. If the buoy fails to appear on schedule, my procedure would be to continue short-tacking until I am certain I had passed the mark. This ensures that subsequent search procedures can be run downwind; they are faster and simpler than an upwind hunt.

Although this diagrammatic approach is fine under ideal conditions, usually it does not include a small boat with a small chart table. Because of this, I have worked out a set of tacking tables which are basically a mathematical solution to the vector diagrams (Fig. 4). They are quicker to use and more accurate, particularly if you are only an amateur draftsman.

Because not all boats tack in 90°, I have included tables for boats tacking in 80° and 100°. My own boat will tack in 80°, but because of leeway and helmsmanship, the 90° table brings me closer to the mark and therefore it is the one I use.

How do the tables work? Suppose we have a modern fin keeler that can tack in 80° and make it stick. The wind is SW, the course to the next mark is 200°; we can maintain an average heading of 180° on the starboard tack and a speed of four knots. Look at the table for 80°. The column of figures at the left represents the number of degrees the heading *deviates* from the desired course. The upper figures are the variance on the tack that heads closest to the mark; in this case it is starboard and the amount off (200° − 180°) is 20°. If we were on the port tack, we could presumably point within 60° of the mark, and would use the lower figure (screened).

Read across from 20° on the left to boat speed four knots. You find 13.2 and 5.2. This represents the number of minutes we should spend on the starboard and port tacks respectively for *each mile* of the distance along the rhumb line. If it is four miles from A to B, spend 13.2 × 4, or 52.8 minutes on the starboard tack and 5.2 × 4 or 20.8 minutes on port. These tables can be copied, perhaps sealed in plastic, and taped near the compass.

Because local circumstances may differ, I should explain why I have presented them in this manner. Most of my sailing occurs where buoys are seldom far apart. On my own boat, I have rounded-off the figures to even minutes. This works well for three- or four-mile distances and makes a very neat and compact table that is easy to use. For longer legs of 10 miles rounding-off could mean an error of four or five minutes. Therefore, I have listed them here to one decimal place.

Similarly, when distances are short, visibility is not too limited, and currents are not a major problem, it is permissible to interpolate fairly casually between the three- and four-knot columns for a boat speed of 3½ knots. However, to be more accurate, I have extended the

Degrees off Desired Course	TACKING ANGLE 100°						
	1	2	3	4	5	6	Knots
10°	60.924	30.5	20.3	15.2	12.2	10.2	
(90°)	10.578	5.3	3.5	2.6	2.1	1.8	
20°	60.000	30.0	20.0	15.0	12.0	10.0	
(80°)	20.838	10.4	6.9	5.2	4.2	3.5	
30°	57.246	28.6	19.1	14.3	11.4	9.5	
(70°)	30.462	15.2	10.1	7.6	6.1	5.1	
40°	52.758	26.4	17.6	13.2	10.6	8.8	
(60°)	39.162	19.6	13.1	9.8	7.8	6.5	
50°	46.668	23.3	15.6	11.7	9.3	7.8	
(50°)	46.668	23.3	15.6	11.7	9.3	7.8	

Degrees off Desired Course	TACKING ANGLE 90°						
	1	2	3	4	5	6	Knots
10°	59.088	29.5	19.7	14.8	11.8	9.8	
(80°)	10.416	5.2	3.5	2.6	2.1	1.7	
20°	56.382	28.2	18.8	14.1	11.3	9.4	
(70°)	20.520	10.3	6.8	5.1	4.1	3.4	
30°	51.960	26.0	17.3	12.9	10.4	8.7	
(60°)	30.000	15.0	10.0	7.5	6.0	5.0	
40°	45.960	23.0	15.3	11.5	9.2	7.7	
(50°)	38.568	19.3	12.9	9.6	7.7	6.4	
45°	42.426	21.2	14.1	10.6	8.5	7.1	
(45°)	42.426	21.2	14.1	10.6	8.5	7.1	

Degrees off Desired Course	TACKING ANGLE 80°						
	1	2	3	4	5	6	Knots
10°	57.252	28.6	19.1	14.3	11.5	9.5	
(70°)	10.578	5.3	3.5	2.6	2.1	1.8	
20°	52.764	26.4	17.6	13.2	10.6	8.8	
(60°)	20.838	10.4	6.9	5.2	4.2	3.5	
30°	46.674	23.3	15.6	11.7	9.3	7.8	
(50°)	30.462	15.2	10.1	7.6	6.1	5.1	
40°	39.162	19.6	13.1	9.8	7.8	6.5	
(40°)	39.162	19.6	13.1	9.8	7.8	6.5	

Figure 4

more accurate, I have extended the figures under the one-knot column to three decimal places. This provides an accurate calculation of the minutes on each tack per mile between marks for any particular boat speed; you divide the appropriate figures in the one-knot column by the speed (expressed decimally) in knots.

For example, if a boat that tacks in 80° can head about 30° from the desired course, and a dependable knotmeter shows an average speed of 4.2 knots: divide 46.674 minutes (from the 30° one-knot column) by 4.2 knots to get 11.1 minutes per mile of rhumb line on the long leg. Then divide 30.462 minutes by 4.2 knots to get 7.25 minutes (per mile) on the short leg. Multiply these figures by the number of miles between marks to get the total time to spend on each tack. In short, the tables can be used as shown or adapted to suit your own purposes.

One word of caution. Both vector diagrams and mathematical solutions give an impression of accuracy and precision that may not survive their practical applications. At the extreme, when winds are light and strong adverse currents multiply any errors, one's judgment and experience may be the most important element in accuracy. However, the more you practice, in clear weather as well as in fog, the more likely you are to find an elusive mark.

When There's Current on the Windward Leg

By William R. Knowlton

In the previous article I described some techniques and tables to use when navigating a small boat on the windward leg with poor visibility. That discussion did not include any compensation for currents. When current is present things not only get a bit more complicated, but the possibilities for error are substantially increased. In fact, considering the number of variables and estimates that are involved, it is a great feat to hit the bull's eye. Even so a reasonable degree of accuracy and consistency should be possible.

A navigator's axiom states that professional maturity can be rated in direct proportion to his cool when his objective fails to appear on schedule. Another proclaims that while practice may not make perfect, it certainly helps. As a corollary, I would urge anyone using the methods I am about to suggest to try them out frequently in clear weather before using them in bad weather.

When sailing to windward, current usually affects a boat's speed and direction differently on one tack from how it does on the other. However, while the problems involved in zigzagging up to a fog-shrouded mark may appear formidable, the vector solution to the problem is fairly simple.

Suppose that Mark B lies 5 miles at 360° from Mark A. The wind is a little east of north and your heading on the starboard tack is 330° or 30° off the course line. Your boat speed is estimated to be 4.5 knots. Current is reported to set 210° at 1.5 knots.

The vector diagram can be drawn directly on your chart or to any suitable scale on a separate piece of paper. Start from Mark A and lay off a line in the direction of the boat's initial heading (starboard tack in this case). Adjust for leeway if necessary. This is the direction the boat would sail if there were no current. Boat speed is 4.5 knots so mark off a 4.5-mile segment from A to point C (Fig. 1). From point C extend a line 1.5 miles (the strength and direction of the current) to F. With no current interfering, in one hour the boat would have sailed from A to C. But the 1.5-knot current has been operating during the same hour and you will, in fact, end up at the point F. Therefore the line AF represents the actual path the boat will follow, and its length will be the distance it will travel in one hour, in other words, the speed it will make good over the bottom.

Next extend a 4.5-mile line from Mark B to point D. This represents the heading on the other tack, adjusted for leeway if necessary. Again extend the line scale 1.5 miles in the direction of current flow, from D to point G. The line BG represents both the speed over the bottom and the direction made good on the port tack.

If line AF is prolonged to meet BG

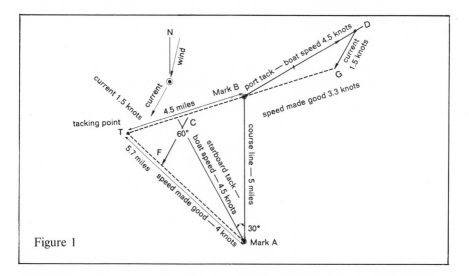

Figure 1

extended *in reverse,* their point of intersection (T) marks the spot where you should tack if you follow the plan in Figure 1. Your speed made good (AF) on the starboard tack can be read as four knots and the distance to the tacking point (AT) is 5.7 miles. Speed on the other tack (BG) is 3.3 knots, and the distance from the tacking point T to the Mark B is 4.5 miles.

By using the formula:

Time (minutes) =
$$\frac{\text{Distance (miles)}}{\text{Speed (knots)}} \times 60,$$

the time you should spend on each leg can be determined. On the first leg AT/AF × 60 = 5.7/4.0 × 60, or 85.5 minutes. On the port tack, TB/BG × 60 = 4.5/3.3 × 60, or 81.8 minutes. In practice, of course, it would not be necessary (and seldom desirable) to sail the course with just two long tacks. As long as a total of about 86 minutes are spent on starboard and 82 minutes on port, the number and duration of the individual tacks can be based on the tactical and strategic considerations. No matter how you slice it though, in

this particular case, it looks like a long afternoon!

I have always found it difficult to achieve pinpoint accuracy from a diagram even under the best conditions; and a small sailboat is far from ideal. Therefore I have compiled some tables that can be sealed in plastic and taped to the deck or bulkhead. A certain amount of arithmetic is necessary, but the need for careful diagramming is eliminated and they do provide reasonable accuracy for distances up to 10 miles or so. I do find, however, that a rough sketch on the chart does help my general picture of things.

In order to keep the tables as compact as possible, I have assumed throughout that the *first leg* refers to the tack that lies closer to the course line. Note carefully that a boat that tacks in anything other than 90° should make the appropriate adjustment to the tacking angles applied in Table 1 used for entering.

To enter Table 1, you must first determine the *angle* the current makes to the boat's heading. In the example in Figure 1 the boat could head 330° and current set was 210°. By subtracting 180° from 210°, you

Table 1
RATIO — BOAT SPEED/CURRENT STRENGTH

Degrees Current off Bow	1.5		2		2.5		3		4		6		8		12	
0°	.33	0	.50	0	.60	0	.67	0	.75	0	.83	0	.88	0	.92	0
	1.20	124	1.12	117	1.08	112	1.05	108	1.03	104	1.01	99	1.01	97	1.00	95
30°	.54	38	.62	22	.68	15	.73	13	.79	9	.86	6	.89	4	.93	3
	.88	169	.87	142	.88	120	.90	113	.93	105	.94	105	.94	101	.96	97
	1.45	76	1.32	87	1.25	89	1.20	91	1.15	92	1.09	92	1.07	92	1.04	91
60°	.88	41	.87	30	.87	23	.88	19	.90	14	.93	9	.94	7	.96	4
	.54	160	.62	142	.68	130	.73	122	.79	113	.86	105	.89	101	.93	97
	1.61	61	1.40	70	1.36	75	1.24	78	1.22	81	1.15	85	1.11	86	1.07	88
90°	1.20	34	1.12	27	1.08	22	1.05	18	1.03	14	1.01	9	1.01	7	1.00	5
	.33	124	.50	117	.60	112	.67	108	.75	104	.83	99	.88	97	.92	95
	1.67	56	1.50	63	1.40	68	1.33	72	1.25	76	1.17	81	1.13	83	1.08	85
120°	1.45	23	1.32	19	1.25	17	1.20	14	1.15	11	1.09	8	1.07	6	1.04	4
	.54	75	.62	87	.68	89	.73	91	.79	92	.86	92	.89	92	.93	91
	1.61	55	1.46	61	1.36	65	1.30	69	1.22	74	1.15	78	1.11	81	1.07	84
150°	1.61	12	1.46	10	1.36	8	1.30	7	1.22	5	1.15	4	1.11	3	1.07	2
	.88	61	.87	70	.87	75	.88	78	.89	81	.93	85	.94	86	.96	87
	1.45	55	1.37	61	1.25	65	1.20	69	1.15	74	1.09	78	1.07	81	1.04	84
180°	1.67	0	1.50	0	1.40	0	1.33	0	1.25	0	1.17	0	1.13	0	1.08	0
	1.20	56	1.12	63	1.08	68	1.05	72	1.04	76	1.01	81	1.01	83	1.00	85

could say the current would *flow* from 030°. For me this analogy makes it easy to calculate that the current is 60° on the windward bow.

The other entry you need is the ratio of boat speed to current strength. In this case boat speed is 4.5 and current strength is 1.5 knots; the ratio is 4.5/1.5 = 3. The bow angles are listed down the left hand side of Table 1, the ratios across the top. Therefore to compute read down to the 60° angle, then go across to the box located under the speed/current ratio 3, where we find:

.88	19
.73	122
1.24	78

Each box contains six figures; three on the left are factors to apply to boat speed. The topmost (.88) pertains to the first leg. The next two relate to the other tack. If the current on the first leg is on the *windward* side (pushing the boat away from the mark), use the middle figure (.73). If the current is on the leeward side use the bottom figure (screened).

To find the speed made good on the starboard tack (first leg) multiply the boat speed through the water by the top figure: .88 × 4.5 knots or 3.96 knots. Because the current is on the windward side, use the black figure to find your speed over the bottom on the port tack: .73 × 4.5 knots or 3.29 knots.

The figures on the right hand side of each box represent angles; the top figure is the number of degrees the boat is deflected from its original heading by the current. In this case, the boat could head 30° from the rhumb line, but the figure, 19°, shows that the track *actually* made good will be 30° + 19° or 49° off course.

If the current had been on the lee side, it would be pushing the boat toward the mark and the angle off course would have been *reduced* by

Table 2
TACKING ANGLE

Angle off Cus	60°	70°	80°	90°	100°	110°	120°	130°	140°	150°
10°	53.07	55.30	57.25	59.09	60.93	62.88	65.10	67.83	71.51	77.13
	12.03	11.09	10.58	10.42	10.58	11.09	12.03	13.60	16.21	20.84
15°	48.99	52.30	55.22	57.96	60.69	63.61	66.92	70.99	76.46	84.85
	17.93	16.53	15.77	15.53	15.77	16.53	17.93	20.27	24.16	31.06
20°	44.53	48.91	52.76	56.38	60.00	63.85	68.23	73.61	80.83	91.92
	23.70	21.84	20.84	20.52	20.84	21.84	23.70	26.79	31.92	41.04
25°	39.74	45.15	49.91	54.38	58.85	63.61	69.02	75.66	84.60	98.30
	29.28	26.98	25.75	25.36	25.75	26.98	29.28	33.10	39.45	50.71
30°	34.64	41.04	46.67	51.96	57.25	62.88	69.28	77.13	87.71	103.92
	34.64	31.93	30.46	30.00	30.46	31.93	34.64	39.16	46.67	60.00
35°	29.28	36.62	43.08	49.15	55.22	61.68	69.02	78.03	90.16	108.76
	39.74	36.62	34.95	34.41	34.95	36.62	39.74	44.93	53.54	68.83
40°	23.70	31.93	39.16	45.96	52.76	60.00	68.23	78.32	91.93	112.76
	44.53	41.04	39.16	38.57	39.16	41.04	44.53	50.35	60.00	77.13
45°	17.93	26.98	34.95	42.43	49.91	57.87	66.92	78.03	92.99	115.91
	48.99	45.15	43.08	42.43	43.08	45.16	48.99	55.38	66.00	84.85
50°	12.03	21.84	30.46	38.57	46.67	55.30	65.10	77.13	98.34	118.18
	53.07	48.91	46.67	45.96	46.67	48.91	53.07	60.00	71.51	91.93
55°	6.04	16.53	25.75	34.41	43.08	52.30	62.79	75.66	92.99	119.54
	56.75	52.30	49.91	49.15	49.91	52.30	56.75	64.16	76.46	98.30
60°		11.09	20.84	30.00	39.16	48.91	60.00	73.60	91.93	120.00
		55.30	52.76	51.96	52.76	55.30	60.00	67.83	80.84	103.92
65°		5.57	15.77	25.36	34.95	45.16	56.75	70.99	90.16	119.54
		57.87	55.22	54.38	55.22	57.87	62.79	70.99	84.60	108.76
70°			10.58	20.52	30.46	41.04	53.07	67.83	87.71	118.18
			57.25	56.38	57.25	60.00	65.10	73.60	87.71	112.76
75°			5.31	15.53	25.75	36.62	48.99	64.16	84.60	115.91
			58.85	57.96	58.85	61.68	66.92	75.66	90.16	115.91
80°				10.42	20.84	31.93	44.53	60.00	80.84	112.76
				59.09	60.00	62.88	68.23	77.13	91.93	118.18

19°. In other words, the boat would follow a path that was 30° − 19° or 11° off.

I don't know if there is a technical term for the two lower angles on the right hand side of the box. The term *tacking angle* usually implies the angular difference between headings on succesive tacks. When this angle is distorted by the effect of current, I suppose it should be called something like *resultant tacking* angle. I will stick to just plain tacking angle, but it is important you know what I mean. Here, the middle figure (122°) represents *tacking angle* when the current is on the windward side and the bottom one is for use when the current is to leeward.

From Table 1, we have now determined that the speed on the first leg, starboard tack, will be 3.96 knots; 3.29 knots on port. Furthermore we know the track on the first leg will be 49° off course and the tacking angle will be 122°. If we assume the visibility is not too bad — say about one-half mile — it probably is safe to round off 49° to 50° and 122° to 120°.

Use these figures to enter Table 2. Read down the left hand side, under *Angle off Cus* to 50° and then across to the box under 120°. The upper figure, 65.10, is the number of minutes that should be spent on the first leg for each mile of distance between the marks at a speed of one knot.

Since actual speed on starboard tack was calculated to be 3.96 knots and the distance between marks was given as five miles, the total time to be spent on starboard will be:

$$\frac{65.10}{3.96} \times 5 \text{ or } 82.2 \text{ minutes.}$$

Treating the lower figure in the same manner but using the calculated port tack speed of 3.29 knots, we find that the total time on the other tack should be:

$$\frac{53.07}{3.29} \times 5 \text{ or } 80.65 \text{ minutes.}$$

These results compare pretty closely with those on the vector diagram: those worked out to 85½ minutes on starboard and 82 on the port tack. A strictly mathematical solution yields 85.6020 minutes on starboard and 81.6007 on port. If the fog is extremely thick, or the distance to the next mark is more than three or four miles, it usually pays to interpolate within the tables.

There are those who feel that, with all the possibilities for error, such emphasis on paperwork is just a form of kidding yourself. My own feeling is that is always pays to be as careful and conscientious as time permits, but when computational accuracy is achieved only at the expense of good boat handling, then some degree of compromise is indicated.

In the example we have been using, if you look at the corresponding figures in the boxes opposite 45° and 50°, the differences are rather small compared to similar differences in the boxes under 120° and 130°. Therefore, if I were hurried I would probably round off 49° to 50° and interpolate horizontally for 122°. This procedure would result in times of 85.23 and 82.7 minutes for the two legs. Further interpolation for 49° would refine the answer to 85.6 and 81.4 minutes, which seems hardly worth the additional trouble.

It might be noted that the largest differences between boxes in Table 1 occur in the upper left hand corner where speeds are low and currents strong; particularly when the currents are on the windward side. Throughout the rest of the table, interpolation, when it is necessary at all, generally can be done in the head.

Tactically I try to aim for a spot somewhat short of the mark, perhaps using up all but 10% of the allotted time for each tack. Then I make a series of short hitches to the mark. These tacks are designed to stay within sight range of an imaginary line extending (hopefully) to the mark. Then, if nothing shows up at the appointed time, I keep short-tacking until I am sure I have gone past the mark; at which point I come around and start retracing my steps in an orderly fashion.

Tacking Downwind

By Jack Nelson

After you have rounded a weather mark, set a spinnaker, and have begun a long downhill run to the leeward mark, you may notice your boat speed has dropped. Should you tack downwind? And if so, how deep should your tacks be?

A new rule of thumb produces an accurate answer, for it tells you how much boat speed you must gain on any given downwind tacking course to break even. And it can give you this information regardless of whether the leeward mark is dead downwind or to one side of the true wind direction line.

This system dispenses entirely with tables, graphs, and paper and pencil calculations. You can call it cockpit navigation, but it is a decided plus for busy crews who cannot take time to go below and dope something out by integral calculus.

For a skipper unfamiliar with downwind tacking, deliberately veering from the rhumb line in the hope of picking up more than enough speed to compensate for the added distance seems to be an uncertain, even foolhardy, tactic. Consequently, he doesn't tack downwind as often as he should, or when he does, with the confidence and accuracy that is needed.

Every good navigator knows the fundamental rule: Distance equals speed times time, or $D = ST$. It follows, therefore, that these factors can be compared as:

$$\frac{D_2}{D_1} = \frac{S_2 T_2}{S_1 T_1}$$

Because our goal is to determine the *added* speed required to cover a greater distance *in the same time*, T_2 and T_1 are considered equal and are constants which can be eliminated from the formula which now becomes:

$$\frac{D_2}{D_1} = \frac{S_2}{S_1}$$

This means that the lines you'll see in the following diagrams represent speed as well as distance. If the length of one line is 10% greater than another, then the speed required to travel that line *in equal time* is also 10% greater.

The downwind tacking problem

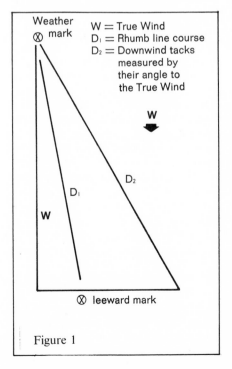

Weather mark ⊗

W = True Wind
D_1 = Rhumb line course
D_2 = Downwind tacks measured by their angle to the True Wind

W

D_2

D_1

W

⊗ leeward mark

Figure 1

can be represented by a right triangle (Fig. 1). In this situation, if you hold to D_2 on a downwind leg, you'll never get to the leeward mark. However, as long as you tack downwind at the same angle to the true wind on

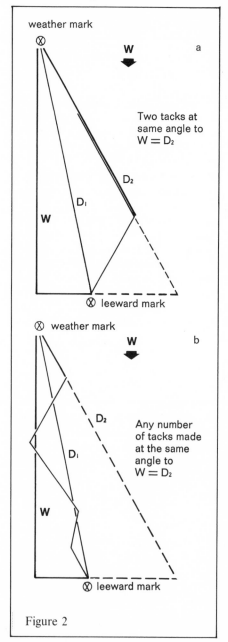

weather mark

W　　　　a

Two tacks at
same angle to
$W = D_2$

D_2

D_1

W

⊗ leeward mark

⊗ weather mark

W　　　　b

D_2

Any number
of tacks made
at the same
angle to
$W = D_2$

D_1

W

⊗ leeward mark

Figure 2

your way to the mark, the total distance (and therefore the percentage of speed increase required) of those tacks equals D_2 (Fig. 2).

Basic trigonometry tells us the relationship of D_1 and D_2 to W, for a given angle at the weather mark is known as a secant. Secants are precisely calculated values, and you can use them to calculate the exact percentage added distance (and therefore speed) required of a given downwind tacking course with the following formula.

$$\frac{Sec.D_2 - Sec.D_1}{Sec.\ D_1} = \%\ \text{speed increase to break even}$$

Since secants are functions of given angles, for simplicity's sake the terms D_2 and D_1 refer to the angles formed by these lines with W.

Although space prevents an exposition of the development and proof of this formula, math buffs can verify it with simple algebra and trigonometry.

Now you don't want to go through computations like this on your boat; and you don't have to. By happy coincidence, the percentages derived from the foregoing formula and those derived from an easily memorized series of numbers correlate remarkably well — and allow you to use this rule-of-thumb approximation.

The series of numbers is 1-1-2-3-4-5-6-7-8. Obviously, all you need remember is to introduce an extra "1" at the beginning of a normal counting sequence.

These numbers represent the approximate speed increases, expressed as percentages, required to break even for each 5° of angle between W and D_2 (your downwind tacks). These numbers are cumulative: for instance, the breakeven

Leeward mark relative to true wind	Downwind tacks relative to true wind	$\dfrac{\text{Sec. } D_2 - \text{Sec. } D_1}{\text{Sec. } D_1}$ % added speed to break even
0° (mark dead downwind)	10°	1.5%
	20°	6.4%
	30°	15.5%
	40°	30.5%
	45°	41.4%
10°	20°	4.8%
	30°	13.8%
	40°	28.6%
	45°	39.3%
20°	30°	8.6%
	40°	22.7%
	45°	32.9%
30°	40°	12.9%
	45°	22.4%
40°	45°	8.3%
1-1-2 numbers added except those in ( )		1-1-2 (% added to break even)
1+1		2%
1+1+2+3		7%
1+1+2+3+4+5		16%
1+1+2+3+4+5+6+7		29%
1+1+2+3+4+5+6+7+8		37%
(1,1) 2+3		5%
(1,1) 2+3+4+5		14%
(1,1) 2+3+4+5+6+7		27%
(1,1) 2+3+4+5+6+7+8		35%
(1,1,2,3) 4+5		9%
(1,1,2,3) 4+5+6+7		22%
(1,1,2,3) 4+5+6+7+8		30%
(1,1,2,3,4,5) 6+7		13%
(1,1,2,3,4,5) 6+7+8		21%
(1,1,2,3,4,5,6,7) 8		8%

Figure 3

speed increase required for a downwind course 15% off true wind directions is 1 + 1 + 2 or 4%.

You can also accomplish the subtraction called for in the secant formula by *not* adding those numbers of the 1-1-2 series that represent the angular difference (in 5° bits) between the true wind and the rhumb line to the leeward mark, when it is off to one side.

To use this 1-1-2 rule of thumb, you use man's oldest computing device: your fingers. You know the course to the leeward mark, the direction of the true wind, and your proposed downwind tacks. Now, follow these steps:

1. Count on your knuckles — by 5° bits — the angle between the true wind and the rhumb line to the leeward mark. For example, if the

155

rhumb line to the leeward mark is 15° to one side of the true wind direction count 5-10-15 on three knuckles.

2. We will assume you have decided to take downwind tacks of 40° to the true wind. Move up to your fingertips and continue counting by 5° bits until you arrive at the angle representing your downwind tacks relative to the true wind.* In this case you would move to your fingers and continue with: 20-25-30-35-40.

3. Go back and count on the same three knuckles again but this time counting "1,1,2," etc. Mentally, throw these numbers away.

4. Move to the same fingertips as in Step 2 and keep counting. But this time continue with 3-4-5, etc., and end on the same finger you did before. Here you count 3-4-5-6-7. Add the numbers you have tapped *only* on your fingertips. In this case the total amount equals 25, and this is the percentage of speed increase you must achieve to break even on this downwind tacking course.

To summarize this example, in a downwind tack of 40° toward a mark 15° off the true wind direction, you must increase your boat speed 25%

---

* Contrary to standard nautical practice, true wind direction in this article is described as 0° (relative) when heading dead downwind. The properly described wind direction would, of course, be 180° relative.

in order to break even. If your boat speed on the rhumb line is 4.0 knots, it must increase to 5.0 knots during the downwind tacking maneuvers in order to arrive at the leeward mark at the same time as would a boat traveling the rhumb line course. Of course, if you achieve 5.5 knots, you'll be considerably ahead.

To reassure you that this system does work, Figure 3 compares precise results from the secant formula (center column) against 1-1-2 results (right hand column). Not all combinations are shown, but intermediate combinations do show the same correlation.

While the discrepancies for 45° tacks on marks dead downwind, or on marks 10° off the wind, may appear large, they really are not. If one's boat speed is 3.0 knots, the error is slightly more than $\frac{1}{10}$ of a knot. Remember too, that you are looking for *substantial* speed increments over the break-even speeds and in that context, a discrepancy of $\frac{1}{10}$ of a knot or so becomes meaningless.

The 1-1-2 rule should pay off. On a five-mile downwind run, if the 1-1-2 rule can help you realize a gain of just $\frac{1}{10}$ of a knot over a 3.0 knot break-even speed, you'll pick up more than three-and-a-half minutes. And that could mean picking up more silver.

5
CHARTS & AIDS

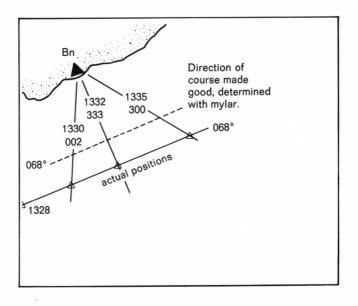

Charts Can Help You Plan Ahead

By Robert H. Gulmon

You can't get very far into any voyage plans before you discover you need navigation charts. The selection, both for planning and later for navigation, is rendered confusing by the vast array of nautical charts now available. Each geographic region is covered by a variety of overlapping charts that differ in scale, the amount of geographic and hydrographic information shown and the purpose for which they are intended. The initial impulse to get one of everything, besides being inordinately expensive, could lead you to stowage, filing and access problems, not to mention the clerical load of entering so many chart corrections. It is wiser to make a careful study of your chart requirements and to purchase only those you are likely to need. Because chart selection is best done in a deliberate manner, it is most sensible to obtain your own copies of the appropriate chart catalogs for leisurely reference at home. These catalogs list all the charts available for indicated geographical regions by title, serial number, scale and price. Additionally, the area covered by each chart is delineated by a rectangle, representing the chart's borders, drawn on a small-scale chart of the entire region (Fig. 1).

Charts can be broken down by scale into several general categories of intended usage. Familiarity with the several categories, their purposes and range of scales, is helpful for selecting the charts you will need. These are summarized below.

World Charts and Sailing Charts (1:600,000 and smaller; or 1 in. = 8.2 n.m. plus) typically depict extensive stretches of coastline, island groups and large portions of ocean basins.

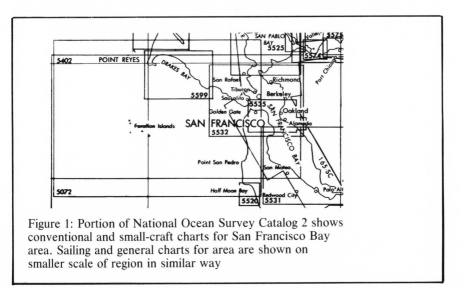

Figure 1: Portion of National Ocean Survey Catalog 2 shows conventional and small-craft charts for San Francisco Bay area. Sailing and general charts for area are shown on smaller scale of region in similar way

The amount of hydrographic and geographic information that can be shown on these charts is limited by their small scale. They are used mainly for laying out intended tracks between distant ports.

General Charts (1:100,000 to 1:600,000; or 1 in. = 1.4 to 8.2 n.m.) are intended for navigating well offshore but within visual range of prominent landmarks and navigational aids.

Coast Charts (1:50,000 to 1:100,000; or 1 in. − 0.7 to 1.4 n.m.) are intended for coastwise navigation inside offshore reefs and shoals, for entering large bays and harbors, and for navigating certain inland waterways.

Harbor Charts (1:50,000 and larger; or 1 in. = 0.7 n.m. minus) contain the greatest amount of detail and are intended for navigating and anchoring in smaller harbors and restricted waterways.

Small-Craft Charts (1:40,000; or 1 in. = 0.5 n.m.) are a special category designed specifically for use on small vessels. These are smaller in size than conventional charts and are issued in packet or folio form similar to road maps. Small-craft charts are now published for the more popular boating areas in US waters and various rivers and restricted waterways, including the Intracoastal Waterway.

Although the selection of charts is a matter of judgment based on the flexibility of your voyage plan and the possible contingencies that might cause you to depart from it, there are a few helpul guidelines.

A single chart covering an area sufficient to contain the track of your entire cruise is useful for planning purposes and later serves as a "howgozit" chart on which you can plot daily positions and keep track of your progress. Usually the scale of this chart is appropriate for plotting the locations and predicted movements of storm centers and other meteorological information received via weather broadcasts. The largest scale chart that will contain your entire track should be selected.

When you select charts for coastwise piloting, bear in mind that the relatively low freeboard of your boat will limit the range of visibility of landmarks and navigational aids, thus dictating a track that lies closer inshore than those normally taken by large vessels. You should choose both your track and the corresponding charts to insure that an adequate number of landmarks and navigational aids for obtaining frequent fixes will be within your visual range. In choosing between Coast and General Charts, pick the largest scale chart that extends far enough to seaward to include your track.

When you are approaching a coastline, as when making a landfall, it is essential that you have a chart that extends sufficiently far to seaward of reefs, shoals and other hazards to permit establishing your position accurately on the chart from visible landmarks or navigational aids while you are still safely outside the area of potential danger. Here again, you must consider your range of visibility and select the largest chart that meets this requirement.

You should have harbor charts for all harbors, bays, inlets or other restricted waterways that you intend to enter — including selected alternate ports in the event you decide to change your itinerary later or an emergency requires you to make for the nearest port.

All charts and publications relating to coastal and inland waters of United States are issued by the US

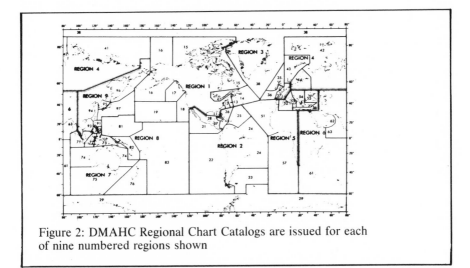

Figure 2: DMAHC Regional Chart Catalogs are issued for each of nine numbered regions shown

National Ocean Survey, a major element of the National Oceanic and Atmospheric Administration. National Ocean Survey (NOS) Chart Catalogs are published for four regions: No. 1 covers the Atlantic and Gulf Coasts; No. 2, the Pacific Coast and Hawaii; No. 3, Alaska; and No. 4, the Great Lakes and Adjacent Waterways. Additionally, each of the catalogs lists all NOS publications, including *Coast Pilots,* maps and charts of other agencies such as the Army Corps of Engineers, and the addresses of all authorized nautical chart sales agents within the region.

Thus, the catalog covering your area of interest contains all the information you need to select and order charts and publications issued by the National Ocean Survey. Best of all, these chart catalogs can be obtained free of charge by sending a letter request to the National Ocean Survey Distribution Division (C44), 6501 Lafayette Avenue, Riverdale, Maryland 20840.

Charts and publications for foreign waters, including *Pilot Charts* and *Sailing Directions,* are issued by the Defense Mapping Agency Hydrographic Center (DMAHC). Because DMAHC is responsible for providing worldwide chart coverage, involving several thousand individual charts, the cataloging system is somewhat more complex than for NOS material. The starting point is Publication No. 1-N-L, *Numerical Listing of Charts and Publications.* This pamphlet, which is free, lists all nautical publications obtainable from DMAHC, addresses of authorized sales agents, locations of DMAHC offices and a numerical listing of charts grouped with the regions and subregions shown on its cover (Fig. 2).

Having identified your region of interest, you should obtain the appropriate regional catalog, Publication No. 1-N-(region number). These are numbered from 1 to 9 to correspond with the regions shown on Figure 2 and are similar to the NOS catalogs in that charts are depicted graphically as well as listed by serial number, title, scale and price. Regional catalogs can be obtained from authorized sales agents (usually the same ones listed in the NOS catalogs) or from DMAHC offices located on the Naval Air Stations at

Norfolk, Jacksonville, and San Diego (North Island); Hickam Air Force Base in Hawaii, and the center at Suitland, Maryland. Publication No. 1-N-L and the appropriate regional catalogs are all you will need for selecting DMAHC material. Although over-the-counter sales are made at DMAHC offices, it is preferred that you deal with authorized agents.

I have dealt with the basic reference material for voyage planning — what is available and where to get it. The plans themselves can be as detailed and as comprehensive as you choose to make them but they should not be regarded as a rigid timetable of events. Flexibility is an essential element of any good plan and viable alternatives ought to be generated by the act of planning. A famous planner, General Eisenhower, once said that plans are nothing — but he then added that *planning* is *everything*. By studying the characteristics of a region and the conditions you are likely to encounter, then considering all the available options, you will have made the best possible preparations.

Don't Forget the Fine Print

By James B. Kane

Someone once said that reading the fine print is educational and not reading it is experience. This statement was probably made in reference to buying a car or a house. But this advice applies equally to piloting your boat. The fine print that occupies the land areas and the borders of your charts has a great deal of data that can help you with your piloting. This fine print has rules about restricted areas and magnetic variation, as well as characteristics of lights and buoys.

What else can you get from your chart? Always look first under the chart title to see whether the soundings on it are in feet, fathoms, or perhaps even in meters. By knowing this basic and important element you will never take one foot to mean one fathom! The difference between one foot and six feet could obviously mean the difference between a happy day and a sad one.

Under the title of the chart you see the stage of the tide from which the soundings were taken. On the Atlantic coast of the United States, the plane of reference (stage of the tide) is *mean low water* (MLW), which is the average reached by water's surface in a lunar month expressed in distance below mean sea level. The Pacific coast uses *mean lower low water* (MLLW), and Canadian charts use Lowest Normal Tide.

The print under the chart title also shows the range of tide for various places on your chart and can warn you of a potentially foul ground and abnormally strong or unusual currents.

Because of constantly occurring changes on charts, you must look at the edition date of a chart, located in the lower left-hand corner of every National Ocean Survey (NOS) chart. It's important you know the date to avoid using or buying an obsolete chart. NOS no longer hand-corrects charts before selling them, and it's up to you to hand-correct them after the printing date shown in the left-hand corner (Fig. 1).

It is my feeling that if you have a choice of buying a *small-craft* chart and a conventional chart, you should think about buying the small-craft chart. They are printed annually and

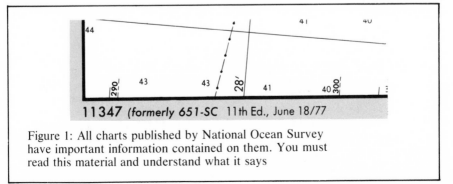

11347 (formerly 651-SC 11th Ed., June 18/77

Figure 1: All charts published by National Ocean Survey have important information contained on them. You must read this material and understand what it says

are folded accordion-style in a jacket that is loaded with such facts as the time and height of the tides, frequencies of stations giving weather forecasts and warnings, phone numbers of the National Weather Service, as well as supplies provided by various marinas and boatyards located on the chart. Its size and style suit it well for use aboard a small boat, though it may not be particularly good for long-distance, point-to-point navigation because of the way it may be laid out. Although small-craft charts are your best buy, generally they cover only those areas used by small boats.

Some oil companies put out maps called "Cruising Guides." They're great for planning trips, but don't try to use them in place of regular charts for they lack some of the detail and accuracy you need for piloting.

NOS has no set time for printing a new edition of a regular chart. When corrections from the *Notices to Mariners* become too numerous, or NOS makes a major change in a chart, it will bring the chart up to date with a new edition. The interval between editions could be one year, or it could be many years. NOS does issue a free pamphlet called *Dates of Latest Editions*, which you should have if you want to know the latest edition of a chart (write NOS Distribution Center, C44, Riverdale, MD 20840). The *Notices to Mariners* also lists new editions as they come out.

To correct your charts, consult both the weekly *Notice to Mariners* and the local *Notice to Mariners*, which is issued free by each Coast Guard District and includes all corrections for that district. You can get the latter by applying in writing to the Coast Guard District in which you're sailing. The number and address of your Coast Guard District

may be found in the phone book under the Federal listings and the Department of Transportation.

Canadian *Notices to Mariners* are also published weekly and may be obtained from The Director, Aids and Waterways, Canadian Coast Guard, Ministry of Transport, Ottawa, Canada. However, you should get your notices from the country you sail in; otherwise you'll run into a mailing problem. If you don't know the charts you need, dealers have a catalog to help you, or you may get a catalog from NOS at the address already listed.

Besides the marked soundings, a chart has depth curves (curves of equal depth usually shown for every six feet) that clearly show the curves of equal depth (6 feet, 12 feet, and so forth). You can always identify submerged and floating features (except soundings) by italic or angled lettering. Conventional vertical lettering describes things that are dry at high water. Green-colored areas show reefs, mud flats, and sand bars that may be covered with water at some stages of the tide. White indicates deep water. Blue indicates shallow water, and buff or yellow colors indicate land.

To interpret a chart fully you must be thoroughly familiar with the sym-

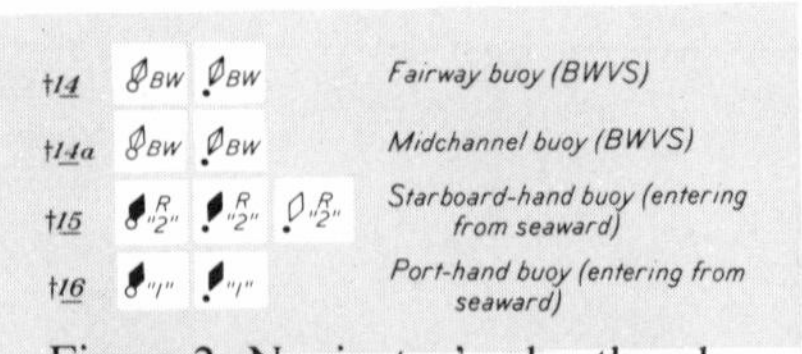

Figure 2: Navigator's shorthand is symbols used on chart. All those working with charts should be familiar with it. Here is detail showing dot and small circle under different types of buoys

bols and abbreviations that are used to show the topography and the structures. These symbols are called the *navigator's shorthand,* and with them you can identify chart detail and relate them to what you see ashore.

You should have a complete list of the symbols used on charts, plus the pamphlet *Chart No. 1, Nautical Chart Symbols and Abbreviations,* which you can buy from NOS for $1.50 (though prices are subject to change). Make your check or money order payable to NOS, Department of Commerce, and mail it to the Riverdale, Maryland, address. Canada also has a Chart No. 1 showing the same symbols and abbreviations as those in the United States. These symbols make no attempt at accuracy either in scale or detail, but they do show the correct location of a large amount of aids and dangers in a tiny space.

Buoys on charts are shown by the symbols in Figure 2. Occasionally

that tiny circle replaces the dot underneath the diamond because rough seas, fixing methods, slope of the bottom and scope of chain on the buoy make it impractical to chart the exact location of a buoy.

Not all the good advice on charts is found over the land areas. Much of it is printed on the water itself. Look for submerged cables or pipelines that could foul your anchor. You find them right at the spot where this danger exists printed in red or magenta.

Horizontal and vertical bridge clearances, both when opened and closed, are shown at the bridges themselves. You find overhead power cables printed on your chart in the same way. Your chart always displays the abbreviations for the characteristic range, and height of lighthouses *at the site of the lighthouse.* Thus Gp Fl (2) 10sec 63ft 13M shown at the lighthouse in Figure 3 means a group flashing light, two flashes every 10 seconds. The lighthouse is 63 feet above high water and has a range

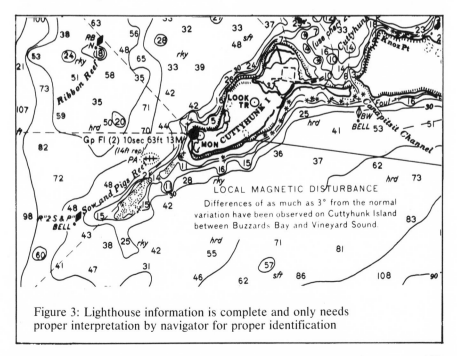

Figure 3: Lighthouse information is complete and only needs proper interpretation by navigator for proper identification

of 13 miles. Because nothing is said here about color, the color of the light is white. A chart indicates the color of a light only when it's something other than white.

Don't be afraid to add your own advice and experience to your chart. Such things as a circle of visibility of a lighthouse for the height of eye aboard your boat might come in handy. Note anything else on your chart you believe could be useful, including ranges, currents, appearances of lighthouses, even sketches of features as they look from the sea.

Always stay away from areas on your chart marked *Fish Trap*. The nets also trap boats! Finally, study your chart *before* you use it, and avoid trying to steer your boat and study your chart at the same time. Familiarize yourself with the features and your course ahead of time so in an emergency everything you need to know is familiar to you.

A chart is a worksheet packed with information on which you may plot courses and position. If you use a chart correctly, it will help you arrive safely at your destination. But read all the fine print first so you really know what you are looking at.

Avoiding Terra Incognita

By Murray Lesser

Four hundred years ago no experienced sailor would venture into a new bay without sending his longboat ahead of him to look for hazards. Each newly discovered small island or hidden rock was then named by the navigator as he updated his chart.

Today we usually don't bother with the longboat. Our reasoning is that a benevolent National Ocean Survey (NOS) has carefully searched all of our cruising waters and has plotted every obstruction on a multicolored chart; the Coast Guard has established markers, also shown on the chart, at every possible place where we might go astray; and every hazard to navigation is so well charted that exploring is hardly worth the candle these days.

Don't you believe it!

There is still a lot of terra incognita left at the bottom of the sea, and you may discover some of it during your next cruise. Even if all the hidden hazards were charted once, coastal waters do change over time. Particularly with stabilized coasts, the underwater contours are continually shifting. The Coast Guard moves its buoys around to conform to the new contours as soon as it discovers any change. New aids to navigation are added as a result of increasing traffic or newly discovered hazards. And periodically a section of buoys and daymarks is renumbered to make order out of the resulting chaos.

As good as the NOS and Coast Guard work may be, none of the natural or manmade changes that have occurred since the edition date of your chart (shown in the chart's lower left-hand corner) are going to be on it unless you put them there yourself. Updating your charts still is an essential part of safe coastal cruising. Only nowadays there is usually an easier way to do it than sending out a longboat.

That easier way is to let the Coast Guard furnish you with new information as it becomes available. You won't learn anything about terra incognita that they haven't yet learned, but at least you will know as much about the changes as they do. You can have all this information delivered to you free each week by subscribing to the *Local Notice to Mariners (LNM)*. Each Coast Guard district publishes an edition covering all the federal water in that district.

To subscribe write a letter to the commander of your local Coast Guard at the headquarters of the district(s) for which you wish coverage indicating that you are a boatowner, sailor, or fisherman and that you want to receive the *Local Notice to Mariners*. You can find the district numbers and addresses of the headquarters in the *Nautical Chart Catalog* or in the appendix to the appropriate coast pilot.

I regularly cruise a part of the coast that covers two Coast Guard districts so I get the *LNM* from both. The *LNM*s are the sole source of data about changes affecting small-craft harbors. The *Notice to Mariners* published out of Washington, D.C., contains only data of interest to ocean-going commercial vessels.

Here are a few examples of what you will find in your *LNM*. Each issue opens with any available "Special Notices," such as the times during which RDF and loran stations are scheduled to be off the air for maintenance. Early each year a "Special Notice" with year-long importance will announce the availability of a new *Light List*.

A later issue of the *LNM* — usually appearing in early March — will contain the corrections you must make to your brand-new *Light List* to take care of all the changes that have occurred during the three months between the time the edition was closed and the time you were able to buy it. While the *Light List* changes also were announced as they occurred, those announcements were all keyed to the numbers in last year's *List*. The annual summary is the only recap of old changes keyed to this year's numbers.

Of course, you could save a few dollars by not buying the new *List*. However, you will then have problems updating your old *List,* because from now on in, the *LNM* changes all will be keyed to the new numbers. The problem can be solved with a lot of work, but it is false economy to continue updating obsolete navigation documents.

An announcement of a newly discovered major hazard will also be carried as a "Special Notice." A not untypical notice reads: "Shoaling exists in Hereford Inlet to such an extent that the inlet is considered unsafe to transit under any condition. All floating aids to navigation in the inlet have been removed. Charts 12316, 12318. LNM 9 (New York) 27 Feb. 80." Shades of the early explorers and their longboats!

Nearly every issue of *LNM* contains a section headed, "Aids Estab-

lished, Discontinued or Changed." Here you find the listings of all the manmade changes that have occurred since the last issue of *LNM:* buoys moved, removed, or renumbered; numbers added to previously unnumbered daymarks; color changes for daymarks; radar reflectors added; and lighthouse characteristics that have changed. Each entry is complete with affected chart and *Light List* numbers so that you can make the corrections.

In order to avoid confusion later in emergency conditions, you should make all your corrections to your charts very carefully. I find the best way is to scrape any obsolete information off the surface of the chart with a scalpel blade and put in the new data using draftsman's india ink and a lettering pen. Making corrections correctly is work, so I usually postpone the inevitable by filing the change information in my navigator's notebook until the week before I am going to need the chart. My procrastination comes from my hope that a chartlet will be issued first.

Chartlets are little sections of chart that are distributed with *LNMs*. If a change has been extensive, NOS may issue a chartlet to be cemented over the changed portions of the old chart. Because the arrival of a chartlet tends to lag the notice of change by about four months, usually I have made my corrections before I receive the chartlet. Even so, I always cement the chartlet on. The reason is that chartlets carry detailed corrections in addition to the ones I have put in by hand. I have plotted courses across a chartlet for a full season, so a permanent bond is best. Rubber cement works well.

The next section of the *LNM* is the "Advance Notice of Changes in Aids to Navigation." Each notice in this section reads the same as it will later in the "Aids Established" portion except that it will say "on or about" and give a date three weeks to a month later than the date of the first notice.

Possibly because of the press of other affairs, the Coast Guard does not always get the change installed on the scheduled date. If this happens the particular "Advance Notice" will continue to run until the change is actually made. However, once that occurs the item moves up one section — to "Aids Established" — after which it may well disappear forever.

I usually don't pay much attention to the "Advance Notices" unless I am going cruising for awhile and will be out of touch with the postal service for a few weeks. Inasmuch as it is better not to be surprised by a strange buoy when piloting in the fog, even an "on or about" warning of what is planned is better than no warning at all.

One very important section of each *LNM* is headed "General." Here you find announcements that new chart editions are available. This listing helps to keep your personal chart catalog up to date. I keep a record of the most recent edition date for every chart I've ever owned. But I don't buy a new one until I'm ready to cruise the region again. This kind of record keeping, incidentally, is a nice application for my home computer. The new chart's availability seems to lag the edition date by about two months. Thus, the chart already could be two months out-of-date before you can buy one.

The "General" section also carries any newly developed information on what was heretofore terra incognita to NOS. For example, *LNM 50* (Boston) 11 December 1979, noted for Penobscot Bay—Muscle Ridge Channel—Little Green Island (Chart 13306) that the correction is "ADD—Sunken Rock and Legend Rep. [reported] in 44°00′59″N,69°03′58.2″W." This note was of especial interest to me because the rock was discovered — the hard way — by a friend of mine. Unfortunately he forgot to give it a name, so the account that follows will be the only historical record of the discovery.

It was very nearly low tide at the time, and my friend was under sail at about 4 knots when he struck. He was carefully avoiding the "... unmarked ledges, but most of them show at high water, and all of them are evident at low water" that the popular cruising guide warns about. This particular sunken rock happened to be one foot under the surface at mean low water, in an area that sounded eleven feet all around its near vicinity.

Not one to let a challenge lie, my friend climbed into his dinghy (longboat) the following day and surveyed the area. He sent the coordinates of his rock to the Coast Guard (and to the author of the cruising guide). The Coast Guard sent the information to the NOS, the NOS gave it a file number and asked the Coast Guard to inform the public. The *LNM* "General Notice" of December 11, 1979, was the result. My friend's anonymous rock will appear on the next edition of the chart.

This episode proves to me that the age of exploration is not really over. Keeping your charts updated from the *Local Notice to Mariners* will not remove all the terra incognita from your cruising area. But at least it may keep you from *rediscovering* a hazard that was already known to the chartmakers.

Setting Up the Universal Plotting Sheet

By Ed Bergin

If you do any kind of offshore sailing, especially celestial navigation, you should be aware of the Universal Plotting Sheet (UPS). One pad of these sheets will spare your expensive charts from several seasons of ruinous navigational chicken scratchings.

On a recent round-trip cruise from the Chesapeake Bay to the Bahamas, six of these sheets, costing a total of 30¢, kept nearly $300 worth

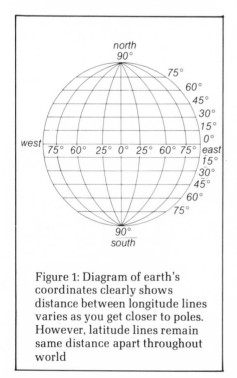

Figure 1: Diagram of earth's coordinates clearly shows distance between longitude lines varies as you get closer to poles. However, latitude lines remain same distance apart throughout world

of charts virtually spotless and ready for the next trip.

When you are using a Universal Plotting Sheet you record all your work on the sheet, then transfer significant events, such as fixes and the day's 24-hour run, to the main sailing chart. I suspect one reason these worksheets are not more popular among sailors is because many simply do not know how to use them. So here is how you can spare your charts without spoiling the cruise. But before I get to the details, let's understand the basics.

We know the world is round and that navigation charts that show a part of the earth's surface as a flat piece of paper are called *mercator projections*.

The UPS is essentially a *blank form* chart you can quickly and easily customize for the area in which you are sailing. You then use the UPS, instead of the chart, for the messy work such as keeping your dead reckoning (DR) and plotting fixes. Because the UPS is essentially a scaled-down version of the big chart, information about key events, such as a fix, can be transferred from the UPS to the chart with great accuracy.

To understand this customizing, look at Figure 1, which is the earth's system of coordinates. First notice how the distance between the latitude lines rèmains the same throughout the world. This fact explains one of the most important things a navigator should know: the distance represented by degrees or minutes of latitude is *the same anywhere on the globe*. In this context, it is important to know that there are 60 minutes in a degree of latitude and that one minute of latitude equals one nautical mile. That is why a chart's latitude scale can also be used to measure distance.

If you look at the longitude lines in Figure 1, you see that they get closer together as they near the poles. Although there are 60 minutes in each degree of longitude, you can see that the distance represented by these 60 minutes varies considerably depending upon where you are in the world.

When you set up a UPS you should always have both the UPS *and* the chart out at the same time because you must see which way the longitude and latitude numbers are increasing. For example, if you are anywhere in the lower 48 states, you can see that latitude increases as you go north and longitude increases as you go west. However, in other areas of the world this may not be the case.

Let's construct a UPS for an area using the Training Chart 1210TR which describes the area of Narragansett Bay, Rhode Island. It covers an area from 41°09′N to 41°45′N and from 70°36′W to 71°35′W. After studying your chart, you determine that the most useful mid-latitude for setting up your UPS is 41°N. This latitude permits you to record the boat's movement north or south of the 41st parallel.

Now take a look at a blank UPS. Because latitude lines are equidistant throughout the world, it's easy to see why these lines, together with the latitude scale in the middle, are already printed on the form. Because the latitude lines are already printed, all you have to do is fill in the missing latitude-degree notations along the

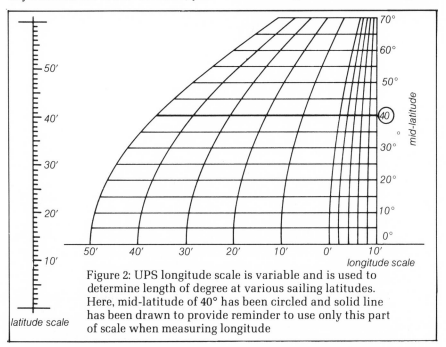

Figure 2: UPS longitude scale is variable and is used to determine length of degree at various sailing latitudes. Here, mid-latitude of 40° has been circled and solid line has been drawn to provide reminder to use only this part of scale when measuring longitude

Navigator's practice session

The following exercise is designed to help you become familiar with the UPS. Check your work by comparing the width of your dividers with the length of the lines under each question. Remember, use the longitude scale for longitude only. Use the latitude scale for *distance and latitude*. *(Use Figure 2 for scale.)*

1. Use the latitude scale to measure 60 minutes.

 ├──┤

2. Use the longitude scale to measure 60 minutes if the 'mid-latitude is 20°.

 ├───┤

 Use the longitude scale to measure 60 minutes if the mid-latitude is 45°.

 ├────────────────────────────────────┤

 Use the longitude scale to measure 60 minutes if the mid-latitude is 65°.

 ├──────────────────────┤

(Notice how 60 minutes of longitude can represent a *different distance*. The same 60 minutes of longitude covers a *greater distance* as you *near the equator* and represents a *smaller distance* as you get into the higher latitudes *nearer the poles*.)

3. What is the distance in nautical miles between these two DR positions? (30 miles)

 ├───────────────────────────┤

4. What is the distance in nautical miles between these two DR positions assuming the mid-latitude is 30°? (18 miles)

 ├────────────────┤

margins. As you write in the latitude values, keep in mind that here latitude increases as you go north and decreases as you go south. Filling these in completes the latitude-labelling portion of your UPS.

Look again at your UPS and you'll see it has one longitude line (the mid-longitude or center line) already drawn. Now refer to your chart and you see that it is appropriate to label this mid-longitude line as 71°. You

can also see from your chart that longitude increases as you move west and decreases as you move east from the mid-longitude point. To find out how far apart to place the other longitude lines take a look at the UPS longitude scale in Figure 2. You'll find this scale printed in the lower right-hand corner of your UPS.

As Figure 2 shows, the length of a degree of longitude varies depending on your particular sailing latitude.

5. Use the longitude scale to set your dividers for 60 minutes, assuming a mid-latitude of 40°.

|————————————————————————————|

6. With mid-latitude 40°, set your dividers for 50 minutes of longitude.

|——————————————————————|

7. With mid-latitude 40°, set your dividers for 8 minutes of longitude.

|————|

8. With mid-latitude 40°, set your dividers for:
58 minutes of longitude

|————————————————————————————|

18 minutes of longitude

|————————|

22 minutes of longitude

|————————|

33 minutes of longitude

|——————————|

9. If your mid-latitude is 35°, how far apart will your longitude lines be placed on the universal plot sheet?

|——————————————————————————|

10. At mid-latitude 35° you find that your DR position must be advanced by 18 miles. Set your dividers for this distance.

|——————————|

Because this UPS is being laid out for a mid-latitude of 41°, you locate and make a mark by the closest printed mid-latitude value on the right-hand margin of the scale. Because 40° is so close to 41° you can safely use 40° as your mid-latitude point. If your mid-latitude were 43° you could interpolate on the scale by marking a point halfway between 40° and 45°, but in this case it is not necessary.

Figure 2 shows how a solid line has been drawn from left to right along the longitude scale at the 40° mid-latitude point. *This solid line is the distance represented by one degree of longitude for this charted area.* The solid line also reminds you that this is the *only* part of the longitude scale you should use.

For example, if your UPS were constructed for a mid-latitude closer to the equator, say 25°, you would draw your line along the 25° area of the scale. If you use Figure 2 and your dividers you can see how much greater the length of a degree of longitude is at 25° than it is at 40° or 55°.

To finish the longitude-labeling portion of the UPS, set your dividers for the distance represented by the solid line at your particular mid-latitude; in this case it is the 40° line. You can now use your parallel rules and a pencil to construct and label the rest of the longitude lines on your chart. Latitude measurements are easy because the scale is printed right on the UPS. Longitude measurements are a little bit tricky, but once you understand how to make them you will have no trouble.

Look at Figure 2 again and you see that the longitude scale is really two scales in one. There is a zero- to 50-minute scale that moves to the left from the zero mark in 10-minute increments. There is also a zero- to 10-minute scale that moves to the right in two-minute increments.

If you require a longitude measurement rounded to the nearest 10 minutes, put your right divider pointer on zero and the left pointer on whatever value is needed: 10, 20, 30, 40, or 50 minutes. However, you often need to find an intermediate value such as 48 minutes. When this happens you put the left pointer of your dividers on 40°, then move the right pointer four "ticks" to the right of zero, because each line to the right of zero is equal to two minutes of longitude. When you are moving the right pointer, be careful to take your measurements only along the solid line you have drawn on the scale because this is the *only* part of the scale appropriate for the mid-latitude.

When using the UPS, disregard the degree markings that are printed on the right-hand side outside the compass rose. These are used with an alternative (and to me cumbersome) method of constructing longitude lines.

Also note that the compass rose printed on the UPS is the true, and not magnetic, rose. I find it useful to mark the magnetic variation from the charted area inside the compass. If it helps, you can also make a pencil reminder of the rules for correcting from true to magnetic and magnetic to true: subtract east and add west when going from true to compass; add east and subtract west when going from compass to true.

Now try the UPS practice exercise I've included with this article. And finally, place a pad of UPS sheets on your navigator's station. When properly labeled they'll help spare both your charts and your pocket book.

Detailing Special Charts

By Lou Hohenstein

Frequently I need charts that are not available from the usual government agencies, or I need one in a different size from those available. I often need a chart of a local cruising or racing area, with additional information that is of special interest to me. It's not hard to convert a chart to another size and to add information. Even the cost of reproduction can be reasonable, and you can develop and print these charts in limited quantities for your own special needs.

A blueprint service can make blue-line prints for large charts in small quantities, and regular printing techniques can be used for small charts in relatively large quantities. For either method, you need to develop a master chart, or *chart manuscript,* from which the copies will be made. This is really the key operation because after you have the master, you can use any reproduction method you want.

The first chart I made was for navigating in the Gulf Stream between Florida and the Bahamas. I designed this chart as a Gulf Stream plotting sheet for Southern Ocean Racing Conference (SORC) racing. The government chart available for this area is too small, and it is crowded with depth soundings, place names, and other extraneous data. All the printing cluttered the offshore water area I needed for plotting. Furthermore, I wanted additional information not shown on the original chart on my chart. Primarily, this was the location of aircraft beacons and key radio-broadcast stations and their frequencies. When I was through, my chart was 3' x 4', made from a section of a National Oceanic and Atmospheric Adminstration (NOAA) chart that was originally 1½' x 1½'.

Here's how you can make a similar chart for an area you are interested in.

First, cut out the section from the printed chart you plan to enlarge or modify. Paste this cut-out section on posterboard to provide a rigid working surface. Cut out the corresponding latitude and longitude scales from the chart and glue them in place. Make sure they are aligned accurately with their correct lines on the cut-out section.

Next, remove all unnecessary soundings, place names, and extra data that is printed on the original chart. Do this with white typing correction fluid. Now you have your *original chart manuscript.*

Now you can enlarge (or reduce) this original chart manuscript to the size you want. A blueprint or advertising photo service can make a photographic enlargement, or reduction, of your chart manuscript. If you plan to add further copy to what is now an enlarged chart manuscript, mount the new size chart on a stiff backing to give you an effective working surface. At this point, you can add:

(1) the chart name, its purpose, and its publication date

(2) the location of navigational aids, such as aircraft beacons and radio-broadcast stations

(3) additional compass roses for easier plotting

(4) other navigational or electronic aids you might use that are not plotted on the chart (loran-C lines or other systems)

(5) any critical bearings, special danger angles, or marks or buoys.

Remember that you can inset an enlarged section of a critical place on this primary chart. You can also delete anything not previously removed.

Once all this has been done, recheck your chart very closely and take it to a blueprint service. Have them make an *autopositive* from your enlarged chart manuscript. An autopositive is a translucent positive copy of your chart. It is like an engineering tracing except it's made photographically from your enlarged chart manuscript, rather than from a drawing. Now you can have low-cost copies duplicated from the autopositive master using the standard blueprint reproduction process.

The autopositive can be made either on thin paper or on heavy-plastic vellum to form a durable master copy. You can use your autopositive to run copies just as you would run blueprints, except the prints will be blue or black lines on a white background. Be sure you specify this. You still can add minor changes directly to a your autopositive without remaking it.

Another chart I have made illustrates a slightly different technique in making the original chart manuscript. A boating organization wanted an accurate chart of Lake Lanier near Atlanta, Georgia, for their students' use when they take celestial sights. The only available source that covered the lake with sufficient accuracy were the topographic maps published by the US Geological Survey. I took six separate topographic maps that covered the lake and aligned and glued them together. The point I make here is that the source for your special chart does not have to be any one original chart. In fact, you may need to make a mosaic of several charts.

I followed the regular procedure of accurately placing the latitude and longitude scales on the edge. I deleted place names and unwanted copy, and I cut off all the unwanted land areas. Then I took this original chart manuscript and had it photographically enlarged to a table-size enlarged chart manuscript. I added a border and made the shoreline of the lake bolder with a heavy line. Finally, a vellum autopositive was made and blue-line copies were run.

In both examples, charts could have been printed with normal printing techniques. But the initial fixed cost of printing them would require that a large number of copies be run before the unit cost would be equal to the cost charged for far fewer copies made by a blueprint service.

You can also make an area plotting sheet by directly tracing needed data from an existing chart. The method is to first overlay a sheet of tracing paper over an existing chart. Next, copy the latitude and longitude coordinates. Trace only the places of primary interest from the original chart, and finally add any other data you feel is important on the area plotting sheet. What you end up with is a chart outline on tracing paper. Use this in place of an autopositive and you can make copies directly from the tracing by the same blueprint process I have previously described.

If you become really interested in charts or cartography, which is the science of charts and chart making, you can read further about charts and hydrography in the *American Practical Navigator* (H.O. 9), also

Where to look for charts

Coastal and offshore United States:
Distribution Division (C44)
National Ocean Survey
Riverdale, Md. 20840
Telephone (301) 436-6990

Foreign waters:
Defense Mapping Agency
Hydrographic Center Depot
5801 Tabor Ave.
Philadelphia, Pa. 19120
Telephone (215) 697-4264

Inland topographic maps for states east of the Mississippi River and Minnesota:
US Geological Survey
1200 S. Eads St.
Arlington, Va. 22202

(For states west of the Mississippi River):
US Geological Survey
Central Region Map Distribution
Building 41
Denver Federal Center
Denver, Colo. 80225

To obtain charts for these regions, check with your local chart store first, or contact the agencies listed above

called *Bowditch*. It's available in two volumes from the Director, Defense Mapping Agency, Office of Distribution Services, Attention: DDCP, Washington, DC 20315. If you want to find out what existing charts or maps are best for your purpose, write National Ocean Survey, Distribution Division C44, Riverdale, MD 20840, and ask for catalogs. Or you can also check with your local chart store; it should have the catalogs on hand.

Obviously, you must be careful about how you prepare your chart as well as whom you give it to. You should put on the chart its purpose, a warning, and possibly a disclaimer.

But if you work carefully and get all the correct information you need on your chart, it can be a great aid in helping you with your own navigation problems. Try making one and see whether you can improve on what is already available.

Understanding Mercator's Chart

By William V. Kielhorn

Almost every chart used by a yachtsman is based on the Mercator projection, and there are some very good reasons for this. The properties of this projection onto a flat piece of paper are most advantageous to the navigator, and the necessary distortions of any such projection are quite tractable — at least in the latitudes more commonly used by sailors. Here I'll discuss the projection as it is used in navigation and describe both the "exact" and the approximate methods of its construction.

To begin with, a chart is simply a means of representing coordinates useful in getting from one intercept to another on a sphere or spheroid. It does not need to have terrestrial or oceanographic topography displayed thereon, although these enhance its value considerably where dangers, seamarks, or landmarks occur. Consider, if you will, the words of a remarkable but shy mathematician, whose works should certainly be sheltered from the eyes of children because of his profound and delightful subtleties:

He had bought a large map representing the sea,
Without the least vestige of land:
And the crew were much pleased when they found it to be
A map they could all understand.

"What's the good of Mercator's North Poles and Equators,
Tropics, Zones, and Meridian Lines?"
So the Bellman would cry: and the crew would reply

"They are merely conventional signs!

"Other maps are such shapes, with their islands and capes!
But we've got our brave Captain to thank"
(So the crew would protest) "that he's bought us the best —
A perfect and absolute blank!"*

The butt of Dodgson's gentle humor was a most remarkable man, born in East Flanders in 1512 as Gerard Kremer (or de Cremer), and who latinized his name later, as was the custom among learned men of those times, to Gerardus Mercator (or Gerardi Mercatoris). He was educated in the best schools and took his master's degree at the University of Louvain, where he was tutored in advanced mathematics by Gemma Frisius. Yet this education got him into trouble later for his university studies in theology gave him some ideas which were contrary to some of those held by the Catholic Regent Mary of Hungary, who, in 1544, ordered him executed for heretical thought. Only the intervention of a persuasive friend saved him from the sword. (Female heretics, incidentally, were sentenced to be buried alive.) Thereafter, Mercator decided not to mix politics with science — for this was clearly dangerous to his health.

We tend to think of Mercator only in terms of the charts we use today

---

* Dodgson, C. L. (Lewis Carroll) "The Hunting of the Snark," Boni and Liveright, New York, 1924. Written in the late 19th century.

and to ignore his other great cartographic accomplishments. In fact, he was the world's foremost cartographer for some 60 years.

He engraved and published his first map (of Palestine) in 1537; this was followed by his 1538 map of the world, based on an unusual and beatiful double cordiform projection used earlier by Finé and Sylvanus. It was on this map that the terms "North America" and "South America" were first introduced. Thus, it was Mercator who finally gave us the recognized name of our own continent. Many years later, in 1569, he depicted the world on the projection with which we are now familiar, adding a great many new geographical features and names.

But Mercator had troubles with his new chart. It never turned out quite right, particularly in the higher latitudes. He had tried to make his chart "conformal," that is, where the expansion of scale of the parallels and the meridians must be proportional, and where the angles are represented correctly for any point. He just couldn't manage to do it, even after trying for 30 years. He managed to create the loxodrome (a straight-line course intercepting all the parallel meridians at a given angle), but no such projection could provide a good solution of the problem of being conformal; and distance measurement could not be determined with accuracy.

It remained for another mathematician, Edward Wright, professor of mathematics at Caius College, Cambridge, England, to solve the problem in 1599. Wright described his method, in popular fashion, with the earth as a rubber balloon encased in a cylinder tangent to the balloon at its equator. Then, as the balloon is inflated, the curved meridians become straightened against the walls of the cylinder. At the same time, each parallel of latitude finally comes to rest against the walls of the cylinder. This process goes on to infinity, because the regions near the poles never quite reach the cylinder walls. Then, the cylinder is cut along any meridian and is unrolled as a flat chart.

Wright's mathematical explanation of this "projection" was his great contribution to cartography. He developed a set of mathematical rules which satisfied the conformal requirements, resulting in the table of "meridianal parts." It must be emphasized that these are *not* based on any geometric or optical projection at all, although they approach a simple projection at low latitudes. I have found no evidence that Wright took into consideration the oblateness of the earth, which magnifies still further the distance distortion at the higher latitudes. The modern tables are given in "Bowditch" (US Naval Oceanographic Office Pub. No. 9), admitting corrections for this factor.

It will be necessary for you to have this publication, or one giving similar data, in order to construct a true Mercator chart, but the general idea of the chart is illustrated in Figure 1. One example will suffice to show its construction. Let us say you wish to construct a chart having a fixed longitude scale of four inches per degree (which is commonly used in celestial navigation plotting) between latitudes 42 degrees and 44 degrees. Proceed as follows:

1. Draw a series of vertical parallel lines four inches apart per degree. These are the meridians. Thus, there are 15 minutes of longitude per inch, so each minute (meridianal part scale) will be $\frac{1}{15}$ inches long, or

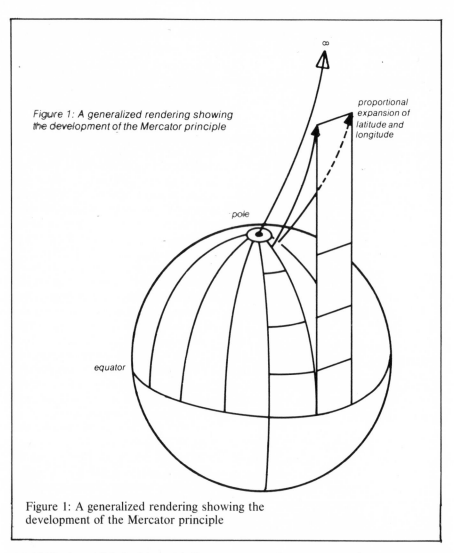

Figure 1: A generalized rendering showing
the development of the Mercator principle

Figure 1: A generalized rendering showing the
development of the Mercator principle

0.0667 inches. This is the multiplier.
2. Inasmuch as the equator will not be used as the lowest latitude reference, but 42 degrees, we will use the meridianal difference (m) between this (42 degrees) and the other latitudes up to our desired limit of 44 degrees.
3. Enter Table 5 of Bowditch (Pub. No. 9), and take out the values you wish to use between 42 degrees and 44 degrees. For simplicity, we shall illustrate only each whole degree. Your table should look like this:

M(43°)	2847.2	M(44°)	2929.6
M(42°)	2766.1	M(42°)	2766.1
m	81.1	m	163.5

The distance, in inches, between the reference latitude (42 degrees) and the next latitudes chosen will be the meridianal part scale (0.0667 inches) times the meridian difference (m) above.

L42° to L43° = .0667 × 81.1 = 5.41
inches

L42° to L44° = .0667 × 163.5 =
10.91 inches

4. Draw the lower latitude (42 degrees) near the bottom of your chart exactly at right angles to your meridian lines. Measure upward 5.41 inches to locate 43 degrees, and 10.91 inches (from 42 degrees) to locate the 44-degree latitude line.

5. Label the longitude lines as may be convenient, as long as they are one degree apart. Divide the longitude segments into six equal parts (10 minutes), and subdivide as desired. Label the latitudes, and divide each interval into six equal parts; or better, calculate each 10-minute interval of latitude and subdivide evenly as desired. You now have constructed an accurate Mercator chart.

There is a much simpler way of constructing a serviceable small-scale plotting sheet approximating the Mercator chart in the latitudes of the United States and lower. These are perfectly suitable for offshore work in plotting celestial fixes. They are particularly well adapted for small-craft use because you need only to draw a few sheets covering the expected latitude range of the cruise. Then you can photocopy or otherwise reproduce as many as necessary, and keep them in a looseleaf folder for use as required. They can be constructed graphically using any compass rose or a protractor, or can be determined mathematically using a table of trigonometric functions. Both are based on the idea that the Mercator chart expands as a function of the secant of the latitude — which it *almost* does in the lower latitudes. We will use the same example as before to illustrate the method, using four inches per degree of longitude and drawing the latitude lines 42 degrees, 43 degrees, and 44

degrees. Figure 2 illustrates this method. You proceed as follows:

1. Take a blank sheet of paper and draw a series of parallel vertical lines four inches apart. These are the meridians.
2. Draw the mid-latitude line at right angles to the meridians about in the center of the sheet. Label it 43 degrees.
3. Using the protractor, draw upward from any intersection of these lines an angle of 43½ degrees. Where this line intersects the adjacent meridian, measure its length, or swing it upward using a drawing compass, and this will be the distance from 43 degrees to 44 degrees.
4. Mark the distance between 43 degrees and 44 degrees into six (or multiples thereof) even parts. This is the approximate latitude scale between 43 degrees and 44 degrees.
5. Using the protractor, draw from the same origin a line at an angle of 42½ degrees downward. Where it intersects the adjacent meridian, measure its length, or swing the drawing compass downwards to your meridian. This will be the distance from 43 degrees to 42 degrees.
6. Divide each different line between intersections into six even parts. This represents 10 minutes of arc for latitude and longitude. Interpolate these divisions 10 times, if you wish to have one-minute scales.

The mathematical method is just as good. Draw the meridians as before, four inches apart, and draw the mid-latitude parallel at right angles to them near the center of the paper.

To find the distance between 43 degrees and 44 degrees, enter any trigonometric table, and find the secant or 43½ degrees. This is 1.379. Multiply this by the distance between meridians (four inches) and this will be the distance between 43

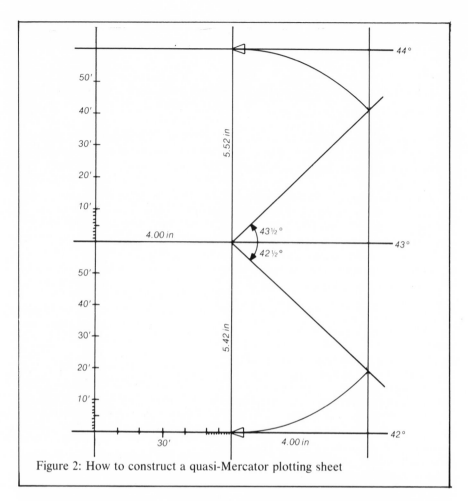

Figure 2: How to construct a quasi-Mercator plotting sheet

degrees and 44 degrees = 5.52 inches.

To find the distance between 43 degrees and 42 degrees, do the same thing, using the secant of 42½ degrees, or 1.356.

1.356 × 4 inches = 5.42 inches

Note that the total distance between 42 degrees and 44 degrees is little different from the true Mercator.

I hope that from this brief article you will have found a new appreciation of this "... chart representing the sea..." which has the most useful attributes for all navigators. There is no other chart constructed where all meridians are parallel, where all latitudes are parallel and normal to longitude, where a single straight line is a single true course from departure to destination, and where distances can be determined with accuracy. It has lasted for more than 350 years and will probably serve as well for many more centuries without significant change.

It matters little that the Mercator projection is not a projection at all nor does it matter that Mercator did not perfect it. But it was he who had the idea that it *could* be done, and for this we are all forever indebted to him.

182

The Pelorus

By James B. Kane

A pelorus is an instrument that will give you bearings and your distance off shore. Some sailors call a pelorus a dumb compass, because its disc looks like a compass card, but it has no directive force. It stays at whatever relative direction you set it.

You can either buy one or make a pelorus yourself — easily and cheaply. To construct a pelorus, you need a nail, a peg the size of a wooden match, a 12″ length of string, a piece of wood ½″ thick by 12″ square (the square must be perfect), a piece of cardboard and a Radar Plotting Sheet (Fig. 1). (The U.S. Naval Oceanographic Office, Washington, D.C. 20390 sells a pad of 50 sheets [H.O. 4665-10] and many nautical instrument stores also sell them.)

To make your pelorus, draw two lines through the center and parallel to both sides (Fig. 2). These are the lubber's lines. Paste the Radar Plotting Sheet to the piece of cardboard, and center it on the wood. Drive the nail through the center so that the sheet can revolve around it. Attach one end of the string to the wooden peg and make the other end fast to the nail. Now you have a pelorus.

To take a bearing, put the edge of the wood base firmly against anything on your boat that parallels the keel. Set the "0" on your pelorus on the forward end of the lubber's line. Now with the string and peg taut, line the peg and the nail up with the object on which you're taking a bearing. Wherever the string crosses the outer circle on the pelorus is the angle of your *relative bearing*. The relative bearing of anything is what it bears from the bow of your boat, either to port or starboard, measured from 0° to 180°.

When taking bearings on your port side, you must change the Radar Sheet readings to measure from 0° to 180° instead of 360° back to 180° as it

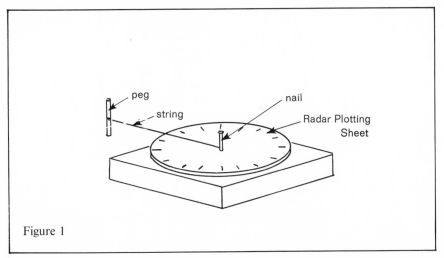

peg   nail   string   Radar Plotting Sheet

Figure 1

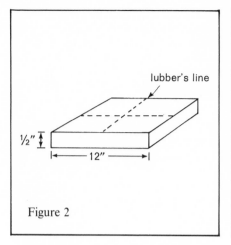

lubber's line

½"

12"

Figure 2

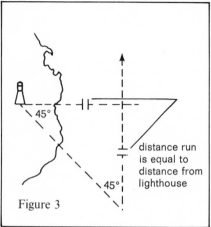

45°

distance run
is equal to
distance from
lighthouse

45°

Figure 3

indicates. Mark the appropriate numbers on the sheet for port side bearings to avoid mistakes when changing from 350° to 10°, etc.

You can use a pelorus to find your distance off lighthouses and other objects ashore. There are several pairs of relative bearings that can give you your distance off. Navigators often use a 45° and 90° bearing off the bow, calling it a bow and beam bearing. The principle behind it is based on the fact that the distance run between the 45° and the 90° bearing of a lighthouse is the same as the distance from the lighthouse to your boat when it's abeam (Fig. 3).

Let's say you're doing four knots and a lighthouse bears 45° off your bow at 0900. At 0930 it is abeam. Thirty minutes at four knots gives you two miles. You've run two miles between the time of the 45° and 90° (beam) bearing which means that you're two miles away from the light.

Another combination of bearings is 26½° and 45°; the distance run between these two bearings will also equal the distance off when abeam. Of course, the distances between 26½° and 45°, and between 45° and 90° should equal each other and one

makes a good check against the other (Fig. 4).

Certain other bearing combinations can furnish you with a quick answer for your distance off. With a 22½°-45° combination, the distance off when abeam is 7/10 the distance run between the two bearings. If the bearings are 30° and 60°, the distance off the object when abeam will be about 7/8 the distance run between bearings.

Other pairs of bearings where the distance off when abeam will approximately equal the distance run between bearings are: 22°-34°, 25°-41°, 27°-46°, 32°-59°, and 40°-79°.

Bowditch (Table 7) lists several pages of factors one can use with a pelorus to figure accurately the distance off.

If you have no compass aboard, you can permanently glue the Radar Plotting Sheet to the piece of wood. But if you have a compass, you can set the pelorus either to the true or compass course, and then you can obtain either true or compass bearings.

Simultaneous true or compass bearings of well defined objects ashore (lighthouses, spires, flagpoles, etc.) that also are on the

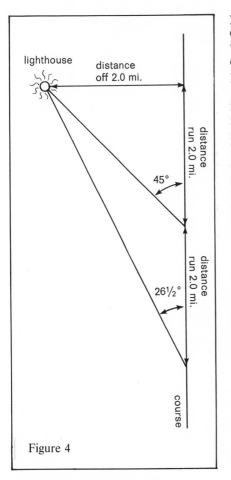

lighthouse

distance off 2.0 mi.

distance run 2.0 mi.

45°

distance run 2.0 mi.

26½°

course

Figure 4

you must be sure to keep on the course set on the pelorus. Otherwise, your bearing will have an error equal to the amount of degrees you're off course.

When taking simultaneous bearings, it's best to take three at a time; if you make a mistake on one bearing, you'll quickly see it. Plot the bearings by transferring the recorded bearing with parallel rulers or a pair of triangles from the compass rose on the chart to the object on which you took the bearing. Wherever the bearings cross (or make a small triangle) will be your fix.

If you are taking two simultaneous bearings, the ideal angle between them should 90°. If the angle between bearings is small, a slight error in a bearing could result in a large error in your position. Also remember to take bearings of nearby objects rather than ones far away; any bearing error always increases with distance.

Finally, always try to get bearings on fixed objects rather than on anchored aids, which may be out of position. But once you know how to use your pelorus, you'll find it is a quick and easy to use device to help verify where you are as you run along a coast.

navigation chart will enable you to plot your position.

When taking bearings this way,

Mylar as an Aid for Navigators

By John Ellsworth

Next time you're near an art supply store, buy a 20″ × 25″ sheet of Mylar, a flexible, transparent woven plastic used for tracing in either ink or pencil.

You can use it to determine distances, courses and bearings. Mylar can also help you obtain a fix using horizontal sextant angles, find the course steered if no simultaneous sightings are available, or determine an LOP using depth soundings.

For example, one is continually measuring distance; gauging the dividers, walking them off between points, and juggling in the mind — Which place? How far? How much time? Of course, it's fun, but it could be easier.

On the dull side of a sheet of Mylar, start from the center and draw a series of radiating concentric circles. Space them by increasing each radius by one, five, or ten scaled miles (depending on the chart's scale). Place the Mylar on the chart with the center at your location or point of departure and you have it — the distance to every port in your range.

You can also make your own direction device with Mylar by ruling a series of parallel line sets all the way across a foot-square, or larger, sheet of Mylar. Draw a set of four or five lines ⅛″ apart, then another set ¼″ apart. Draw the sets alternately until the sheet is filled. It is best to draw them in India ink.

This lined sheet will give you a compass direction fast and quite accurately. Simply place the Mylar on the chart so that one line is over your planned course or bearing line.

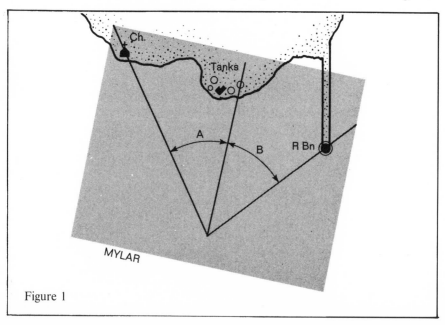

Figure 1

186

One of the other lines will fall across the center of the compass rose and give you the correct true or magnetic direction.

This device is especially helpful in a wet cockpit or on a rolling or pitching deck, where obtaining a reading with parallel rulers, triangles or a protractor could cause fumbling and loss of time.

Mylar can help you plot a fix by measuring the two horizontal sextant angles obtained from three fixed identifiable objects. To get a fix, first measure the angle between the center object (a tank in Figure 1) and the object to the left. We'll call this angle A. Then quickly measure the angle between the same tank and the object to the right; here it is the radio beacon, or angle B.

Draw a straight line on the Mylar. From one end of the line, plot angle A on one side, B on the other. Place the Mylar on the chart and maneuver the tri-legged diagram about until all three lines pass through the centers of the sighted objects. Your position at the time of the sextant reading is at the common junction of the lines.

This method is reliable because the sextant is not affected by compass error, but it should be noted that care must be taken in selecting the objects. A circle can be formed through three objects that are not in a straight line and the closer you are to this circumference, the less accurate the fix. If your sailboat happens to be ON the circle, a fix will be indeterminable. So select objects that are nearly in a straight line, or try to have the center one closer to you than the other two.

Perhaps you can't get a reliable two or three point fix. As you know, when simultaneous observations are not available a running fix from a single navigational aid can provide a slightly more reliable position. But advancing earlier bearings ahead to the time of the latest observation can't always account for an unknown current. And if the current is strong, a running fix can be quite unreliable.

Whatever the current is, though, the *direction* of the course made good can be determined; and this can be most helpful when plotting a running fix. Again Mylar is very useful in this situation. Plot your bearing lines on the chart (Fig. 2). Then take a piece of Mylar and draw a straight line on it. Use any assumed speed and, using the time difference, mark the distances run between bearings.

Here I have used six knots, and

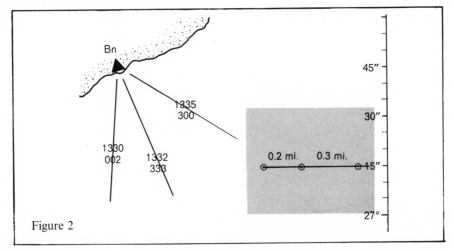

Figure 2

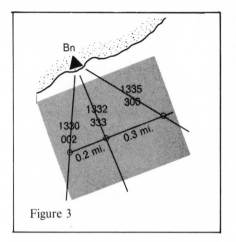

Figure 3

therefore the boat would sail 0.2 of a mile between the times of the first two bearings and 0.3 of a mile from the second to the third.

Now maneuver the Mylar with these distances around on the chart until all the distance marks fall on the bearing lines (Fig. 3). The direction of the line will be the *course* being made good: it is *not* an LOP, and of course any other assumed speed would have resulted in a parallel line a proportional distance away.

If a reliable fix was obtained within a reasonable time before the first bearing of the running fix, a track can be determined by drawing a line from

the fix in the direction of the course made good (Fig. 4). An actual position would be wherever the track intersects a bearing line.

Mylar can also help you establish an LOP via a chain of soundings. And with this method, you'll also get a rough estimate of the boat's position along an LOP.

First write down a series of soundings made at short intervals; the length of the series would be dictated by the chart scale and the existing situation.

For example, the eight soundings in Figure 5 were taken at five-minute intervals starting at 1300 (64 feet). As you can see, longer intervals would have been necessary if the soundings were farther apart, or if the boat was moving slower.

Draw a straight line on a piece of Mylar. Superimpose the line over the latitude or chart distance scale and mark the line at the respective distances (according to your speed) at which the soundings were made. At each mark, record the time and corresponding depth; correct the soundings for the prevailing height of tide.

Now check the chart for a fathom curve that is the same depth as one of

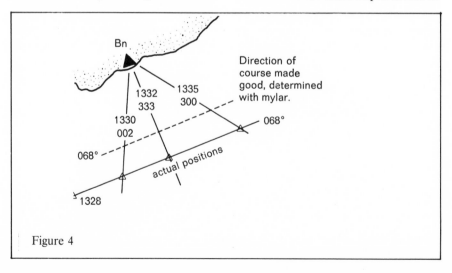

Figure 4

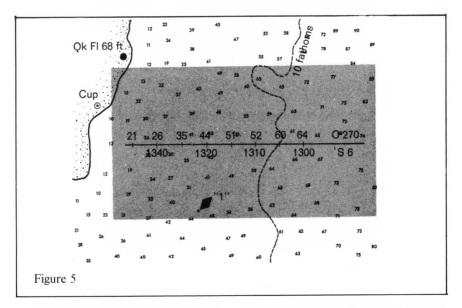

Figure 5

your readings (in Figure 5 the 10-fathom curve and a 60′ recording match). Place the Mylar on the chart a reasonable distance north of your assumed position and align the two equal depths. Keep the Mylar line parallel to the course, the two matched readings aligned and slide the Mylar south until the Mylar readings match the actual chart soundings.

It is possible that an unknown current may have affected the course a bit. So when searching for the match, it may be necessary to seesaw the Mylar slightly, using the fathom curve and its matched reading as the fulcrum.

Because it may be possible to fit the line of soundings to several places on the chart, this method should be used with *great caution*. Keep in mind that exact concurrence won't occur at all times for sounding inaccuracies, incomplete chart data, etc. may affect the match. But by seeking a general agreement, you should get a fairly adequate LOP.

I've covered several uses for Mylar in piloting and I hope you'll practice their application. Don't forget that Mylar is also very good as an overlay on your chart to preserve it.

There are many more uses for Mylar in piloting, and no doubt you'll discover many of them yourself as you become more proficient in its use.

Homemade Instruments

By James B. Kane

When working with navigation charts, what two instruments do you use more than any others? If you said parallel rulers and dividers, you'd be right. Parallel rulers and dividers are in constant use, for without them you cannot plot courses, bearings and positions. But you can navigate without these tools, and this article will explain how you can make substitutes and how to use them.

To make a substitute for parallel rulers, first get a flat thin piece of wood or Plexiglas about ⅛″ thick and cut it into a perfect square; an eight-inch square is a good size. Saw this square exactly in half, cutting from one corner to the opposite corner.

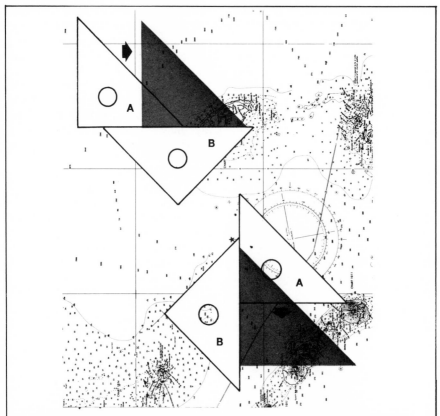

Figure 1: The long edge of triangle A is set to 50° true. Triangle A is moved by sliding it along B's long edge. The setting on A's long edge remains the same. By using a combination of these movements the bearing or course on A's long edge can be moved anywhere on the chart

What you now have are two identical isosceles triangles. These triangles can do anything that parallel rulers can do.

Let's plot a bearing to demonstrate their use. Call one triangle A and the other triangle B. We'll use a bearing of 50° true. First, lay the longest edge of triangle A at 50° on a compass rose, just as you would with parallel rulers. Now determine in what direction you want to move this bearing.

Place the long edge of triangle B firmly against whatever edge of triangle A is appropriate to plot the 50° bearing on the chart. By sliding the edge of one triangle against the other, the bearing of 50° is maintained on the long edge of triangle A. When you get close to where you want the bearing plotted, shift triangle B to another edge of triangle A so you can slide A's long edge to where you want it.

Remember, no matter how much one slides the triangles around the long edge of triangle A will always be on the correct bearing. But don't get confused and plot the bearing with the wrong triangle *or* the wrong edge.

You may have to pick up and move triangle B several times before finally getting triangle A to where you want it. Be sure B is always firm-ly against A before you slide it along B's edge. If it is loose, A may slip, and the original bearing may be lost.

Most people use dividers to measure distance but one of these triangles can work just as well.

All National Oceanic Survey charts have a scale printed below the chart's title. You'll notice that on almost all NOS charts the scale is 1:20,000, 1:40,000 or 1:80,000. Take one of the triangles and permanently mark these three scales on the three edges. If you prefer, you can cut the scales from old charts and actually glue them to the edges. To measure distance along a course line all you need is the appropriate edge of the triangle. A few important charts have a scale of 1:400:000. To use this scale, simply add a zero to each distance obtained from the 1:40,000 scale.

You can learn to use triangles skillfully with about five minutes practice. They have no moving parts and therefore will not wear out. Another advantage is that they require less room to use and consequently are extremely handy on small chart tables.

So give them a try. They are easy to make, easy to use, and are only as expensive as you yourself want to make them.

Utilizing the Almanacs

By Joe Consolmagno

You don't need a sextant to make good use of either the *Nautical Almanac* or the *Air Almanac*. Although both these navigator's references published by the U.S. Naval Observatory are intended primarily for celestial navigation, they contain much information of value to recreational sailors who have no occasion to use celestial.

These almanacs can help you plan a single outing, a vacation cruise, or a whole season of sailing activities. They can spot-check a compass on one or numerous headings. Both can serve as guides for general position orientation, and they can even provide a basis for navigation in an emergency if nothing more reliable is available.

Both almanacs provide essentially the same information, and which one you choose is largely a matter of preference. You can determine the exact geographic position of the sun, moon, navigation stars, and planets for every instant of every day of the year with either one. You can find the phases of the moon or the time of sunrise, sunset, twilight, moonrise, and moonset for wherever you plan to be, whenever you plan to be there.

The *Nautical Almanac* even tells you when and where you can see an eclipse of the sun or moon. In 1980 it promised that on August 10 the shadow of a solar eclipse would brush the United States on a diagonal sweep from northern California to southern Florida.

Both books have detailed instructions, and some thoughtful reading will tell you how to use them. If you can identify principal constellations and navigation stars you will expand each almanac's usefulness even more. Some aides to star and planet identification are included in both books, but the *Air Almanac* is perhaps superior in this respect because of its monthly sky diagrams.

For general planning purposes, however, those guides are not necessary. The sunrise/sunset tables, for example, require minimum involvement with celestial navigation, but they can be helpful in planning a voyage where the principal means of navigation is piloting. They can also help schedule an estimated time of arrival at a hazardous inlet in daylight, or help determine whether you can use effectively any lighted aids to navigation along a course.

For example, you'd like to spend Thanksgiving Day, 1980, sailing from Key West, Florida, to the Dry Tortugas. You calculate the distance at 62 nautical miles, and you anticipate a speed of advance of five knots. You want to arrive while it is still daylight, so what is the latest time you should leave Key West?

The *Nautical Almanac's* sunset table for November 27, 1980, indicates that sunset occurs at 1719, local standard time, at latitude 20°N and longitude 75°W, which is the zone meridian for the Eastern Time Zone. To be more precise, you follow the *Almanac's* directions and adapt this information to Eastern Standard Time at the coordinates of your destination: 24°38'N and

Eastern Daylight Time (Aug. 31) 10:00 PM
corr. to 24-hr. time   +   12:00
                       2200
corr. to GMT   +   0400
                       2600 =
(Sept. 1) 0200

GHA Aries 02:00 GMT
   (daily page)   10°23′
                   + 360°
                  340°23′
Longitude (W)   (−) 82°00
LHA Aries   288°23′

Azimuth *Polaris* for Lat. N40°
(*Polaris* Azimuth table)   1.0°

By referring to *Nautical Almanac's* tables, items such as azimuth for *Polaris* can be determined, then used to check compass accuracy

82°52′W. You find sunset occurs there at 1741 Eastern Standard Time and civil twilight ends at 1807.

At your projected speed, your trip will take 12 hours and 24 minutes. Work back from the time of sunset at the Dry Tortugas, and you find you must not depart from Key West later than 0517 to arrive by sundown — with 26 minutes of deepening dusk to spare.

A sunrise check at Key West (24°33′N, 81°48′W) also shows you will be leaving before daylight, for morning twilight doesn't begin until 0627 with sunrise at 0652. All is not dark, however. The *Nautical Almanac* also says that you will have a gibbous moon to help you until sunrise.

Moonlight, incidentally, is something you might also want to check in the almanacs when you choose vacation dates or schedule sailing events for the upcoming season. The data on phases of the moon, moonrise, and moonset can assist you in scheduling a night race, planning a cruise with nighttime passages, or even concocting a romantic moonlight sail.

If, for example, you wanted your vacation cruise in the summer of 1980 to include some moonlight passages, the moon listings in both almanacs indicated that your prime choice was a period that brackets one of the three dates of summer full moon: June 28, July 27, or August 26. On the other hand, if you had a little covert action in mind, the almanacs advised that you set out July 12, August 10, or September 9, when there was no moon at all to illuminate your clandestine capers.

Both almanacs can also give you directional guidance, as both carry azimuth tables for *Polaris* — the North Star — indicating how far off true north it is for any given time and latitude. For the latitudes encompassing the continental United States, in one run of the earth the azimuth of *Polaris* swings the short arc between 358.7° and 1.3° when viewed from the 50th parallel, and between 359.1° and 0.9° from the 20th parallel. For most purposes, the difference from true north is hardly worth thinking about, even at its greatest. But it is a useful value to have if your compass accuracy is in doubt or if you are in an area of unusual magnetic interference.

For example, it is 2200, EDT, August 31, 1980, and the moon has not yet risen to outshine the stars. You are on Lake Huron, at 43°30′N, 82°00′W. You head your boat directly at Polaris and get a compass bearing of 006°. Does your compass have any deviation on that heading?

The almanacs show an azimuth of 1.0° for *Polaris* for that time and place. The chart shows a variation of 5° west, and you have no deviation for that heading. So your compass reading matches the *Polaris* azimuth plus the westerly variation. If it read 001°, a deviation of 5° east could be involved (see Table).

Polaris, with its second magnitude brightness, is not the ideal body to use for swinging a compass by celestial azimuths, particularly if you are trying to read bearings at the higher latitude. But it does have advantages. It is the only body with its azimuths listed in the almanacs, and its azimuth changes only slightly as the night progresses.

There are other azimuth indicators available, and the daily pages of the *Nautical Almanac* list the times of meridian transit for the sun, moon, and navigation planets. All of these can provide directional reference, for a body on your meridian is always due north or south of you depending on its declination and your latitude.

If the sun, moon, or planets are not available at the desired time, you still can calculate the time of the meridian passage of a star with the help of the daily pages and the *Nautical Almanac*'s star list.

One problem with azimuths at meridian passage is that they change most rapidly at that point. In Key West, the sun's azimuth changes at the rate of about one degree in three minutes at transit. In our Lake Huron example, the star *Altair* changes at the rate of one degree in two minutes transit.

However, azimuth changes occur far less rapidly at the time of rising or setting. If you have a pocket calculator that handles trigonometric functions you can use a formula, not in the almanacs, that converts almanac data to azimuth at rising or setting.

The formula is:

cosine Z_n + sinD/cosL

where: Z_n is the azimuth at rising

D is declination of the body (+N, −S)

L is latitude of the observer.

You can get azimuth at setting by subtracting the rising azimuth from 360°.

One word of caution is in order for these ancillary uses of the navigator's almanacs. They can become addictive.

6

EQUIPMENT

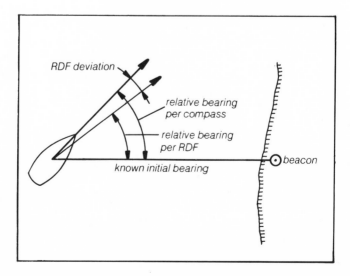

Plan Ahead for Safety

By William V. Kielhorn

Each year about this time I sit down and review what I have done during the past sailing season. I go over both the delights and the errors. I take notes and plan ahead for the coming year of adventurous voyaging. And even though we all know that anticipation is greater than the realization, nevertheless I believe you should enhance that anticipation by planning. So I'd like to put forth a few thoughts that may make your coming season a little better than the last one.

I assume that you carry aboard your boat all the equipment required both by Coast Guard regulations and by common sense. If you have not had a courtesy inspection by the Coast Guard Auxiliary or by U.S. Power Squadron volunteers, it's a good idea to do so. They are helpful people interested not only in guiding you in legal aspects of sea law, but more importantly in your own well-being and safety. You should have aboard fire extinguishers, Coast Guard-approved Personal Flotation Devices, and safety lines, buoys and cushions.

What about your compass? Is it in a convenient place, and is it properly corrected? Some people say, "Oh, I know about the deviations, and I know the courses out and back, so why should I worry about the compass?" There are some good reasons why you should. In 50 years of experience in this field I have never seen a captain expressing such thoughts who really does know what his compass deviations are, all around. Few, if any, know that when significant deviations are present, the directive forces on the compass needles vary with the heading, and this causes erratic behavior. You must remember that the *integrity of your course* is the basis of navigation. Upon this you must add your leeway and current drift. But, if your compass is in error you may very well find an unexpected barnacle-encrusted rock playing footsie with your keel.

You may have a good electronic echo-sounder, but like all electronic gadgets, it can suffer from the ravages of salt water, or even salt air. So plan to have a little three-pound hand lead and a properly marked $\frac{3}{16}$-inch line for a backup. This can keep you out of a lot of trouble when the weather gets thick. Furthermore, it's a handy device for all sorts of other things such as holding charts down, or tapping a boated bluefish, bass or barracuda in the head. It's a great $5 investment.

You probably have a radio, too. It may be part of your normal shipboard gear, or it may be a small portable system. If it is a portable AM system, then you also may have a reasonably accurate backup to your radio direction finder (RDF) because the built-in antennas of these radios are highly directive to AM radio signals. Determine whether or not your radio does have these qualities. If it does, practice using it for homing on marine and commercial radio stations. But you must know the location of the *transmitting* antenna of the station, *not* the studio location. Some of these are noted on the National Ocean Survey (NOS) charts but others are not. A couple of telephone calls to the radio stations in your sailing area will get you their antenna locations. If you happen to have a multiband radio receiver there are still other possibilities, especially in the marine and aircraft bands. You will find many aeronautical radio ranges and non-directional beacons on aeronautical charts that can be extremely useful for marine navigation. Check this out with your flying friends or at your local airport.

Speaking of radios, there is one that few small boats carry, but it can be a real life-saver: the Emergency Position Indicating Radio Beacon (EPIRB), which is available from retail stores. It transmits a distinctive distress signal simultaneously on 121.5 and 243.0 MHz. Both are aeronautical radio frequencies. Ordinarily, the first frequency is guarded by aircraft flying over water, including commercial airliners. The second is guarded by various Navy patrol aircraft. Usually Coast Guard patrol aircraft are equipped to carry both. But don't rely upon this alone. When you are in distress, an aircraft hearing your signal may not be able to see you as a tiny dot upon the sea. Handheld or launched flares are a great help in further pinpointing your location for an aircraft.

You can make no better investment than one in a good up-to-date chart. They are expensive, but the charts published by the National Ocean Survey (formerly USC&GS) are the best in the world, and in US waters they are updated and corrected frequently. Don't throw away your old charts, though. They are printed on very good paper that is designed to withstand much abuse

from folding, wear, and salt water. They make excellent book covers, and can be used for a variety of other uses when they become outdated. But even these excellent charts will fail you if you do not make all the corrections that appear in the Coast Guard's *Notice to Mariners*. Some sailors are not aware that they can have a free subscription to this most important publication if they write to their own Coast Guard District and request it. Do so now and you will be ready for the coming season.

Do you have a pair of dividers, a set of parallel rules (or their equivalent), and pencils and paper? You should have. There is little that is more useful on a small sailing craft than some unallocated space and some empty pads of paper. Of course, a nice electronic calculator is handy, but then, a cheap six-inch slide rule may be far more dependable under all circumstances.

Some years ago, I wrote about the desirability of having a sea anchor. After having had many experiences with them, I am still a strong proponent of their use. A small anchor is useful when it is streamed astern to reduce violent yaws while you are surging forward under bare poles or a storm jib. A large one is more useful when it is streamed from the bow chocks, and for most sailing craft it seems best to use a large one, streamed forward. By large, I mean nothing less than a parachute of at least nine feet in diameter for boats 20 feet in length, and up to 24 feet in diameter for boats 100 feet long. You really have to try one of these in order to appreciate its usefulness. Otherwise no words of mine can possibly convince you.

Do you have a spare or emergency anchor? If you are in waters with kelp, weed, or rocky bottom, a good bet is a plough anchor, such as the

CQR. If you are sailing in areas having a sandy or muddy bottom, I recommend the Danforth type of imbedment anchor that has at least a 7:1 scope (for which it is designed) and, in very shallow waters, at least at 10:1 scope. A five- to 10-pound anchor will do well for a 30-foot boat. I have successfully anchored a 2,500-ton ship with a 500-pound Danforth anchor in 10,000 feet of water with 1:1 scope, using a small wire rope, but this is not in the techniques available for most small-boat sailors. The principle, however, is that the shallower the water, the more scope you should have.

You should also retain onboard a couple of lengths of $\frac{3}{8}$-inch three-strand nylon warp. You may find that two 50-foot lengths of this stuff is a useful addition your craft. It is good for mooring, anchoring, and towing. The breaking strength of this material is about 4,000 pounds — far more than most bits and chocks can stand. Rarely, even in a gale, will your mooring or anchoring system be subjected to more than one-tenth of that amount of strain.

Too many sailors use an unbalanced mooring rig. They believe the heavier their anchor line or mooring line the safer they will be. Not so! You must think of the physics involved and also realize that the characteristics of nylon warp permit it to stretch nearly 30 percent before it reaches its breaking strength. This is a most powerful spring and it evens out the load of several surges. A $\frac{3}{8}$-inch nylon three-strand warp has repeatedly held a 137-foot ship at anchor in the open ocean in 18,000 feet of water. It's very tough stuff, as long as you use chafing gear to reduce the wear around the bits and chocks.

What if you are caught offshore at night? This is really a beautiful time to sail, particularly if the wind is fair and the moon is full. Too many sailors fail to enjoy this delightful experience, and they are really missing something. On the other hand, night sailing does take preparation. Not only should your running lights be in good order, but so should the lamps that light your compass and your charts. Most important, perhaps, are navigational aids you must illuminate in order to enter your snug harbor and anchorage. The Coast Guard, somewhat belatedly, discovered how useful reflective numbers and marks could be on buoys and fixed markers. Now these are on a great many aids to navigation, and they can be spotted from great distances (a mile or more) if you have a good spotlight to train on them. Because of this (and for several other good reasons), you should have onboard a good-quality high-intensity floating spotlight powered by its own heavy-duty lantern battery — not just a few flashlight cells — that can turn night into better-than-day for the navigator. There are many spotlights to choose from on the market. The helmsman can benefit from wearing a little necklace-type flashlight having both a red and a white mode. Use the red to prevent night blindness, and the white for more urgent matters.

There are some items you should consider getting for next year. For example, how's your first-aid kit doing? Have you checked it out for corrosion and for dated materials? Chances are you will not have to use it at all, but when the time comes, as sooner or later it will, it becomes very important and you had better know exactly what you have, and how to use it. It may be hours or even days before professional help might arrive for a sick or injured person. Meanwhile, the responsibility rests with the person in command — both legally and morally.

Even what some consider to be non-essentials are worthy of attention. Most weekend sailors are unfamiliar with, and unpracticed in, the art of celestial navigation. For some reason many consider it to be a kind of black art to be able to steer by the sun, the moon, and the stars. If the facts were more generally known, you would find that celestial navigation is really the easiest of navigation. It is piloting that demands the greatest skill. However, celestial navigation, like playing the piano, does require constant practice. It requires practice with the sextant, the stopwatch, and the use of whatever method you might choose for reducing sights to a line of position. I have my own preferences for sight reduction tables, and I have used nearly a dozen different methods.

If you want to become really proficient in this area, you should obtain several things this winter, then become familiar with their use. First, a sextant. You will soon learn that when you have a precision sextant you will *never* lay it down except in its own padded box, nor will you permit anyone else to use it until they are thoroughly proficient in its care and use.

Second, you need a chronometer. Nowadays this is easy to come by for the quartz-crystal, liquid crystal watches are better than the finest marine chronometers available only 20 years ago. They can give you Greenwich Mean Time (GMT) to an accuracy of ± one second over extended periods once you have established their rate of change by time signals from your radio.

Third, you must have onboard either the *Nautical Almanac* or the *Air Almanac*, both published by the US Naval Observatory and available through the Government Printing Office in Washington, DC, or your local chart store.

What do you know about the biology of the sea? If you do not study the life in the ocean, you are missing out on much of its fascination. There are so many textbooks on this subject that you will have little difficulty in finding one that is pertinent to your sailing area. You will find that the sea life is not confined to only the blue water, but is even more varied and prolific at the seashore. There are tens of thousands of animals and plants in and on the sea; there is more adventure to be found in a cubic centimeter of ocean soil or in a liter of ocean water than you ever dreamed of.

To examine a tiny bit of this, all you need is an old nylon stocking for a net, a little hoop of wire made from a coat hanger to keep the stocking open, and a little glass or plastic medicine bottle into which you can rinse or pour the catch after towing the net for a few minutes. A simple magnifying glass will reveal some of the strangest, most wonderful and important life in the sea — plankton.

How about rigging your sailing craft so that you can fish in the sea and in the bays? It has always been perplexing to me that so few sailboats are trolling in waters that abound with all kinds of game fish. Some say, "Oh, we're going too fast (or too slow) to troll." The more active of the pelagic animals are not very choosy about speed, or even the lure. I have caught bluefish trolling at one or two knots, and bonito, tuna and albacore cruising in a motorboat at 11 knots. In Hawaii they catch billfish while trolling even faster. You don't need any great length of line overside. A 50¢ Japanese feather trailed on a 20- or 30-pound test line 15-50 feet astern will catch all these species and more. And it won't bother your sailing a bit.

I could go on with ideas that might strike a responsive note as you sit by the fireside and contemplate the coming joys of the next season. But the really important ideas must come from you alone. My objective has been to titillate your imagination about the things you *might* want to do this coming year. The rest, of course, is up to you!

What Equipment Should You Have?

By Lou Hohenstein

Between the extremes of a piece of yarn on a dinghy and wall-to-wall instruments on a Grand-Prix racer or large offshore cruiser, all of us must decide what kind of navigation equipment to install aboard our boat. This is almost always a compromise between what is ideal and something less.

The need for navigation equipment aboard a sailboat first appears when you sail beyond the familiar landmarks or buoys you use for orientation. At this time you need other ways to establish your position and to find the safest and best route to your destination. The equipment you need depends not so much on the size of the boat as how and where you will sail. A 45-footer on a day sail in familiar waters doesn't need (on that day anyway) much more navigation equipment than does a dinghy used in the same way.

On the other hand, even the smallest ocean racer—a Half-Tonner competing in an all-out level rating competition—would benefit from the same navigational equipment found on 50- to 60-foot boats.

Generally speaking, large boats have more equipment, not just because they are larger, but because they have the capacity to sail to destinations that require more precise means of position-finding. Given two otherwise identical boats, one used for racing and the other for cruising, the racing boat usually, though not always, will have more elaborate navigating gear only because it needs more precise navigation to assist racing strategy.

Now let's discuss the navigation problem in terms of purpose. I divide it into four general categories:

(1) very protected and familiar waters; in sight of known and familiar objects;

(2) alongshore; still sailing in protected waters, in open bays, and in sight of visual aids to navigation, in weather conditions that usually permit visual sightings of these aids;

(3) coastal offshore; out of sight of land but generally sailing alongshore, or going from island to island; and

(4) high-seas sailing; sailing well offshore including transocean sailing.

Appropriate navigational equipment varies somewhat for racing and for cruising but the stated purpose of getting as much information as possible should remain the same. Then the only requirement is how much information is needed—and how quickly it is needed.

Protected and Familiar Waters

Cruising. The absolute minimum equipment here is a compass and a chart during periods of good visibility, but when fog, heavy rain, or darkness reduces visibility, you have to be prepared to shift immediately to dead reckoning. It is easy to overestimate your ability to pilot by sight alone. For safety, you should have basic plotting equipment aboard and should know how to use it. To this, add a set of parallel rules or plotter, watch, dividers, lead line and a knotmeter. A depth-sounder is nice to have depending on how well you know the area, and binoculars always help in sighting objects.

Racing. The racing boat cannot stop for reduced visibility so you must always be ready to dead reckon and to plot. This means plotting equipment is required for any racer, no matter where he sails. The depth-sounder is useful both for things like getting a line of position and for keeping track of the bottom contours. A hand-bearing compass provides more accurate lines of position for accurate piloting than does sighting an object over the steering compass. A knotmeter can provide additional speed information for dead reckoning.

Alongshore

Cruising. For unfamiliar waters, all the dead-reckoning equipment previously included is the minimum necessary but a radio direction finder (RDF), which provides lines of position from marine beacons onshore, is a good item to add. Use the RDF properly; its accuracy depends on your knowledge of its bearing errors. You'll also need to develop judgment in using RDF bearings, particularly in tight quarters and when they are unsupported by other data. A radio for receiving local weather broadcasts will alert you to changes in wind direction and velocity that can affect your navigational decisions. Although most RDFs pick up broadcast band stations and low-frequency aviation weather, the continuously broadcast weather on

VHF is more convenient and oriented to boating needs. With a little practice, the RDF is a useful, extra piece of information-producing equipment.

Once you are out of familiar waters, all the appropriate charts, *Coast Pilots* and cruising guides should also be aboard.

Racing. In addition to all the equipment you would use for cruising, both omni and loran are useful additions for position finding. Omni is an aircraft navigating system with a range of line-of-sight that depends upon antenna height. Offsetting the limited range, omni is extremely accurate, to about one degree. Its usefulness, however, also depends on the number and location of omni transmitting stations in the boat's operating area.

Loran is also useful for alongshore and offshore racing whenever other visual aids for navigation are not available. And for dead reckoning, an odometer can provide a more accurate measure of distance run than you can get by relying on the knotmeter alone.

Coastal Offshore

Cruising. For coastal sailing beyond the sight of visual navigation aids, the cruising sailor must have offshore systems for position finding, and these would include, in addition to the equipment already mentioned, light lists, tide tables and all other publications. As sailing offshore becomes more frequent, loran-C receivers will become even more useful. Barometer and other weather instruments help assess changes in weather patterns. You also need a radio to keep you informed of local weather.

Racing. The competitive offshore racing sailor needs as much equipment as he feels he can carry. Some

Sailing Category	Navigating Equipment for Cruising Sailboats	
	Minimum	**Optional**
Familiar and protected waters	compass charts	depthsounder/lead line plotting equipment knotmeter watch binoculars
Alongshore	All the above plus: plotting equipment depthsounder knotmeter watch binoculars RDF	All the above plus: hand-bearing compass light lists tide and current tables odometer cruising guides *Coast Pilot* publications radio for local weather
Coastal offshore	All the above plus: spare compass light lists tide tables pilot publications radio for local weather	All the above plus: loran relative wind direction and velocity instruments sextant *Nautical Almanac* and tables
High seas	All the above plus: sextant *Nautical Almanac* and tables accurate watch or chronometer	All the above plus: patent log broad-band radio receiver loran omega

Minimum and optional equipment for sailboat navigation

racing sailboats carry two-station automatic-tracking loran to allow continuous display of two loran lines of position. The ability to sail with a continuous fix helps when you are racing in places like the Gulf Stream off Florida. Omega, actually designed for high-seas use, is useful if you are racing or cruising in an area out of range of loran. You can use a permanently installed water-temperature indicator to help identify the location and axis of major ocean currents like the Gulf Stream, and an odometer can help you in determining the distance run. You can catch high-seas weather broadcasts and time signals for back-up celestial

Sailing Category	Navigating Equipment for Racing Sailboats	
	Minimum	**Optional**
Familiar and protected waters	compass charts plotting equipment watch knotmeter	depthsounder/lead line hand-bearing compass binoculars odometer

Alongshore	All the above plus:
	spare compass
	depthsounder/lead line
	knotmeter
	binoculars
	hand-bearing compass
	RDF
	light lists
	tide and current tables
	odometer
	cruising guide
	Coast Pilot publications
	radio for local weather
		All the above plus:
		relative wind direction
		  and velocity
		  instruments
		omni
		loran
		pocket calculator

Coastal offshore	All the above plus:
	loran
	relative wind direction
	  and velocity
	  instruments
		All the above plus:
		two-station loran
		omega
		water temperature indicator
		automatic tracking RDF
		magnetometer
		course-heading instrument
		strip-chart heading recorder
		sextant
		Nautical Almanac and
		  tables
		broadband radio receiver

High seas	All the above plus:
	sextant
	Nautical Almanac and
	  tables
	accurate watch or
	  chronometer
		All of the above.

Minimum and optional equipment for sailboat navigation

navigation on a broad-band radio receiver. And a sextant, *Nautical Almanac* and *Sight Reduction Tables* are going to be very helpful if your electrical power fails and your primary offshore navigating device, loran for example, is lost.

You could also have sophisticated racing options such as a *magneto-meter,* a course-heading instrument, and course-heading recorders. The magnetometer is a compass device that reads out the boat's heading, left or right of a desired course. You can use it with a course-heading instrument so that when you are sailing off the wind the helmsman can keep a needle on-center of the course-heading instrument rather than steering a specific compass heading. A magnetometer can also drive a course-heading strip-chart recorder which enables the navigator to derive a more precise dead-reckoning plot than he can get by relying on what is in the helmsman's written log.

High Seas

Cruising. For offshore cruising, the sailor must add all the gear necessary for reliable celestial position finding.

Loran and omega are useful to have for cruising but be sure you can deal with the maintenance problems if they should occur far from home. Chances are the sextant and related tables and equipment will be a primary form of position finding if the problem can't be solved right away.

Racing. The ocean racer's needs are the same as the cruiser's, except the racer usually has omega and/or loran as required equipment. Otherwise, the equipment is essentially the same as is needed for coastal-offshore racing, but it includes additional celestial position-finding gear.

Navigational skills. By simply possessing a lot of navigation equipment, you are not guaranteed a safe passage. The operator must know how to use the equipment, and any navigator must have all the required skills for piloting, for dead reckoning, for offshore work, and for celes-

tial sight reduction. One skipper I know bought an omega unit for the Southern Ocean Racing Conference's St. Petersburg-to-Fort Lauderdale race believing that an omega receiver alone was adequate. When he was well offshore, he lost power for the omega and the memory used for updating the boat's position also went blank. Without a log, skills for DR navigation, or other back-up methods for position finding, the boat wandered around more or less lost before finally finishing at Fort Lauderdale in an obviously non-competitive position. You should learn three points from this:

- You need to understand both the capability and limitations of any navigation equipment on which you depend.
- You must have a contingency plan for failures that can happen.
- The navigator must have all the skills necessary to navigate in whatever conditions exist.

Loss of electrical power aboard a sailboat can happen anytime the engine (or generator) won't start or the batteries run down. Think about the equipment and skills you would have to fall back on if this should happen. You will find yourself back to basic equipment: chart, compass, lead line, plotting equipment, watch, sextant, *Almanac* and tables. And your own navigational knowledge and skills.

Understanding the Radio Direction Finder

By Burt Sauer

It is reassuring to have a radio direction finder (RDF) just in case you get socked in by fog, because, next to the marine compass, the portable RDF is probably the most useful and affordable instrument available to small-boat skippers for navigating in limited visibility.

But how effective will yours be when condensation is dripping off the sails and the night is darker than a stack of black cats? Like all good

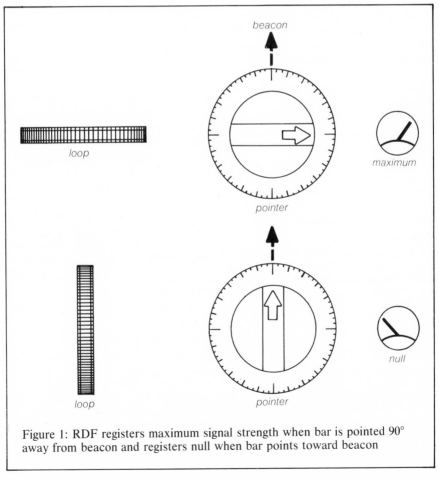

Figure 1: RDF registers maximum signal strength when bar is pointed 90° away from beacon and registers null when bar points toward beacon

tools, the RDF only does the job when you understand how it operates and when you learn to use it properly.

Basically, a radio direction finder is a radio receiver with an antenna that turns (Fig. 1). Just as you turn your portable AM radio one way or another to get best reception, on an RDF you turn the antenna. At least two brands of RDFs have built-in antennas, and you point the whole radio to tune for the best reception and to find the *null*.

The apparent strength of the signal received by an RDF varies with the relative orientation between the antenna and the transmitting station; an RDF uses this principle to determine the direction of the beacon. The signal will come in strongest when the antenna shell is perpendicular to the transmitter and will be least or *null* when the antenna shell is end-on to the direction of the transmitter. Under proper conditions an RDF receives no signal at all with the antenna at the null position. However, the point of maximum signal strength is more difficult to determine because, theoretically, even if the antenna is rotated 10 degrees away from the optimum angle, the received signal strength drops by only two percent.

The signal-strength meter indicates the null more accurately than does the audio signal, particularly when a set is picking up ignition noise from the engine. The indicator on one end of the rotatable antenna is matched with a graduated azimuth ring to find the bearing of the transmitter (Fig. 2).

Most portable RDFs permit you to tune in transmitters from two or three frequency bands—the beacon band from 150 to 415 kilohertz (kHz), the broadcast band from 525 to 1600 kHz, and the marine band

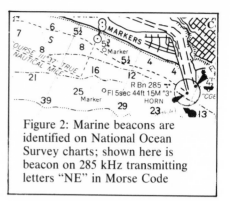

Figure 2: Marine beacons are identified on National Ocean Survey charts; shown here is beacon on 285 kHz transmitting letters "NE" in Morse Code

from 1600 to 4750 kHz. Marine beacons and low-frequency aircraft beacons are on the beacon band, not the marine band, which is principally for voice communications.

You should consider several things when choosing an RDF. First, you want *sensitivity* so that you will be able to pull in a very weak radio signal. Sensitivity measures the minimum discernible signal of your set and is expressed in microvolts per meter (μV/m). Lower numbers indicate more sensitive sets that are able to receive signals from farther away. The specs are always poorest in the beacon band (typically 30 to 45 μV/m) although you need the most sensitivity here because marine beacons transmit at very low power. The marine-beacon system is designed so that an RDF with a sensitivity of 75 μV/m or less should receive the beacon signal at the nominal range of the beacon.

Sensitivity is not the same as *signal-to-noise ratio,* which measures how much a receiver can enhance the signal it receives more than it amplifies the non-signal noise, including any noise generated in the set itself. This ratio is expressed in decibels (dB) and the more dB, the better.

Another important quality is *selectivity,* the ability to discriminate between the desired signal and signals on nearby frequencies. This is particularly important if the station you want is weak relative to one nearby on the dial. Selectivity, too, is measured in dB, and large values are better than small ones. In comparing RDFs you should be sure the same frequency separation is used in the selectivity measurement. The selectivity of portable RDFs is usually based on a difference of 10 kHz between competing frequencies (which is the minimum frequency separation of AM broadcast stations). The quoted selectivity may be something like 25 dB. This means that a receiver tuned to a signal separated by 10 kHz from a station with equal strength should receive the desired signal 17.5 times more strongly than the unwanted station's signal. However, marine beacons are designed for selectivities of about 73 dB/10 kHz.

An RDF rated at 25 dB/10 kHz will function satisfactorily unless conditions require a higher selectivity. For example, at the maximum range of two equally strong beacons whose frequencies are less than 10 kHz apart, an RDF would not distinguish between the two frequencies. It would produce a radio bearing somewhere between. Fortunately, adjacent beacons of equal power are usually separated by 20 kHz or more, and beacons with nearly the same frequencies are separated by considerable distance.

Regardless of the manufacturer's specifications, you can compare various receivers on the dealer's counter by tuning them all to a local beacon, then checking for clear reception and sharp nulls. If possible, tune in a more distant beacon (for example, a long-range marine beacon) and test them all again. Do the same at several stations on the broadcast band. With each set, detune the broadcast stations slightly on each side of the correct frequency. listen for interference, and see if the null will shift. These simple tests should indicate which RDFs perform satisfactorily.

An RDF should be easy to use and easy to read. The tuning dial, control knobs and null meter all should be conveniently located. The azimuth ring underneath the pointer should be legible *even in dim light,* with numbers and degree markings in a contrasting color to the color of the ring itself. The tuning dial and the

Ferrite Core Antennas

The RDF's rotatable loop antenna consists of about 50 turns of copper wire wound around a ferrite bar approximately seven inches long. The wire constitutes the "loop." The ferrite bar can be magnetized by an electrical current to a greater degree than a bar of soft iron. When it is used in the center of the loop it gives the loop an effective diameter equal to a much larger air-core loop. The loop makes electrical connections with the receiver by slip rings on the end of a shaft that extends into the case and engages brushes with electrical leads to the tuner. The antenna is covered by a shell having a mark to show one end of the ferrite bar.

A loop antenna brings in the strongest signal when the loop is aligned with the direction the radio waves are traveling, so the bar and its cover will be perpendicular to this path when reception is strongest. Thus the indicator on one end of the shell will point directly toward the signal source or directly away from it when the loop is nulled.

null meter should both be lighted (and it would be great if the azimuth ring were, too). A battery-condition indicator is very useful and often is incorporated on the null-meter dial.

A good RDF will have separate controls for the *audio volume* and the *gain,* permitting you to suppress the sound and to concentrate on the null meter once you've tuned in the transmitting beacon. Some sets have earphones which are useful when the watch below is asleep.

In addition to the horizontally rotatable antenna, some sets have a telescoping vertical antenna which can distort the signal pattern of the rotatable antenna to distinguish between a null *toward* the tuned transmitter and a null *away* from the transmitter.

An RDF should, but rarely does, feature rugged waterproof construction and a provision for locking it in place with a quick-release arrangement. You'll see why these features are desirable if you picture yourself at night trying to align and hold down an RDF while clutching a flashlight in one hand, rotating the antenna with the other hand, and trying to protect the set with a raincoat. And as far as I am concerned, an instruction book explaining more than just how to turn the set on would be a welcome addition.

An RDF must be properly *calibrated* for use on a particular boat. To calibrate it, check for deviations from true bearings just as you would with a compass. These deviations result from currents induced by incoming radio waves in the metal rigging.

National Ocean Survey charts mark each marine beacon with a magenta-colored circle, the letters *R Bn,* the frequency used and the identifying signal broadcast (Fig. 2). Figure 2 shows that the marker beacon at West Jetty Light No. 3 transmits continuously the letters "NE" (− · / ·) in International Morse Code on a frequency of 285 kHz. To use this beacon, you tune the RDF to 285 kHz and listen for the "dah-dit (pause) dit" repeated over and over while you rotate the antenna for the strongest signal.

It is best to learn the technique for getting the sharpest nulls at the dock or in an open space. But remember that in actual use, an RDF must be placed, and if possible clamped, so the azimuth ring can be aligned parallel to the boat's keel. This line should be established carefully and marked so the instrument can always be operated from the same position. Any slip of an RDF introduces error in the next bearing to be read.

For bearings relative to the boat's heading, the 0-degree and the 180-degree marks on the azimuth ring *should line up precisely* fore and aft with the line parallel to the keel. If you want the actual compass bearing of the beacon, rotate the azimuth ring until the boat's heading lines up with the keel line on the *forward* side of the RDF and the reciprocal lines up with the keel line on the aft side of the RDF.

There is a definite procedure you should follow to get a good null (which is what you need to determine direction). First, turn on the set and tune for the clearest reception of a local beacon, rotating the antenna as needed. After identifying the station and achieving the best possible tuning, reduce the audio volume to a non-distracting level and adjust the gain to produce a reading about midway on the null-meter dial.

Now, rotate the antenna fairly slowly to point the indicator in the general direction of the beacon while you watch the meter. The needle will probably fall gradually as signal reception begins to dwindle; increase

Sky Wave

When you and your RDF are only a few wavelengths away from a vertically transmitting antenna you will receive only vertically polarized radio waves because only that component of the transmitter's output that follows the surface of the earth, called the *surface wave,* will be present. However, as your distance from the transmitter increases, the radio waves may also be reflected from the sky (ionosphere) as depicted in the figure. This detracts from the accuracy of an RDF in two ways. First, because of the longer path from transmitter to receiver via the ionosphere, the *sky wave* will arrive slightly later than, and out of phase with, the counterpart surface wave. Likewise, as the signal is turned back towards earth by the layer of electrons in the ionosphere, its electrical polarization may become twisted from the original vertical alignment.

If the late-arriving, out-of-phase sky wave is relatively weak, it will add to the background noise and will reduce the operating range of the RDF by making the null wider and shallower. However, if the sky wave is stronger than the surface wave it will replace the surface wave as the direction-finding signal. Not only will the nulls be shallow and broad but an appreciable phase shift will result in more noise when you use the sense circuit, wiping out the null completely. If the down-coming wave no longer has strictly vertical polarization, the loop antenna will receive energy at all positions around the azimuth ring and no null will be found.

Sky-wave effects are most noticeable at night (particularly at dusk and dawn), at increasing distance from the transmitter, and with signals of higher frequency—especially commercial broadcasts. Generally, if you can get a sharp null without the sense circuit, you will also get good results when you switch in the sense circuit.

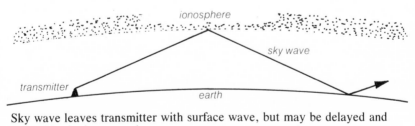

Sky wave leaves transmitter with surface wave, but may be delayed and twisted by its longer path

the gain to keep the needle at its original setting. Eventually you should notice a point where the needle falls suddenly and sharply. *Without adjusting the gain,* continue to turn the antenna. Watch for the point where the signal level begins to increase again. That means you have passed the null point.

Go back until the needle again registers at the minimum. Now increase the gain so the needle registers above zero and see if you can define the null more precisely as you swing the antenna a little bit each way. With a clear signal, the meter will drop to zero at the null, even at full gain. Observe the reading from the azimuth ring but go past the null point several more times in each direction

Sense Circuit

The propagation of a radio wave along its path can be represented *conceptually* as in the figure where horizontal movement indicates increasing time or distance and vertical direction represents oscillation amplitude of the energy propagated into the air by the alternating current in a transmitting antenna. The portion of the wave above the straight horizontal line is its positive phase, the portion below the line, its negative phase, with the two halves making one wavelength (measured from the point of zero amplitude). The wave does not stand still; at beacon frequencies it takes a wave about 1/300,000th of a second to sweep past an antenna.

When this propagated energy strikes a vertical wire antenna like the sense antenna on your RDF, it induces a voltage in the antenna directly proportional to the energy it receives. The output of the vertical antenna is an alternating current with the same frequency as the generating radio waves. The maximum voltage in the omnidirectional vertical antenna occurs at maximum amplitude of the radio wave; there is no voltage induced in the omnidirectional antenna at the point of zero amplitude.

However, when radio energy strikes the coils of a loop antenna, the loop output voltage represents the *difference* between the voltages induced in the front and back sides of the loop. For this reason at any point along the wave path the loop produces the most voltage when it is pointed directly along the path of the radio signals and it produces no voltage when oriented perpendicular to this path.

The loop in the figure will generate maximum voltage when the center of the loop is at the point of zero amplitude of the radio wave or half a wavelength (provided the sides of the loop line up with the wave path). Maximum voltage in the omnidirectional antenna occurs at one quarter and three quarters of the wavelength, the points of greatest amplitude. So the points of maximum voltage in the two antennas are a quarter of a wavelength apart. Because the two antennas are physically side by side, their output voltages are 90 degrees out of phase.

Although the voltage induced in the loop in any position around the azimuth ring is equal in magnitude to that induced at a position 180 degrees away, the voltages at the two positions are of the opposite sign. For example, if the voltage at 60 degrees is plus, the voltage at 240 degrees would be minus. This property can be used to distinguish actual bearing from its reciprocal bearing.

The sense circuit incorporates a phase-shifting device that changes the phase of the vertical antenna output by a quarter of a wavelength to match the loop antenna when a

and jot down or remember the bearing of the null each time. Average these and use the average as the RDF bearing from the boat or dock toward the transmitter.

After obtaining a null always rotate the antenna 180 degrees and check for a similar null. If you don't detect this second null, the signal you've picked up may be very weak, scattered or fading and shouldn't be relied on. Find a different transmitter on some other frequency and begin again.

On the subject of uncertainty, you shouldn't expect dockside accuracy at sea even with a good strong signal because no helmsman can hold a perfect course. Besides fluctuations in the boat's heading, the boat's yaw

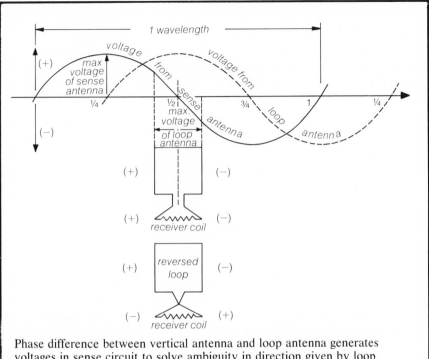

Phase difference between vertical antenna and loop antenna generates voltages in sense circuit to solve ambiguity in direction given by loop antenna alone. Increasing time or distance is on horizontal axis; oscillation amplitude is on vertical axis

particular side of the loop antenna is nearest to the transmitter. When this output is added to that of the nulled loop by pressing the sense button, it produces an output voltage once again so the loop is no longer nulled.

The loop usually can be nulled once more by rotating it to a point where the loop voltage and the sense voltage will cancel. The rota-tion will be in one direction when the original null was obtained with the phase-matched side of the nulled loop to one side of the signal path (pointer toward the transmitter) and in the other direction when the phase-matched side of the loop was to the other side of the signal path (pointer away from the transmitter). The 180-degree ambiguity is thus resolved.

and roll will also affect accuracy in reading the boat's compass (which is how you determine the relative bearing). An accuracy of ±2 degrees at dockside would translate realistically to more like ±4 degrees in relatively smooth water and ±6 degrees, or worse, in rough seas—which, often as not, represents the sea conditions in which you will use an RDF.

You get two nulls 180 degrees apart, so how do you know which null points *toward* the beacon? Normally, marine beacons are on the shore, and although you may be uncertain of your position you should still know the general direction of land. However, sometimes the beacon will be located on a peninsula, an island or perhaps on a long jetty and you will need to be absolutely certain which side of the beacon you are on.

This is why the telescoping sense antenna is provided on many RDFs. It also receives the beacon or broadcast signal, and its output can be coupled to that of the horizontal (rotatable) antenna by pressing the sense button. To use the sense antenna, extend it all the way and press the sense button while the horizontal antenna is nulled. If the meter indicates increased voltage, reset it to zero or slightly above zero with the gain knob. Note azimuth reading; and rotate the horizontal antenna clockwise about 20 degrees. Should the meter again show increased voltage your original null indicated the actual bearing to the beacon. If the needle stays at zero, rotate the horizontal antenna 180 degrees from the previous null and press the sense button again while rotating the antenna clockwise. If you get the proper response, the second null indicated the actual bearing.

It is possible that on some RDFs the sense circuitry connects with the loop output in such a way that the correct meter response occurs when the horizontal antenna is rotated *counter-clockwise*. This is easily determined at dockside by tuning in on your local beacon.

With these RDF operating principles and procedures mastered, you are ready to choose an operating station on your boat. Your first concern is where to situate your RDF to get clear undistorted reception. On most sailboats, large and small, results with an RDF always seem to improve if it is brought on deck or into the cockpit. I believe the layout of the mast, shrouds, chains, etc., substantially interferes with reception when an RDF is belowdecks.

Because position finding with a manual RDF is definitely a two-person job, the RDF operating station has to be within communicating distance of the helmsman—but not too close. Don't forget that an RDF has electrical circuits and a permanent magnet inside which can cause compass errors that will invalidate the whole operation. You should check this out carefully on different compass headings, but generally a separation of three feet or so from the boat's compass should be enough to avoid this problem.

You must be able to mount your portable RDF precisely fore and aft each time you use it, so mark a permanent line for aligning the azimuth ring and also provide some secure mounting to keep the RDF aligned during use.

With these criteria in mind, select various possible locations. At each location, test for reception and sharp nulls with the transmitter bearing 0°, 45°, 90°, 135°, and 180° port and starboard from your bow. What this means is that you will have to turn your boat in its slip, tie up to a mooring and kedge the boat around or sail various courses past a beacon to obtain these eight relative bearings. Don't be concerned yet with measuring deviation at these relative bearings, only with the quality of the reception. Be sure there are no tall buildings or hills between your boat and the beacon that might distort the signal while you are making this test.

After you have gone through all this preparation you are ready to chart the deviation of your RDF.

Correcting the Radio Direction Finder

By Burt Sauer

To use a portable RDF correctly, you need to chart the deviations that your RDF will always have because of induced currents in your mast and rigging. This is analogous to preparing the deviation card for your compass (which you should already have, since any bearings you get from an RDF depend on the compass readings).

You need a clear and relatively calm day, one or, better yet, two willing helpers, and a good bit of patience. Although you naturally want to get the job done quickly and easily, accuracy is the prime consideration. Make a worksheet like the one shown in Figure 1. It can save you a lot of RDF time and possibly avoid some undetected errors that can later foul up your navigation. Don't make any hasty computations; just fill in the first four columns. You can do the rest ashore and double-check your arithmetic.

Note that Figure 1 calls for RDF readings every five degrees. Sailors who swing their compasses for deviation only every 15, 30, or 45 degrees may object to the tedium of making 72 separate measurements for their RDFs. They know that if the

INITIAL COMPASS BEARING TO BEACON	COMPASS HEADING (Boat's Course)	RELATIVE BEARING PER COMPASS STBD = + PORT = −	RELATIVE BEARING PER RDF STBD = + PORT = −	RDF ERROR STBD= + PORT= −	RDF CORREC-TION STBD = + PORT = −
		0			
		+ 5			
		+ 10			
		+ 15			
		+ 20			
		etc.			
		+175			
		+180			
		0			
		− 5			
		− 10			
		− 15			
		etc.			
		−180			

Figure 1: Worksheet for recording RDF errors

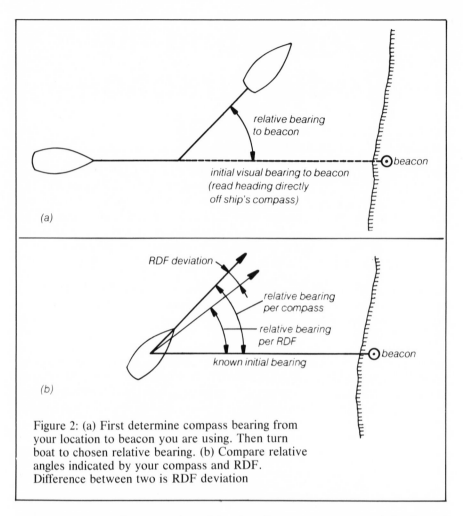

Figure 2: (a) First determine compass bearing from your location to beacon you are using. Then turn boat to chosen relative bearing. (b) Compare relative angles indicated by your compass and RDF. Difference between two is RDF deviation

compass errors discovered at 24 headings around the complete circle are plotted on graph paper and a smooth curve is drawn through the points, the curve will reliably show the deviation at the intermediate headings. But this isn't so with RDF deviation. The deviation could be zero at 285 degrees and zero at 315 degrees but five or 10 degrees at 300 degrees. You have to measure it.

Be careful that the deviation of the compass doesn't crank in large errors in the supposed relative bearing (Fig. 2). You need to know the actual angle between the boat's heading per compass and the line of position (LOP) from the marine beacon. The helmsman cannot, realistically, correct a one- or two-degree deviation when steering by a compass graduated in five-degree increments. So don't worry about such small compass deviations, but do study the compass deviation card and avoid steering courses requiring helm corrections of five degrees or more to get the intended magnetic course.

Also avoid courses where the actual angle between the course and the beacon increases or decreases considerably from the intended angle because the compass deviations are in opposite directions. For example, in Figure 3, if a visual bearing of 005° per compass is really 007° magnetic when heading directly toward the beacon and later, when you are checking for RDF deviation, a course of 240° per compass is really 237° magnetic, your intended relative bearing of 125° is actually 130°. To avoid this difficulty choose a different location on the water so you get a different initial bearing to the beacon.

Consult your chart and select a marine beacon situated close to some easily recognized landmark. A beacon located in a tall tower is ideal. Make certain from the chart and from on-the-spot inspection that there are no hazards in the area. You don't want to hit a sewer outfall or a sandbar while the helmsman concentrates on his compass and you concentrate on the RDF.

There are three problems in getting good bearings for your deviation chart. First is the heavy traffic close to the entrance to any harbor or marina. If your beacon marks a harbor you may have to wait while both your visual and radio bearings clear up. Second, often you can't wander over the whole ocean while recording bearings, even with no boats around, because of the navigational hazards already mentioned. Third, when operating within line of sight of the marine beacon, your relative bearing will change rapidly when you are taking relative bearings near the beam. This makes it difficult to get accurate radio bearings.

The first problem is resolved with patience; the second and third require prior thought. Plan in advance the pattern you will follow when taking the RDF bearings. While avoiding hazards, you still want to get visual bearings on the beacon. Plan to stay as far from the beacon as you can while still keeping it in sight when you are taking relative bearings between 60 degrees and 120 degrees port and starboard to minimize

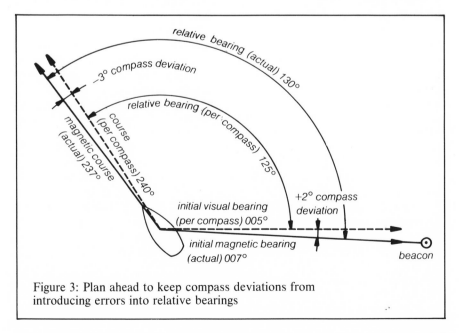

Figure 3: Plan ahead to keep compass deviations from introducing errors into relative bearings

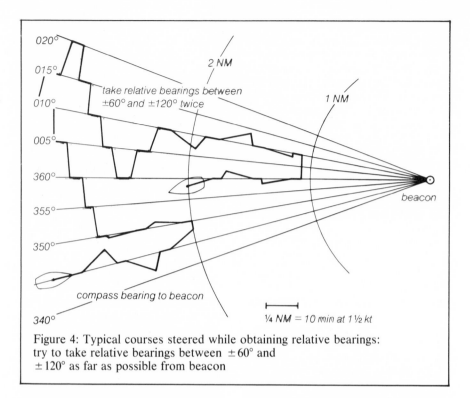

Figure 4: Typical courses steered while obtaining relative bearings:
try to take relative bearings between ± 60° and
± 120° as far as possible from beacon

the rate at which the actual bearing to the beacon shifts aft. Even so, you probably should run these bearings a second time.

Don't use a hand-bearing compass for any of the bearings unless it is the compass you steer by. RDF bearings must be related directly to the boat heading which is most easily and accurately read off the main compass. You don't have to take the RDF bearings in any particular sequence, but you do have to take them at known precise relative bearings from the target beacon, based on the compass.

Figure 4 typifies courses steered when finding the corrections for RDF bearings with a manual RDF. In actual operation, one initial bearing may be enough if it is more appropriate or convenient to keep returning to this original LOP. Note from Figure 4 that small relative

bearings can be measured close to the beacon while beam and near-beam bearings are best taken farther away.

If you can find a good position in sufficiently shallow water, you can set out some anchors and swing your boat by five-degree increments through a full circle. This eliminates the problem of a rapid bearing change while you determine the relative bearing.

Now you can proceed with the actual work. When you are two or three miles to sea, but still within view of the landmark, get everything ready. Your RDF should be correctly mounted, the zero of its azimuth ring should point *exactly* forward, the previously checked-out compass should be in the binnacle, and all gear should be stowed where you normally carry it in times of limited visibility (for example, your anchor

The RDF deviation occurring as the boat turns is called *quadrantal error* (a circle has four quadrants). Reference books depict this error as a smooth curve but deviation errors do not always follow the classic quadrantal curve. Such curves are based on data from large vessels which can employ a variety of techniques to erase induced currents in rigging, masts, funnels, and derricks. They only need to compensate for the predictable effects of the metal hull on radio signals. Wood or fiberglass hulls will not produce these effects. The errors caused by currents in the mast and shrouds are not very predictable or correctable on small boats.

should be ready on the bow). I suggest you use only the motor and have it running at "dead slow" to keep water flowing past the rudder at minimum speed for steerage way.

Now, with your RDF turned on and tuned for maximum reception, have the helmsman point the bow toward the beacon while you or your second helper watch the compass. Each time the forestay lines up with the landmark representing the beacon the helmsman should call out *mark*. The helmsman should maneuver so the landmark and forestay line up exactly on one of the degree markings on the compass. (For relative bearings per compass greater than 90 degrees the helmsman must head away from the beacon while someone sights the landmark across the mast and backstay.)

Now start heading off on the various relative bearings and try to tune the RDF for a null just as the helmsman yells *mark* to indicate he is on the chosen course. When you have a null just as he yells, log the apparent bearing on a scratch pad. Take

several readings, average them, and record the result in column four, "Relative Bearing per RDF," of the worksheet.

Some old hands might tell you to steer in a circle while you record RDF bearings. However, the bearing to the beacon will change constantly as the boat moves around and with a manual RDF you may never get a proper null.

Even if the helmsman maintains a steady compass course or a controlled course change, the bearing to the beacon will change unless the boat is bow-on or stern-to. For example, in Figure 5, the initial bearing of 340 degrees to the beacon has changed to 025 degrees at position B after a series of nine five-degree course changes. The true relative bearing of 90 degrees at B would be calculated *incorrectly* as 45 degrees using the original beacon bearing of 340 degrees. For this reason, try to take the relative bearing per RDF from as close as possible to the initial LOP from the beacon. Otherwise, imagine the catastrophic effects of a 45-degree error when you are lost in the fog.

Radio beacons are usually located with Coast Guard-operated lights that should be visible on a clear day. However, if you can't find a marine beacon located adjacent to a visible landmark, you will have to run your RDF deviations the hard way. That means you must determine your offshore position with visual bearings on other landmarks first and then plot on your chart a precise LOP to the beacon transmitter. This can slow you down and provide additional opportunities for error.

Also, you will have to "uncorrect" the true bearing from the chart by adding or subtracting local magnetic variation and compass deviation. After a few passes toward and away

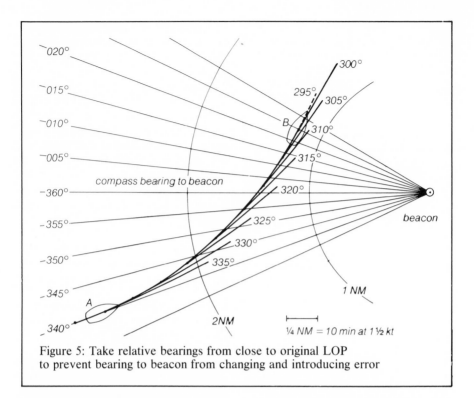

Figure 5: Take relative bearings from close to original LOP
to prevent bearing to beacon from changing and introducing error

from the beacon, take new visual bearings to be sure you are still on the plotted LOP. Take all the same precautions as when you use visual bearings directly to the beacon.

The signal path from the transmitter should not pass over any land or within 15 degrees of a coastline or you may get a false reading. The transmitter must be at least two wavelengths away which, at beacon frequencies, means a mile or farther.

You can also use one of the high-powered marine beacons if you are within its range. These are intended for use by ships approaching from seaward and typically have an effective range of 100 miles or more. However, close inshore you may have trouble receiving one clearly because of land attenuation.

Most high-power beacons are sequenced and operate in groups of three or six. With these you must work quickly because the particular station you are monitoring may be on for only one minute out of six. You may have to wait through many cycles until you get a good null at the same time the helmsman calls *mark*. Your actual position is less critical when the beacon is many miles away, for being one-half mile off the intended LOP will introduce less than a full degree of error at 30 miles from the beacon. You still need a precise boat heading, however.

For getting the most accurate source of radio bearings, my first choice is a local beacon I can get visual bearings on. My second choice is a LOP from an unseen local beacon. The distant high-powered beacons would be my last choice, although I certainly appreciate having them when I'm sailing offshore.

Every Coast Guard district has some special RDF calibration sta-

RDF REL BRNG	RDF CORREX	RDF REL BRNG	RDF CORREX
0°	0	0°	0
− 5°	+1	+ 5°	0
−10°	+1	+10°	−2
−15°	+1	+15°	−2
−20°	+2	+20°	−2
−25°	+3	+25°	−3
−30°	+4	+30°	−4
−35°	+5	+35°	−2
−40°	+3	+40°	−3
−45°	0	+45°	−3
−50°	0	+50°	−6
−55°	−1	+55°	−1
−60°	−2	+60°	−2
−65°	−3	+65°	−3
−70°	−3	+70°	−3
−75°	−2	+75°	−4
−80°	0	+80°	−4
−85°	0	+85°	−1
−90°	+2	+90°	0

Figure 6: Example of RDF Deviation Card (front side)

tions that operate by special arrangement. Low power (nominal range about two miles), they transmit at special frequencies not used by regular beacons. Although they are provided to permit large ships to check equipment, the Coast Guard's *Aids to Navigation* section assures me that this service is equally available to small boats. The locations and instructions for using these stations are printed in the *Light List*.

As for using aircraft beacons or stations in the broadcast band, use them for direction finding, but don't construct an RDF deviation card based on these types of signals. For technical reasons, RDF bearings from aircraft beacons and broadcast stations are not so accurate as bearings from marine beacons. Strictly speaking, you should prepare a deviation card for each frequency band on your RDF (beacon, broadcast,

and marine), but for practical purposes it's best to carefully prepare one for the beacon band and then allow for decreased accuracy on the other bands.

When all 72 RDF bearings have been taken, turn off the RDF and re-stow it securely. Pass out refreshments as you return to the harbor; all hands have earned a generous reward. Besides, you may need them again to resolve a few questionable bearings once you have completed your worksheet.

The fifth column of the worksheet, "RDF Error," is "Relative Bearing per RDF" subtracted from "Relative Bearing per Compass." Naturally, "RDF Correction" equals "RDF Error" but is of the opposite sign. When you have filled in all the columns, check your arithmetic to eliminate any mistakes.

You still need an RDF deviation card (Fig. 6) to put the information into its most useful form. I find that both sides of a 3x5-inch card make a handy pocket-sized record of the RDF corrections. The *corrected bearing* is the actual bearing of the beacon from your bow. However, as this is the LOP to the beacon, the RDF bearing must be converted from boat compass azimuth to chart azimuth. Adding or subtracting 180 degrees gives you the *reciprocal* bearing from the beacon toward your boat (Fig. 7). You plot this LOP *from* the beacon and cross it with another LOP to find your approximate position.

I prefer to convert all courses and bearings to true azimuth before plotting them. The LOP conversion involves five steps:

Course per compass
(1)   ± Relative RDF bearing per compass
       = Apparent bearing per compass

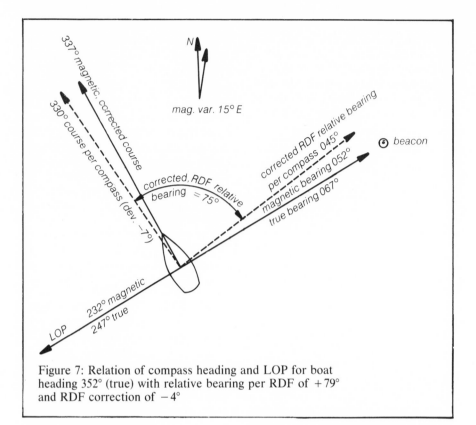

Figure 7: Relation of compass heading and LOP for boat
heading 352° (true) with relative bearing per RDF of +79°
and RDF correction of −4°

(2) ± RDF correction
    = Corrected RDF bearing per
    compass
(3) ± Compass deviation
    = Magnetic bearing
(4) ± Magnetic variation
    = True bearing
(5) ± 180 degrees
    = Line of position

Naturally, if you do your chart work directly from the magnetic ring of the compass rose, you can skip step 4.

In preparing an RDF deviation card, you want to know the RDF deviation at each five degrees of RDF relative bearing. But you recorded the RDF relative bearing at five-degree intervals per compass, which is not the same thing. Imagine the following row of entries on the worksheet:

360 335 +25 +29 +4 −4.

This row was intended for the relative bearing per RDF of +25 degrees and was recorded by sailing a relative bearing per compass of +25 degrees. However, because of RDF error, the relative bearing per RDF is actually +29 degrees. This is close enough for the +30-degree column of Figure 6 but now you have no data for the +25-degree spot.

One or more of these gaps in your data are almost bound to appear. You will have to go out to take data again, this time making special allowance for compass and RDF deviations.

Now, can you (at last) use the RDF effectively in fog? Yes. You certainly will use it more accurately than most RDF owners, for very few bother to prepare a deviation card. Also, by now you probably have had

222

more practice in taking RDF bearings than most skippers.

Remember that obtaining a *fix* from radio bearings is not so precise as getting one from visual bearings. For this reason it is a good idea to chart two lines of position for each radio bearing. For example, if your presumed error margin is ± two degrees, draw a LOP two degrees on either side of your indicated bearing. You can be anywhere within these LOPs.

Operating Your Magnetic Compass

By William V. Kielhorn

The basis of all surface navigation on our planet is the direction from a known point of departure to a known destination. Time, speed, and distance also are of great importance to be sure, but without being able to steer reliably in the proper direction you cannot hope to reach your destination with assurance.

The primary tool used to figure the desired course is the simple magnetic compass. Meridian-seeking gyros, inertial systems, and a host of other electrical and electronic devices can also greatly aid and simplify navigation, and I do not mean to minimize their usefulness. But there is only one reliable, zero-power device that is nearly indestructible and good in fair weather and in foul that can provide this essential guidance — the magnetic compass.

Unfortunately, for all its simplicity there remains some misunderstanding, misconception, folklore, and even downright nonsense about magnetic compass operation and use. I hope to dispel some of these false notions, explain some of the underlying physical principles by which the compass operates so admirably, and show why you have to know what is going on with your compass.

Understanding the nature of terrestrial magnetism goes a long way to helping you appreciate how your compass operates. Basically, the earth has a weak magnetic field that is somewhat aligned with its geographic or rotational axis. The strength of this field varies considerably, being strongest near the magnetic poles and weakest at the magnetic equator. The lines of magnetic force are parallel to the earth's surface at the magnetic equator, but become perpendicular to the surface at the magnetic poles.

This change of direction in the vertical plane is not directly proportional to the change of magnetic latitude. The change of angle of a freely suspended magnetized needle from the horizontal, called *magnetic dip,* occurs rather rapidly as you leave the magnetic equator and proceed toward the magnetic poles. Along the east coast of the United States this angle, or dip, amounts to about 73° at a latitude of about 42°N and is about 58° at a latitude of 25°N. At Callao, Peru, which is near the magnetic equator, the dip is only about 3°, and it is downward toward the north even although Callao is at 15°S. The north-south discrepancy is because the magnetic equator does not coincide with the geographic equator, but happens to be quite a bit south of it at Callao's longitude.

As we all know, magnetic direction differs from the geographic, or true, direction, with the magnitude of difference depending on your general location. This difference, called *variation,* is indicated on every nautical and aeronautical chart either by means of broken lines indicating the value and direction of the difference or on the compass roses imprinted on the charts. In the United States, from the Mississippi Valley east, the north-seeking end of the compass is pulled to the left, or west, of the true direction, and the magnetic compass course or bearing reads a greater number of degrees than does a true compass. In the western United States the opposite happens, with the north-seeking end of the compass needle being pulled to the right, or east. The former is called *westerly deviation;* the latter is called *easterly deviation.* And this is not all. Lines of equal variation are not constant, but change slowly with time. For example, immediately after World War II the variation at my home in Florida was about 1°E. Now it is about 1°W. In general in the United States, these lines of variation drift to the west about 25 miles every year. This is but one reason to sail with an up-to-date chart.

Occasionally I find a student trying to understand the intricacies of magnetism who confuses it with some of the phenomena of electrostatics. There are some similarities, but also some great differences. In electrostatics you can have charged particles that repel each other, much as do similar poles of a magnet. But electrostatic particles can be isolated so that you can collect all positive or all negative charges. Rain falling through the air separates these charges very effectively. When the voltage or potential reaches a high enough state, the result is lightning.

In magnetism you cannot isolate one pole from another. They always exist in exactly equal and opposite states in the same matter. They are called north and south poles, or more commonly red and blue poles, because of the semantic confusion caused by the directional designation. The north-seeking end of a compass is always designated as having red magnetism, and the north magnetic pole of the earth is called blue.

We all know that opposite poles of a magnet attract each other and that similar poles repel. But if this is so, why isn't the north end of a compass needle actually drawn toward the north pole of the earth? It does line up with the magnetic lines of force toward the pole, but it is not pulled toward it for a simple reason. The magnet you hold in your hand is extremely small compared with the magnet that is the earth. The north-seeking end of the magnet (or compass) is comparatively about as far from the pole as is the south-seeking end. So both the attracting and repelling forces are equal and opposite.

Try a simple experiment. Magnetize a steel needle by rubbing or striking one end of it with one end of a very strong magnet. This will induce in the needle what is known as a *subpermanent magnetism.* Now stick the magnetized needle into a bit of cork so it will float, and put it in a dish of water. Sure enough, the needle orients itself exactly and precisely to the earth's magnetic meridian. But it will not be drawn to the north by any magnetic forces. It will stay right in the middle of the dish as long as it is undisturbed by other forces. You have made as good and as accurate a magnetic compass as ever was designed. In fact, it would be considerably better than fifteenth-century compasses of similar design, which relied on natural lodestones (an iron ore of the chemical composition Fe_3O_4) as the sensing agent. Of course, your experimental compass is not very practical for use at sea,

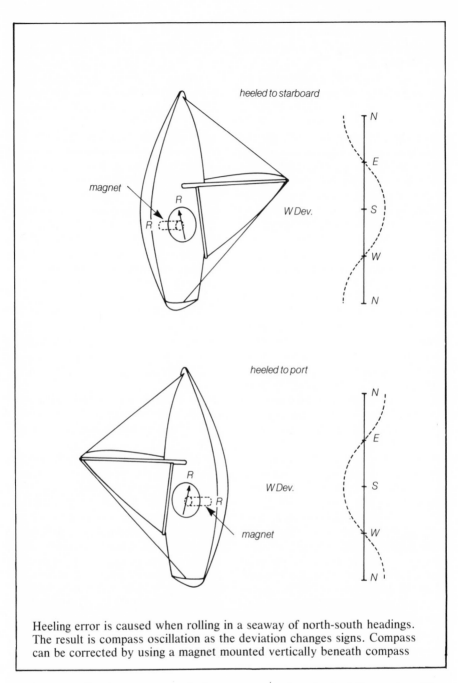

heeled to starboard

heeled to port

Heeling error is caused when rolling in a seaway of north-south headings. The result is compass oscillation as the deviation changes signs. Compass can be corrected by using a magnet mounted vertically beneath compass

and eventually that compass design was improved upon. A compass card was attached to the needle or lodestone, and the card and needles were kept from the sides of the bowl by means of a pivot at the center. The card was inscribed with a system of points, usually numbering thirty-two, about the circle and was called in Latin the *stella maris,* or "star of the sea." Your own modern compass may well have one of the derivatives of this ancient symbol.

A modern magnetic compass is but a slight refinement of the floating magnetic needle. It relies on strong construction and almost-frictionless bearings of the card on the needle. To achieve this combination, compass designers use an extremely sharp and well-ground needle and an extremely hard and durable jewel bearing to rest upon it. Usually the bearing is made of an artificial sapphire resting on a metal alloy needle hardened by the element iridium.

This metallic needle serves two purposes; it provides a very sharp and durable point, and it dissipates *heat* caused by the tiny amount of friction. Yes, I said heat. Although the needle and compass card may impose only a fraction of an ounce of weight they still impose pressure on the pivot point to a degree where it is best described in terms of *tons* per square inch. Compass needles need not be strongly magnetized in order to sense magnetic direction, and some of the best are very weak needles. It is the bearing that counts.

So much for the facts; now for a few myths. Over the years there has been some talk in sailing literature that your compass card balance must be adjusted when you are cruising over a wide range of latitude (because of the changing direction of the earth's lines of magnetic force). *This is simply untrue.* A compass constructed in Tasmania will work just as well, without rebalancing, in Brazil or Iceland. But don't the lines of force change and don't compass needles tend to align themselves with these lines? The answer is yes, if you have a freely suspended magnetized needle. But the mariner's compass is *not* freely suspended. The center of gravity of the card/needle system is well below the pivot point, which acts to restore the needle to the horizontal at all times. Because of this gravitational restraint compass needles only respond to the horizontal component of the earth's field. A magnetic compass may become almost useless near the earth's magnetic poles but not because of card tilt. It is simply because the horizontal component it is designed to sense approaches zero.

Stated another way, the magnetic forces on the needle, both vertically and horizontally, are extremely small. But the gravitational forces holding the card level are, by comparison, extremely large. Magnetic field strength does increase with increasing latitude, but so does gravity, although not in the same proportion. For all practical purposes, your compass card will remain horizontal no matter where you cruise.

This brings me to a second major problem area. I know of nothing that is so misunderstood as the heeling error of the compass. One reason may be that most modern fiberglass, lead-keeled sailboats have comparatively little heeling error. On a big steel ship, though, the heeling error is ordinarily the greatest of all the errors and must be accounted for with great care. However, if your boat has an iron keel or a large auxiliary engine beneath the compass, or even a radio speaker or ammeter above or beneath the compass, you may have a very significant heeling error that will not appear until you sail heeled over on north-south courses.

Most compasses do not provide for a simple correction — presumably because many boats do not require the correction and its complexity and cost might render a compass noncompetitive on price. I will also submit that not all professional compass adjusters who specialize in yacht compass compensation are equipped to make the proper adjustments.

Just as the east-west magnets and the north-south magnets in the correcting system take care of subpermanent magnetism in the horizontal plane, an adjustable heeling magnet corrects for the errors in the vertical plane. This latter error is caused by having the keel, speaker, ammeter, and so on acting as a vertical magnet placed beneath the compass. The effect is illustrated in the figure. You compensate for this error by installing beneath the compass another magnet oriented in the opposite direction to such a degree that it cancels the opposing field.

In practice, a compass adjuster corrects for the heeling error by using a *dipping* needle, which is a magnetized steel needle mounted so it responds only to the vertical component of the magnetic field. He carefully levels and balances the instrument ashore in the general location where the adjustment will be made. Then he takes it aboard the boat, places it in the exact position to be occupied by the ship's compass, and relevels it using the vertical heeling magnet.

On a big steel ship there are additional important corrections to be made in the releveling process. If the sources of the heeling error were entirely of the subpermanent variety the correction would be good for any latitude. Unfortunately this is rarely the case. More often the heeling error results from a combination of factors, including magnetically "soft" iron and materials that exhibit permanent magnet characteristics. An iron engine block, for instance, or an iron keel may be magnetically permeable. In this case the vertical component of the magnetism will be affected by the strength of the earth's magnetic field and the magnetic latitude or dip.

Thus, if you are on a long voyage that covers a wide range of latitudes, sailing from New York to Brazil, for example, the heeling error *will* change, and the compass will tend to oscillate when you are on north-south headings. As you proceed south the heeling error will become *overcompensated*. Now, in order to keep the compass steady, you must *lower* the heeling magnet(s). As you proceed still further into southern latitudes, it may even be necessary to reverse the magnet(s) and then begin to raise them in the reversed position. One early edition of *Bowditch* did recommend that the heeling magnet be reversed at the magnetic equator, but this is usually not correct and subsequent editions have been properly amended.

But what if you have no heeling corrector? You may be lucky by having little of this type of error on your boat. And what there is of the subpermanent variety can perhaps be corrected simply by placing a couple of magnets (same end up) low down on the binnacle stand. But if you do have that iron keel or that big engine beneath the compass you would be very prudent to install a full correction system, including adjustable heeling magnets.

You probably have heard about or read about another corrector — the Flinders' Bar. This is a rod of soft iron that usually is mounted forward or abaft the compass. It is designed to correct for induced magnetism of a certain type that affects the compass as a function of the changing magnetic latitude. But unless you have a boat with a big iron rudder post near the compass, as Captain Flinders did, you may fortunately forget this additional complication.

I would like to emphasize one last thing. The semicircular correctors (your north-south and east-west correctors), if they are properly balanced magnetically and are geometrically symmetrical, will have *no affect on the heeling error*. I have read recent accounts to the contrary that have been written by people highly respected in sailing circles. It is too bad they choose to extend their good knowledge in some fields to areas beyond their expertise. You must always stick to physical principles when you consider the physical problem of compasses.

In conclusion, if you understand your magnetic compass and its principles of operation well, you minimize its errors and know what they are. Then you can sail all the cruiseable waters of the world with assurance. The compass, after all, is your true *stella maris*.

Compensate Your Compass

By William V. Kielhorn

Chances are good that you have added some equipment to your boat this past year — perhaps a new engine, a new generator, some new instruments or even some new wiring. Any of these additions can have an important effect on your magnetic compass if the compass is located near the addition. And, although you should check your compass at least annually, additions of the sort I have mentioned make it even more important that you recheck and correct your compass before you sail anywhere.

Checking your own compass is not that hard. With practice you can correct the instrument with great accuracy. But before you start, make sure your boat is rigged completely and stowed with all the sailing gear that you would normally have aboard during the season. That way, when the ship is swung, you can be sure that your compass will not have any influence placed on it that is not already accounted for.

It is always helpful to understand the *why* of a procedure as well as the *how*. In the case of earth magnetism, I can't give you all the whys because all the answers are not known. It is known that large, rotating bodies, such as the earth and the sun, have magnetic fields. The fields are not constant. Ordinarily, the earth's field varies slowly and predictably, causing the compass variation from true north to change a fraction of a degree per year at most locations.

Superimposed on this are the so-called *magnetic storms,* which are of solar origin, that can cause significant, erratic compass behavior at very high magnetic latitudes.

In addition to this there may be *magnetic events,* which can cause the entire earth's field to reverse suddenly, making the north magnetic pole the south, and vice versa. But you needn't worry about these events. They take several thousand years to happen, and the last one took place about 700,000 years ago.

We can make a model of the earth as a magnet in order to aid in visualizing the earth's field. It is scientifically acceptable to make such a simplified model of nature provided the limitations of the model are recognized. Thus, although we know that stellar and planetary magnetism is extremely complicated, we can still make the assumption that the earth contains a big magnet imbedded deep within and is cocked off-axis significantly. Such a model, viewed as an apple sliced along a meridian near the east coast of the United States, would look something like Figure 1. The geographic latitude of Boston, Massachusetts, is about 42½°N; Key West, Florida, is about 25°N; and Callao, Peru, is about 15°S. The dip of a freely swung magnetized needle, which is sometimes called the magnetic latitude, is about 73° at Boston, 58° at Key West, and 3° at Callao. By another definition, .the magnetic latitude is measured from the magnetic equator to the magnetic poles, and the

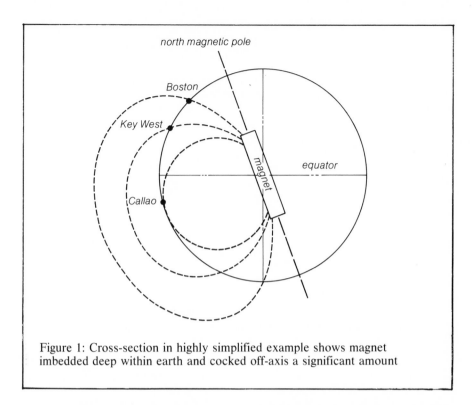

north magnetic pole

Boston

Key West

equator

magnet

Callao

Figure 1: Cross-section in highly simplified example shows magnet
imbedded deep within earth and cocked off-axis a significant amount

approximate dip is described as: tan
dip = 2 tan mag. lat.

If the lines of magnetic force of the
earth are directed downward so
greatly, and the compass needle
tends to follow these lines, why
doesn't the compass card tilt downward in the bowl? The compass card
doesn't tilt downward because the
compass needles, attached to the
compass card, are heavily balanced
and remain horizontal with respect
to apparent gravity. The magnetic
forces of the earth's field are a lot
less than the gravitational forces on
the card, so the card does not tilt at
all, regardless of magnetic latitude or
dip. The compass needles are responsive only to the horizontal component of the total earth's field. This
is why the compass becomes less
and less sensitive in sensing magnetic direction as it approaches the
magnetic poles of the earth. There is

also another effect. If your craft had
a maximum compass error of only
five degrees at Tampa, Florida, this
error would magnify about four
times should you cruise up toward
Greenland. Obviously, a compass
error of zero at low latitudes will remain at zero at higher latitudes, if
you are dealing only with subpermanent magnetism. This is but one
reason for having a well-adjusted
compass.

Most of us are concerned with
modern fiberglass or wooden vessels, in which the structure contains
little *soft* iron. *Hard* and *soft* are
terms used in the magnetic sense to
describe whether or not the material
is susceptible to magnetic induction
from the weak earth field, and
whether or not it can retain its
magnetism for a comparatively long
time. For example, a steel screw-
driver once magnetized acts as a

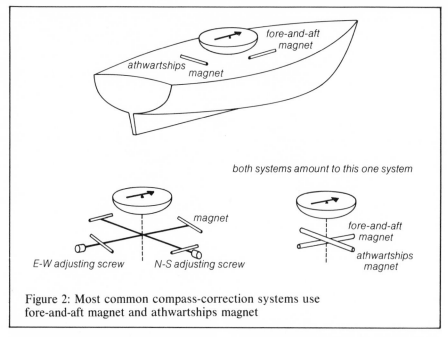

both systems amount to this one system

E-W adjusting screw | N-S adjusting screw

magnet

fore-and-aft magnet

athwartships magnet

Figure 2: Most common compass-correction systems use fore-and-aft magnet and athwartships magnet

strong permanent magnet and is almost unaffected by the earth field. It is physically and magnetically *hard*. On the other hand, a common nail, or a piece of cast iron, has magnetism induced in it easily by the earth field, but it does not retain the magnetism very long. So it is magnetically *soft*. Most of the compass adjustment complications come from the proximity of soft iron, so we can ignore it for our immediate purpose.

The object of compass compensation is to neutralize all the extraneous magnetic forces in the boat, such as those caused by engines, piping, braces, plates, radio speakers, etc., leaving only the earth field to direct the compass needles. Every wire carrying direct current, every electric motor, and many types of electric gauges also act as magnets which can affect the compass. Any compensation procedure must be carried out with all equipment near the compass placed in its usual loca-

tion and with all electrical apparatus that is normally in use when you are cruising turned on.

The magnets used to neutralize the extraneous fields come in a variety of forms. Some consist of simple bar magnets placed fore and aft or athwartships near the compass; others are arranged as rotating or spreading magnets beneath the compass. The most common system consists of two short magnets attached to a brass rod under the compass with one oriented fore and aft and the other athwartships. Each arrangement is magnetically analogous to having two bar magnets placed directly below the compass (Fig. 2).

Why can't you neutralize the ship's magnetic field in the vicinity of the compass with a single magnet? You can. A single permanent magnet located beneath the compass (or above it) can correct not only for the E-W and N-S errors, but for heeling error as well. But in order to locate the magnet correctly, you have to

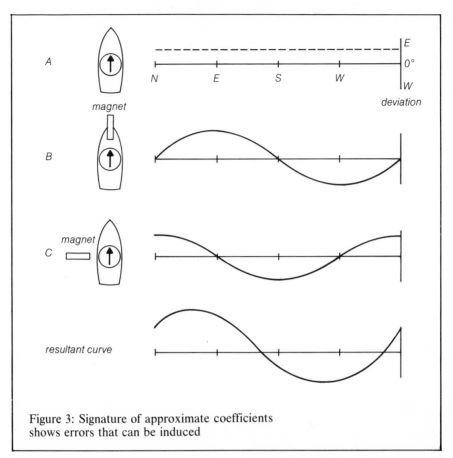

Figure 3: Signature of approximate coefficients shows errors that can be induced

make a careful magnetic survey of the compass location and calculate exactly the angles of orientation (in three dimensions) and the distance from the center of the compass system. This would be tedious and probably inaccurate. I have never known of its being done in nautical practice.

It is far better, and much simpler, to break the compass error into its several major components and then to correct each component separately. In small sailboats the deviation of the compass may be described for any heading as follows so long as the ship remains upright and at constant speed:

$$\text{Deviation} = A + B\sin z^l + C\cos z^l.$$

In this formula I have left out all the terms that have to do with the bothersome soft iron. So for our purpose the equation describes all our major errors. The capital letters in the equation are called *approximate coefficients*. They are determined quite accurately, but are called approximate because they denote the effects of magnetic forces, rather than the forces themselves. The little z^l is simply a conventional symbol signifying *compass* heading rather than *magnetic* heading. You will recognize that these two are somewhat different when deviation is present, but they are the same when the compass is perfectly corrected.

The coefficient A is the constant

error from the magnetic meridian that your compass might have. In big steel ships it may have its origin in some of the soft iron arrangements near the compass, but in modern yachts it is almost invariably caused by the lubber's line not being in perfect alignment with the ship's centerline. Thus, it is a mechanical error and is removed simply by rotating the whole compass assembly clockwise or counterclockwise until the error disappears.

Coefficient B has its maximum values on east and west compass headings. You correct it by using the E-W correction screw or by placing fore-and-aft magnets alongside, or under, the compass. In big-ship binnacles there are wooden trays running fore and aft and athwartships beneath the compass. Magnets placed in these trays serve the same purpose.

Coefficient C has its maximum values on north and south compass headings. You correct it by using the N-S correction screw, or by placing athwartships magnets ahead of, behind, or under the compass. In correcting B or C using bar magnets, it is usually best to use strong magnets far from the compass rather than weak ones near it. If correcting screws are there, you can only hope that the manufacturer has installed well-matched correctors. Figure 3 illustrates the signatures of the several errors discussed, but be aware that the sign of the errors can be either plus (E) or minus (W) for any of these coefficients.

In almost any good yachting textbook you will find some method for correcting your compass. Usually, it consists of getting on a magnetic cardinal point (N, S, E, W), taking out all the error, then reversing course, and taking out one-half the remaining error. These methods are all right

and will work for you. However, I'm going to give you another method which is also very simple, is inherently more accurate, and offers you a little more knowledge of your compass than before. I'll call it the *Analysis Method.*

First, rig and stow your boat in her normal cruising configuration. Turn on radios and other electrical apparatus you normally have in use most of the time. Keep pocket knives, screwdrivers, metal cap grommets, etc., well away from the compass. Proceed in calm, clear weather to a sheltered area where plenty of distant objects can be seen, and find about a dozen that are plotted on your chart. The more distant the objects the better, and never use floating aids to navigation unless they are very far away (at least several miles).

Get a reference point (also on the chart) and stay as close as possible to it. Aim the bow precisely at the distant object, let the boat steady upon it for a few moments, and then read the compass carefully. Record this heading (z^1) and also the chart plot of the magnetic bearing to the object from your location. Do this all around the compass. *The more data the better.* You don't have to do this all in one day or even at one general location. Take a couple of weekends to do it if you like. Soon, you will have enough data from which to draw a good deviation curve. Then you can analyze the curve and make your corrections with the correcting magnets.

Draw the curve on a piece of graph paper to some convenient scale. The horizontal axis should be the *compass headings* in degrees, and the vertical axis should be the *observed deviations* in degrees. Conventionally, easterly deviation is (+), and westerly deviation (−). If you have taken many observations (as you should), you may find that observations made on identical or nearby headings may differ a degree or two in deviation. In drawing the smooth curve, average out these discrepancies by eye. Figure 4 is a sample table of observations and the resulting curve. From this curve, pick off the deviation values to the nearest degree at the cardinal and intercardinal points. Now you are ready to analyze the curve and correct the compass.

To determine A, simply find the mean of the algebraic sum of the deviations at the cardinal and intercardinal points. In our example in Figure 4 we have:

$$
\begin{array}{l}
+6 \\
+10 \\
+9 \\
+4 \quad \text{Mean} = \\
-3 \quad +15/8 = +1.88° \\
-6 \qquad A = 2°E \\
-5 \\
\underline{0} \\
+15
\end{array}
$$

On the *average*, the compass reads two degrees too little all the way around. So loosen the binnacle screws and twist the whole compass assembly clockwise two degrees. You can do this at the dock, on any heading.

To determine B, take the mean of the deviations at east and west compass headings as determined from the curve, reversing the sign at west. In our example:

Reversing the sign at west: $+9$
090° = +9° $+5$
270° = −5° $\overline{+14}$
Mean = +14/2 = +7.0
    B = 7°E

Put the boat on an easterly or westerly heading, either when you are under way or at a pier, and re-move the seven-degree error, using the E-W correcting screws or the fore-and-aft magnets *only*.

To determine C, take the mean of the deviations at north and south compass headings as determined from the curve, reversing the sign at south. In our example:

Reversing the sign at south: $+6$
000° = +6° $+3$
180° = −3° $\overline{+9}$
Mean = +9/2 = +4.50°
    C = 5°E

Put the boat on a north or south heading, either when you are under way or at a pier, and remove the five-degree error, using the N-S correcting screws or the athwartships magnets *only*.

Now you have a compass which is as well compensated as possible using the limited correction systems that are furnished. Unless there is something very wrong with the compass itself, such as a broken bearing, it should be accurate within a degree or two for the rest of the season, unless some magnetic change is made near the compass. If the compass appears to operate smoothly, but it still shows significant deviation, consult a professional compass adjuster.

Some advantages of the ordinary magnetic compass are that it works well under sail or power and requires absolutely no outside energy for it to function properly. Fancy, expensive true-meridian gyros are just grand — until the power fails or it tumbles. Then, you can thank the stars above for the simple, reliable little magnetic needle. Even so, the magnetic compass is not altogether perfect for it is subject to some errors for which correction is not ordinarily provided. These are *heeling error*, *northerly turning error*, and *acceleration error*.

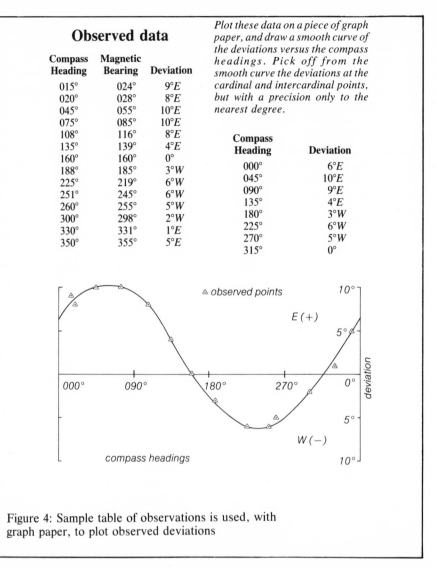

Observed data

Compass Heading	Magnetic Bearing	Deviation
015°	024°	9°E
020°	028°	8°E
045°	055°	10°E
075°	085°	10°E
108°	116°	8°E
135°	139°	4°E
160°	160°	0°
188°	185°	3°W
225°	219°	6°W
251°	245°	6°W
260°	255°	5°W
300°	298°	2°W
330°	331°	1°E
350°	355°	5°E

Plot these data on a piece of graph paper, and draw a smooth curve of the deviations versus the compass headings. Pick off from the smooth curve the deviations at the cardinal and intercardinal points, but with a precision only to the nearest degree.

Compass Heading	Deviation
000°	6°E
045°	10°E
090°	9°E
135°	4°E
180°	3°W
225°	6°W
270°	5°W
315°	0°

Figure 4: Sample table of observations is used, with graph paper, to plot observed deviations

Heeling error is extremely important in a large ship, and is often the greatest of the errors. It is semicircular in nature, like *B* and *C,* with maximum error for rolling being on compass north or south, and maximum error for pitching on compass east or west. It acts as if there were a magnet mounted vertically under the compass. Indeed, it is corrected by employing just such a magnet. Usually it is not significant in small boats, but it can be if the compass is mounted

directly over a large engine or an iron keel. Let your compass adjuster handle this one.

Northerly turning error is not much of a factor in cruising sailboats but is sometimes noticed when you maneuver high-speed multihulls. Earlier I mentioned the reaction of the compass card to apparent gravity and also the surprisingly steep dip angles of the earth's line of magnetic force. When a high-speed craft makes a turn, the compass card responds to the *apparent* gravity and assumes an angle of bank whether the boat herself does or not. This angle from the true horizontal subjects the compass to the vertical component of the earth's field, and it can cause very large temporary errors. One way of avoiding this error is to install a surplus aircraft directional gyro which can be set to the magnetic compass from time to time when the magnetic compass is steady. This is the technique used in almost all small aircraft, where this kind of error is extreme.

Acceleration error, sometimes called *speed error* (erroneously) occurs when the boat is accelerated while on an east-west heading. You may have noticed it when you surf downslope, or suddenly butt into a steep wave. In either case, the compass card, responding to apparent gravity, tilts from the true horizontal, and is affected by the vertical field component as in the northerly turning error. Again, the best solution is a surplus directional gyro.

A total system, which consists of a magnetic flux-gate compass that is gyro-stabilized, is also available and is nearly free of deviation. These are beautiful instruments, as they should be at about $10,000 per copy, but if the power goes off, so does the compass. It is really more fun to watch the simple compass card that rotates cleanly in a binnacle. And it is especially reassuring to know that whatever errors it has, you already know about — and have compensated for.

Determining Your Speed

By William V. Kielhorn

Time, speed, distance and course — these four quantities comprise the essence of navigation from one known position to another. Here we will consider one of these factors in particular, *speed*. Determining speed is not so easy to come by as you might think.

Speed is merely distance per unit of time. It may be expressed as nautical miles per hour (knots), centimeters per second, inches per year, or whatever scales of distance and time may be convenient for the problem involved. Until we go entirely to the metric system, ships will continue to use the nautical mile per hour as being by far the most convenient unit for speed.

In ancient times, the nautical mile was quite unheard-of. Instead, a variety of distance units were used. Among these were the *stadium,* or *stade,* a measure of distance that originated in Attica. Scholars dispute the exact conversion of this distance to modern linear measure, but they have generally accepted its approximation as being 10 stadia or one mile. The measure described as a "day's run" for a sailing ship was often used, but it could mean a variety of things to different sailors from different lands.

For example, the Phoenicians reckoned a day's sail to be the theoretical distance a ship would go in a 24-hour run with a fresh, following breeze. According to the *Periplous* (circumnavigation-book of the Mediterranean Sea) of Scylax, this would be about 1000 stadia, or about 100 to 125 Roman miles, according to the value one used for the stadium.

On the other hand Herodotus, with respect to the Caspian Sea, used as a day's voyage the distance one could travel in an oared boat — about 40 miles. The Norsemen and ancient Irish also used the term, a *day's sail,* but here, too, there is ambiguity about just what they meant by it.

Even the Arabs had troubles in defining speed and distance. In the Red Sea a "day's journey" by Pilgrim Boat to Jidda meant what one would do on camelback ashore — about 20 to 25 miles. But a sea-going Arab, Al Marwazi, gave a day's sail as 150 miles, or the equivalent of about six knots. No wonder the ancient maps were so inconsistent!

Perhaps the earliest of the ship's logs was that of a Roman engineer, Pollio Vitruvius. He had invented the odometer for use on land vehicles in the first century, AD, and tried to apply the principle to ships. His paddle-wheel ship odometer simply didn't work, because of friction, water-slippage, and the usual marine gremlins. This was the first recorded case of a land-based engineer trying to get his feet wet — ocean technologists take notice! It is interesting to note that some successful modern yacht-logs are based on the Vitruvius principle.

In Columbus's day, ship speed determination was already an art, and those who were expert in this phase of navigation were highly prized as pilots. Columbus himself learned what he knew of navigation during his years in Portugal, but his methods for determination of speed and distance seem unclear. It probably consisted of pacing (i.e., walking aft a given number of paces, or counting paces in a given time) in concert with an object thrown overboard at a point forward in the ship.

This was a variation of what now is known as the Dutchman's log, although there is no evidence that the Dutch had any inventive priority in this ancient method of speed determination. However, the Dutch did popularize this method in a strange way. They imprinted upon pocket-sized copper tobacco boxes tables of ship speed to be used for timing between marks 40 feet apart on the ship. One such box, made in 1754, was designed so that a person counting evenly at the rate of 54 in 30 seconds could consult the table and read his speed directly. If the count were eight, for example, the table would show that his speed was four miles an hour.

Later — no one can say just when — someone had the idea of tying a light line to a chip of wood, and measuring the amount of line played out in a given time that would be measured by a sand-glass.

This *chip-log* was pretty good for determining speed through the water. It did suffer from the problem that fathoms and leagues were commonly used as the distance-units, and these varied in value from one country to another. Not until the nautical mile became standard (more-or-less) was there any real consistency among ships of different nations.

A further improvement in the chip log came when some seaman suggested tying knots in the line spaced seven fathoms (42 feet) apart, and counting them as they passed overboard. But as the nautical mile became better known, a mathematician and seaman, Richard Norwood, suggested in 1637 that the knots be made at 50 feet, rather than at 42 feet. This represented a sea-mile of 6000 feet, rather than 5000 feet, or quite close to its proper value. Now, the number of knots passing overboard in a 30-second run was about right to give the speed in nautical miles per hour:

$$\frac{50 \text{ ft.}}{30 \text{ sec.}} = \frac{6000 \text{ ft. (1 mile)}}{3600 \text{ sec. (1 hour)}}$$

But sailors, being remarkably conservative as a group, continued to use the old 42-foot knots for nearly 100 years more! And in Spain and Portugal, and among some French sailors, too, the log line simply wasn't used at all, or was secondary to their traditional reckoning for *singradura,* or day's sail, which depended upon the estimated force of the wind.

During the 18th and 19th centuries, all sorts of speed logs were developed, some by well-known scientists who had great depth of theory, but not always of practicality. For example, the famous astronomer Edmund Halley suggested using a "log" consisting of a metal ball suspended overside from a boom, and dragged submerged a few feet below the surface. He reasoned correctly that the "wire angle" from the vertical would be a function of ship speed. But he had not considered the errors introduced by the surging, rolling ship, so nothing practical developed. Another method was to tow a submerged sphere astern and measure the towing line tension related to ship speed. This concept too suffered from much the same difficulty.

The towed rotating log became popular around 1800. There were many designs, but all consisted of having a streamlined metal "fish" with angled rotor-blades towed well astern, usually from the ship's taff-rail. At first, the distance recording mechanism was contained within the fish, and the distance was indicated on small dials. This required the watch to retrieve the log every time it was to be read. Later, the recording dials were placed at the inboard end of the line at the taffrail — much to the liking of the watch, no doubt.

These were good logs as long as the ship maintained enough way. But they were quite useless at very low speeds. Also, they tended to foul in patches of floating seaweed, and once in a while a hungry shark would make a mistake in food identification to the detriment of the rotor.

Early in the 19th century Vicomte de Vaux designed a pressure-type log based on the theory advanced in 1732 by the French engineer Henri Pitot. This consisted of a tube pro-truding through the ship's hull, the tube having a short right-angle bend with the orifice facing forward. The dynamic pressure in the tube, as measured on a manometer, was a function of ship speed, and therefore could be read directly.

But this was only instantaneous speed, and did not average out the surges of the ship as did the taffrail and chip logs. Advances in electrical engineering later permitted the odometer feature which was so im-portant, and "pitometer logs" were commonly used in US warships dur-ing World War II.

In 1915 Captain Basil Chernikeeff of the Imperial Russian Navy de-veloped a different kind of sub-merged log. This consisted of a cleverly designed, almost friction-less rotor or impeller attached to a shaft protruding from the hull. Elec-trical signals from the rotor were transmitted to speed indicators and distance recorders. This type of log has long been in use by the British Admiralty and is similar in many re-spects to some modern yacht logs.

When you look at all the different types and brands of yacht logs being marketed today, think back upon this short history of their develop-ment. All the principles have been employed before, and only the tech-nology — electrical, mechanical and material — has improved.

Well, what can a yachtsman do to measure his speed through the water accurately but without acquiring some of the more expensive equip-ment available today? First, list what should be the desirable attributes of your speed log.

1. It must be inexpensive — less than $20, and perhaps not over $5.
2. It must be compact — there's no extra room on most small sail-boats.
3. It must be accurate — as good or better than most patent speed logs.
4. It should not consume battery power — there's rarely enough.
5. It must be convenient — labo-rious duties are anathema to a one-man deck watch.

With these five criteria in mind, how does one select the right sys-tem? First, eliminate all those that cannot qualify. This includes all the pressure logs, strain-gauge logs, im-pellor or propeller logs, and any other logs that give only instan-taneous speeds. A log giving only an instantaneous speed can (properly) indicate one knot one instant, and six or seven knots a few moments later. This is particularly apparent in a fol-lowing sea where the boat "surfs" ahead on the face of a wave, then "squats" in the trough. In order to obtain an accurate run, the observer

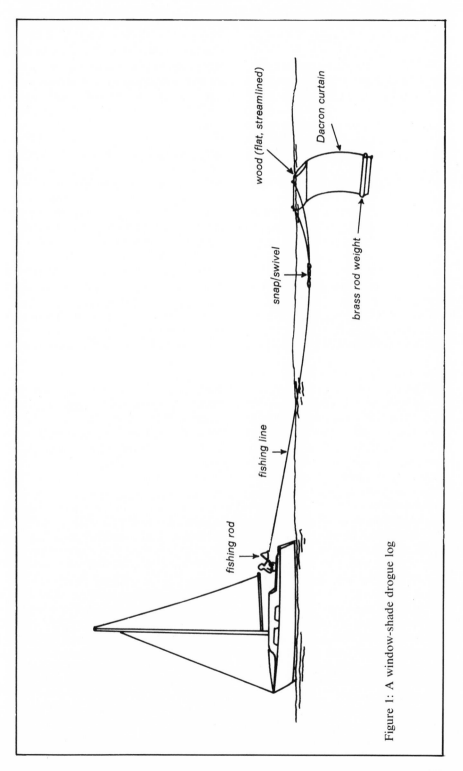

Figure 1: A window-shade drogue log

must interpolate or average by eye over this range of speeds. The result can be significantly in error.

So, one of the few types of logs which can meet our criteria adequately still must be the old chip log. By using a little imagination we can make some improvements, and increase its adaptability to small sailing yachts. I shall present one such scheme; no doubt you can think of others more suitable to your own needs.

First, let's start with the outboard end — with the "chip." In earlier times this was a quadrant of wood weighted barely to float and had a wooden peg that released under tension so that the chip had less drag upon retrieval.

Why not have a much more compact device? Figure 1 illustrates a *window-shade* drogue that has a high drag coefficient at low tensions, and a low drag coefficient at higher tensions — just the quality we want. Also, it can be rolled up and stowed easily. The size of the drogue is up to you, but I would suggest starting with one about 4″ × 4″, weighted so that it barely floats or, if you wish, is suspended a couple of feet below the surface supported by a small slim fishing bobber.

Now get an old spinning-reel with a fast retrieve and a short fishing rod. An old, cut-down spinning rod will do fine. You could even use your regular spinning-rod and reel and have a replaceable spool containing the log-line. Put at least 100 yards of Dacron or nylon fishing line on the spool: 20-pound test line is ample. Tie a figure-eight knot in the line at least 25 feet from the drogue. This becomes the "start knot." Then tie in another knot every 25 feet for the whole length of line.

To employ the rig, unwrap and cast the drogue overboard, leaving the reel on free spool. The moment the start knot slips through your fingers (keep almost no tension on the line), pay out the line for 30 seconds, counting every *second knot* as one knot of speed. If you are going faster than three knots, pay the line out for only 15 seconds, counting *every* knot as a knot of speed. The easiest way to stop the line is to flip the reel-bale, but have the drag set up firmly.

This is an accurate log. It is so good, in fact, that it may be used not only by itself for good navigation, but also as a means of calibrating your speed/odometer log, should you be so fortunate to have one, or your engine tachometer.

But this log, just as with other yacht logs, will only give you your speed and distance through the water: it does not consider the current vector. In order to obtain speed or distance *over the bottom,* you would have to go to acoustic doppler logs (shallow water only), or to inertial navigation systems of the type used by modern submarines. These, of course, are beyond the scope of this discussion.

Oceanographers frequently have to deal with current speeds that are comparable to the cruising speeds of sailboats, and they too have found that accurate speed measurement is sometimes elusive. They now have hopes that an entirely new kind of speed (or current) meter can be developed, one that uses very little power and has no moving parts. The commercial development of this device may be a few years away but at least we now have hope for something *really* new since Columbus, Bourne, and de Vaux.

Electronic Depthsounders: The Versatile Helpers

By James B. Kane

When you hear the word *fix,* you probably think of bearings, lines of position, and other traditional methods of establishing your location. But what you may not know is that you can also help find your boat's position by using an electronic device called the depthsounder. A depthsounder is a very handy device not only because it tells you when you are heading into shallow water, but also because its versatility can help you find your own position.

One way of finding your position with a depthsounder is by a method called a *chain of soundings.* To find your boat's position by a chain of soundings, you first must record a series of soundings over a period of time. Then, by placing a piece of tracing paper over the latitude or distance scale on your chart, space the individual soundings at the proper distance apart. For example, if you're making five knots and you want to space your soundings every 500 yards, you would write down a sounding on your tracing paper every three minutes. When traveling at five knots, 123 minutes equals one mile; three minutes equals a quarter mile or 500 yards (Fig. 1).

On the tracing paper, next to the sounding, mark the time you took it.

Orient the chain of soundings to your course line and allow for the effects of any current or leeway. Keep the tracing paper correctly aligned with your course and slide it around until the soundings you have written on the paper coincide with a string of soundings printed on the chart. Where they match is where you were at the times you took the soundings. Naturally, when you do a chain of soundings you must start from a reasonable dead reckoning (DR) position if you are to have much luck.

Don't expect the tracing paper to agree *exactly* with the charted bottom every time. It won't. And it's going to be difficult and even misleading if you use this technique where the area has an even bottom. On the other hand, a sharp bump or ledge on the bottom is perfect to give you the big slope difference you are looking for.

A second way to use the depthsounder is to take a bearing on any charted object and simultaneously to get a sounding. Plot the bearing on your chart and look down along that bearing. When you find a sounding that is the same as the one you took, there you are with a pretty good fix. You can also use this method in fog by using a radio direction finder (RDF) bearing instead of a visual

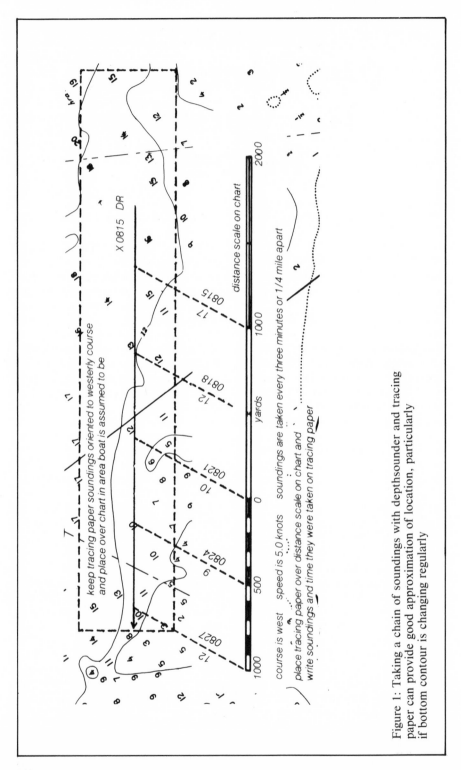

Figure 1: Taking a chain of soundings with depthsounder and tracing paper can provide good approximation of location, particularly if bottom contour is changing regularly

course is west   speed is 5.0 knots   soundings are taken every three minutes or 1/4 mile apart

place tracing paper over distance scale on chart and write soundings and time they were taken on tracing paper

keep tracing paper soundings oriented to westerly course and place over chart in area boat is assumed to be

X 0815 DR

distance scale on chart

0815
0818
0821
0824
0827

yards

2000   1000   0   500   1000

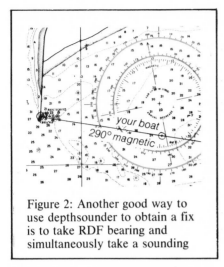

Figure 2: Another good way to use depthsounder to obtain a fix is to take RDF bearing and simultaneously take a sounding

bearing on a lighthouse, tower or some other readily identifiable object.

For example, let's say you're heading 290 degrees magnetic and it's thick fog. Your depthsounder is on, and you've been staying in depths over 30 feet (Fig. 2). You want to pass to seaward of the jetty, and your DR track tells you that you must be getting close to it. Shortly after you cross the 30-foot curve, you take an RDF bearing on the beacon at the end of the jetty and simultaneously read the depthsounder. It shows 27 feet. The RDF bearing shows 290 degrees magnetic. Plot this bearing to the beacon and look along it for a 27-foot sounding. About halfway between the 24-foot sounding and the 30-foot curve is your most probable position. But make sure when you are doing this that there aren't several similar depths to the one you're using along the bearing line.

If you want to get a line of position (LOP) with your depthsounder, look on your chart for contours of equal depth. They're shown on your chart by usually broken or dotted lines. Now as you are moving along note the time you cross a bottom contour (12, 18 feet, etc.). Place your parallel ruler so the edge follows the general trend of the contour. Advance or retard this line along your own course

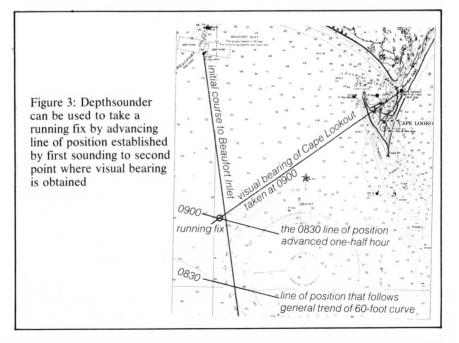

Figure 3: Depthsounder can be used to take a running fix by advancing line of position established by first sounding to second point where visual bearing is obtained

line as you would with any other LOP such as a bearing.

You can use the LOP you get with a depthsounder with another bearing to obtain a fix or you can advance the line until you have an opportunity to obtain another LOP. You then would have a running fix, but one produced partly by a depthsounder.

To simplify how you do this, Figure 3 shows a course heading from sea to the Beaufort Inlet sea buoy. You note the time (0830) you cross the 60-foot curve and take your parallel ruler and draw a straight line following its general trend. This is your LOP. At 0900 you sight Cape Lookout light and take a visual bearing on it. Now advance the 0830 LOP ahead the distance run in one-half hour to 0900. Where the LOP and the bearing cross is your running fix.

Another way to use your depthsounder is to keep your boat in safe water by using a *danger sounding*. A danger sounding will differ depending on your boat's draft and the slope

of the bottom. When you've decided what you want to use for a danger sounding, connect these soundings on your chart by marking a line in red pencil.

To illustrate, let's say it's thick fog and you're off the south coast of Long Island in the vicinity of Short Beach (Fig. 4). You're heading west and you want to pass south of the Jones Inlet Buoy — thereby keeping clear of the shoal water to its north. As you can see, the 30-foot contour is slightly to the south of the "JI" Buoy. By staying south of the 30-foot curve, you automatically keep yourself clear of the abrupt shoal off Jones Inlet.

So far all this sounds good. But the depthsounder, like any piece of good electronic equipment, does have limits, and you must use it correctly. Let's look at a few things you must watch out for. Really rough seas can cause turbulence under your boat, sometimes affecting your depthsounder's accuracy.

And before you use your depthsounder, be sure you know whether the person installing it adjusted it to allow for the distance the transducer (instrument at the bottom of the boat receiving the echoes) is below the surface of the water (Fig. 5). The adjustment is made so the indicated depths you get from your sounder are compatible with the soundings you read on your navigation chart.

If your sounder is giving you the actual water depth from the transducer, you must add the additional depth of the transducer from the surface to the depth you receive — otherwise you can't currently match or compare your depths with those on your chart.

Furthermore, always look under the title of the chart you're using to find whether the soundings on it are shown in *feet* or *fathoms*. Charts of

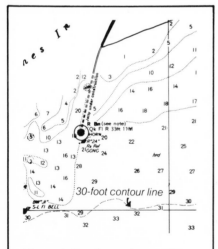

Figure 4: Depthsounder can be useful to establish danger soundings and therefore keep boat off in deeper water or away from known obstructions

areas near shore show the depths in feet; depths on charts of offshore areas generally are in fathoms. Of course, six feet equals one fathom.

You also must consider the range of tide where you're piloting. Soundings on charts always are near the lowest levels you can expect, such as *mean low water* on the Atlantic Coast of the United States, *mean low water springs* for the West Coast including Alaska, and *lowest normal tides* for Canada. National Oceanographic and Atmospheric Administration (NOAA) charts generally show the range of tide for several points on the chart.

Sometimes your depthsounder will show more than one echo. With digital displays this will show up as a mixture of soundings, usually five or six feet apart. If this starts to happen, check the *gain* knob if your set has one. You may have it tuned up too high. If this isn't the trouble, then the most probable cause of this double reading is a soft mud or silt bottom over a hard rock bottom. A rocky bottom reflects almost all sound while mud or silt tends to let the sound go through it thus returning a weaker echo. If this happens, always use the lesser depth as your sounding. The lesser depth is the depth from the top of the mud.

On depthsounders that show depth by a flash on a screen, the flash always has some width. Read the *trailing* edge or the least depth that is indicated. Schools of fish can return an echo. While this is useful to anyone fishing it's an annoyance to anyone seriously navigating, so be alert to that possibility.

Because a depthsounder doesn't forecast depths ahead of you, it's of limited use in predicting what is ahead when you are approaching any shores strewn with rocks, or other places where the bottom changes suddenly.

The depthsounder is a modern refinement of the world's oldest navigational instrument, the hand lead. But the depthsounder gives you far more readings per minute than a lead. A depthsounder is safer, too. You don't have to worry about a per-

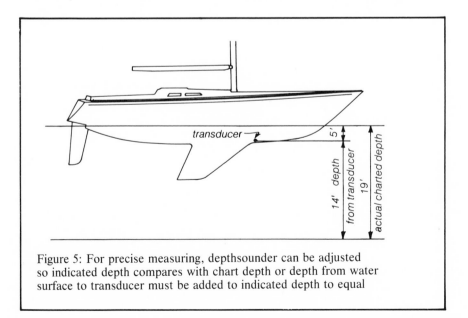

Figure 5: For precise measuring, depthsounder can be adjusted so indicated depth compares with chart depth or depth from water surface to transducer must be added to indicated depth to equal

son falling overboard when he is using one. And, of course there is no danger of anyone's getting conked on the head with a flying hunk of lead.

Of the problem areas I've mentioned only two are really tough ones to handle: sudden bottom changes and rough seas. If you bear these two in mind and remember what to do when you're faced with them, you'll find your depthsounder to be a good and reliable friend. In fact it's one of the most useful piloting tools you can have aboard.

The Lead Is Not Dead

By Dag Pike

The average sailing yacht is not designed to take the bottom, so whether you are under way or stopped you are always concerned about the amount of water underneath your keel. The advent of the echo sounder has made life a lot easier; all you have to do is switch on and there is the depth.

The leadline, the only means of finding the depth before the echo sounder came on the scene, has largely disappeared from the inventory of yachts but there are things you can do with a leadline which you can't do with an echo sounder, and it is well worth carrying one. The obvious use of the leadline is to check the readings of the echo sounder, a thing you must do now and again if you are going to have faith in its readings.

The method is simple. Find an area where there is a hard bottom, measure the depth with the leadline and then compare it with the depth shown by the echo sounder. Remember that the echo sounder is probably set to measure the depth of water under the keel or from the bottom of the hull, so add the distance between the transducer and the surface to the echo sounder reading.

A hard bottom is essential so that the echo sounder reading gives a nice firm, clean, line and the lead will not sink into the bottom silt. The leadline reading will be accurate only if your line does not stretch. When the lead was in general use a special type of hemp leadline was available. Even

then it was towed astern for a while to stretch it before measuring, and it was measured when it was wet.

A suitable modern rope for the job would be the type of braided polyester used for sheets and halyards. These have low-stretch properties and are easy to handle even when wet. It is still a good idea to tow the rope astern before measuring it to give it a chance to bed down and settle in a natural length. There are traditional markings to use on the line, but you may find it easier to make up your own code, particularly now that metric measurements are on their way in.

The traditional shape of the lead includes a hollow in the bottom which is armed with tallow. When the lead touches the sea bed samples of the bottom stick to the tallow so that the navigator can find out what it is composed of. Different areas have different bottom materials, and the information can give the navigator a clue to his whereabouts.

When you are at anchor or moored the lead comes into its own. Something it can do that the echo sounder can't is give readings showing the difference in depths between bow and stern or on each side of the boat, particularly useful if you happen to go aground and want to find the best way to get off.

The leadline can tell you if your boat is dragging its anchor, particularly useful at night when it can be difficult to check dragging by shore marks. The leadline is lowered to the bottom with a little slack to allow for the rise and fall of the tide. If the

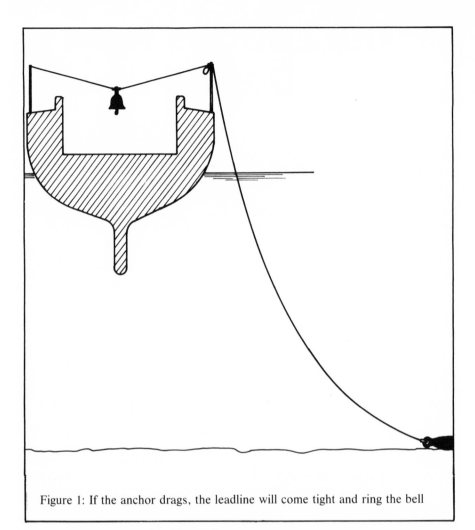

Figure 1: If the anchor drags, the leadline will come tight and ring the bell

anchor drags then the leadline tightens and you know your boat is moving. The amount of movement can be judged by the feel of the lead being dragged across the bottom.

Used in this way the lead can be made to operate an alarm, but it will want careful setting up if it is not to give you a sleepless night. The leadline is brought on board through a block fixed to the rails or shrouds and led across the boat where it is made fast. A bell is fixed to the section of the line between the rail and its fastening (Fig. 1).

When the boat is static the leadline is slack and the bell rests on the deck. If the boat drags its anchor, then the leadline tightens, the span supporting the bell becomes taut and the bell rings. It will continue to ring as the line jerks with the lead being dragged across the bottom. The only snag with this system is that the bell will probably ring when the boat swings with the tide or the wind, but then you may want to have warning of this anyway.

If you are one of those sailors who prefers small harbors to marinas then you may have to cope with your boat's drying out when it is lying

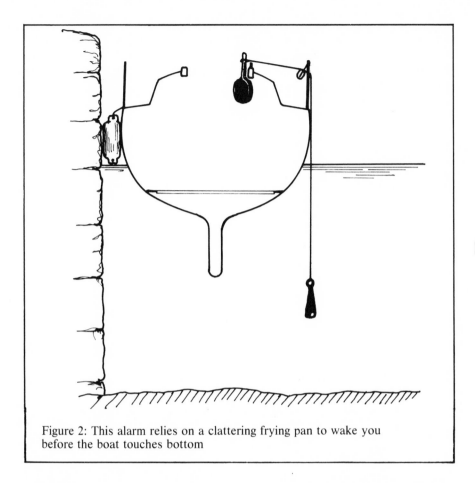

Figure 2: This alarm relies on a clattering frying pan to wake you before the boat touches bottom

alongside a harbor wall. This is a time when you want to be about to check the mooring ropes and make sure the boat settles comfortably. Inevitably, it will take the bottom at some time during the night, and you may not be sure of the exact time because of lack of tidal knowledge. The lead can be used to give you warning in time to get up to attend to things.

As before, the leadline is led on board through a block. The length of line left overboard is a foot or six inches greater than the draft of your boat. A loop is tied in the inboard end, which is just long enough to reach the edge of the hatch coaming. If you put the handle of a frying pan

or saucepan through the loop this will be sufficient to hold things in place when the line is taut, but when the lead touches bottom, the line becomes slack, the pan is released and drops with sufficient noise to wake you (Fig. 2).

The crude device can be improved depending on the layout of your boat. The ingenious owner can devise an electrical system connected to the line, and for the heavy sleeper the pan can be allowed to fall onto a collection of other pans. One point to remember is to make sure that the leadline cannot run out through the block when released or you may find yourself waiting for the tide to go right out in order to recover the lead.

Using the lead for these purposes is not applicable to every yacht, but using it as a standby in case your echo sounder fails is a universal requirement. Modern electronic instruments are reliable, but the marine environment is harsh and the cautious navigator always tries to keep a few tricks up his sleeve. The leadline is one of these.

Get the Most Out of Your Loran-C

By Parker Boggs

The age of loran-C is upon us! A combination of forces — including government decree, microcomputer technology, production efficiency, and competition — is pushing radionavigation systems into the 1980s. If you are the kind of navigator who likes to know exactly where you are at any time, you will be glad to have loran-C aboard.

In case you haven't been keeping up with the US loran situation, this is what's happening: the Coast Guard has been replaced its aging loran-A equipment with loran-C, which is more reliable, more accurate, useful over long distances, and less costly to operate.

Until recently, though, the cost, size, and power demands of a loran-C receiver that could take full advantage of the new system were too high for the average cruising sailor. Even so, fishermen and offshore racers changed over to loran-C as it became available, and they can attest to its usefulness—as well as the growth pains that the system has had. But the Coast Guard anticipated some shakedown problems and left the loran-A system running in tandem with loran-C to allow for a gradual changeover. Now, however, loran-A is off the air, and if you want any loran at all it will have to be loran-C.

Fortunately for the cruising sailor, the timing couldn't be much better. The cost of receivers has dropped rapidly in the past two or three years (with accompanying reductions in size, weight, and power consump-

tion), while the sophistication of the units has been on a corresponding upswing. Loran-C coverage has been improving, too; virtually all US waters are covered by good-to-excellent loran-C signals.

Like any navigational aid, though, loran-C is only as good as the navigator's understanding of it. Nearly anyone can turn on a receiver, wait a few minutes, and jot down some numbers—but if you know what those numbers are really telling you, you can plot your position with exceptional accuracy.

Before you can get reliable loran-C position fixes, you've got to install a receiver on your boat. This may seem obvious, but a leading cause of loran-C problems is *improper installation*. If you pay for professional installation, then you'll probably get it. If you are installing the receiver yourself, though, you should know that the problems tend to fall into two categories: faulty groundings and poor antenna placement.

If your boat has external, bolted-on ballast, all you normally have to do is run a heavy ground wire (AWG 10, for example) to a keel bolt. With internal ballast, you can try going to the engine block with the ground wire, but you may find that you need to install an external grounding device at your next haulout. If you've chosen your loran-C dealer with care (as you should have), you can trust his judgment in this area.

Antenna placement is often the most troublesome part of the installation. Since loran-C operates in a very low-frequency band (90-110

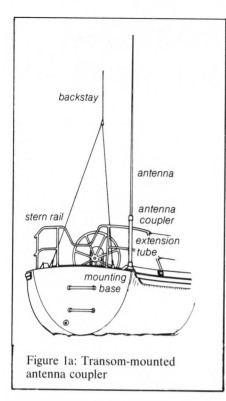

Figure 1a: Transom-mounted antenna coupler

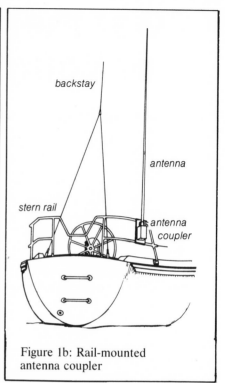

Figure 1b: Rail-mounted antenna coupler

kHz), your loran antenna must be well clear of all other antennas, stays, shrouds, and so forth. On two-masted vessels, this is no problem; you can have your VHF antenna on one mast and your loran antenna on the other. Sloops and cutters, however, do have a problem. Most sailors want to have their VHF antenna at the masthead, and there's simply not enough horizontal separation up there to hang on the loran-C antenna too.

What are the choices that remain? For best reception, you can use your backstay as a long-wire antenna. This means going to your local rigging loft to have insulators put in it, but if you want the best possible reception, this is what you have to do. On the other hand, if you seldom venture more than a few hundred miles offshore, you can probably get fine results using the arrangement shown in Figure 1a. This setup uses standard antenna mounting hardware and an extension tube set as close to the outer edge of the transom as possible to get the antenna well clear of the backstay and stern rail. Some manufacturers may not offer the screw-on type of antenna coupler shown here. If you plan to use this mounting arrangement, be sure that the receiver you are buying comes with the right kind of coupler.

If you are buying a receiver with a "box" type of coupler, the mounting arrangement shown in Figure 1b usually gives satisfactory results. Note that the box is mounted as high as possible to get most of the antenna above the stern rail.

When everything is installed to your satisfaction and the dealer has shown you how the receiver operates, you have the opportunity to navigate your boat with incredible

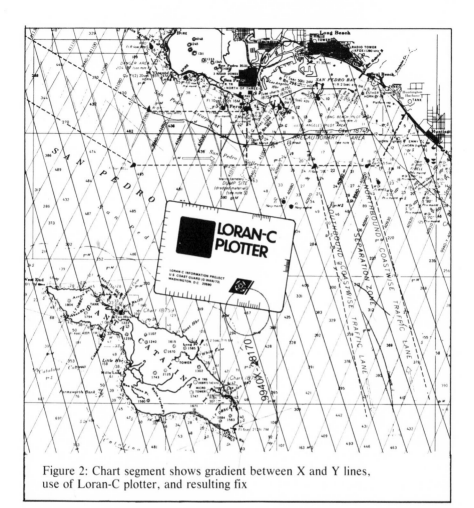

Figure 2: Chart segment shows gradient between X and Y lines, use of Loran-C plotter, and resulting fix

precision. The techniques we'll look at next will show you how to get the most out of your receiver.

Interpolation. Once you've got some numbers flashing away on your receiver, you need to relate them to the loran lines that are printed on your chart. As you can see by a glance at Figure 2, the lines on your chart are laid down in multiples of five or 10 microseconds. What you need to do when your actual time difference (TD) line doesn't fall right on one of these printed lines is *interpolate*.

The most common method of interpolation finds you hauling out

your dividers and using the Loran Linear Interpolator on the chart. (If you've done this for loran-A, it's the same for loran-C.) But there is an easier, faster way that you ought to know about—the loran-C plotter. The plotter shown in Figure 2 is available from your local Coast Guard Aids to Navigation branch, free for the asking. The back side of the plotter tells you how to use it, but the print is pretty small. The basic procedure is this:

1. Pick a scale on the plotter that is as close as possible to the loran time difference (TD) lines on your chart. You can use the plotter at an

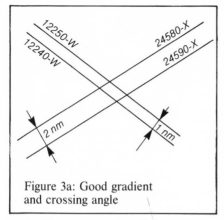

Figure 3a: Good gradient and crossing angle

angle, if necessary for alignment, as shown in Figure 2.

2. Put the ends of the scale on the lines that bracket your actual loran TD, and mark your TD with a pencil point at the appropriate spot on the scale. For example, suppose your receiver is displaying TDs of 28170.0 and 40977.0. Figure 2 shows how you would plot the 40977.0 line. You would plot the 28170.0 line the same way. By drawing a line through each point, parallel to the bracketing TD lines for each, you can fix your position where the lines intersect.

After you've done this for a while, you become practiced enough so you can interpolate fairly well with a quick inspection of the chart.

Gradient. The loran-C gradient is a measure of how much the time difference (TD) changes in a given distance. It is gradient that provides the main limiting factor for the accuracy of your position fix. (Another factor is the crossing angle of the TD lines, which we'll look at next.) Gradient is usually described as some number of microseconds per mile, with a large gradient defined as one in which a small change in time difference corresponds to a large change in position. (This is also called a poor gradient and often occurs near a baseline extension. Try to avoid using TDs near baseline extensions, which are clearly marked on your charts.)

The effect of gradient accuracy is illustrated by this simple table, which assumes that your loran-C receiver displays TDs with a resolution of 0.1 microsecond:

Gradient in microseconds/ mile	Distance represented by 0.1 microsecond
1	600 feet
5	120 feet
10	60 feet

By inspection, you can see that a gradient of 10 microseconds per mile is 10 times more accurate for your position plotting than one of one microsecond per mile.

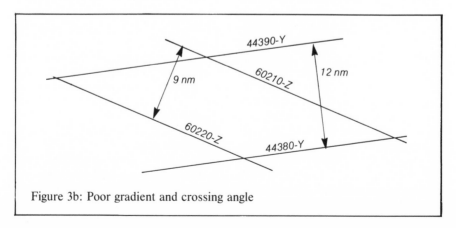

Figure 3b: Poor gradient and crossing angle

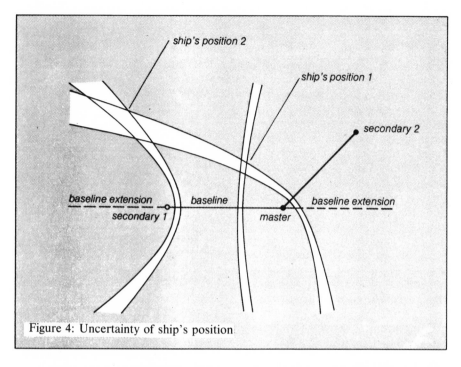

Figure 4: Uncertainty of ship's position

Another way of looking at gradient is to think of it as determining the significance of the error in your fix. For example, if your receiver has an error of 0.1 microseconds, the gradient you are working with determines the actual distance that error could be. Looking at the chart segment in Figure 2, you can see that the gradient off Long Beach for 9940-X is about 2.9 microseconds per mile (or ± 210 feet in 0.1 microseconds). The 9940-Y lines have a much better gradient of about 5.9 microseconds per mile (or ± 102 feet in 0.1 microseconds).

Off the coast of Southern California, you don't have much choice. You use the 9940-X and 9940-Y lines because that's all there are on the chart. In other areas of the United States, you may be able to receive up to four TDs quite reliably and be able to select the ones with the best gradient for your position plotting.

Even off Southern California, you may be able to receive other loran-C signals. You can still use these TDs, even though they aren't marked on your chart, as we'll discuss later. Figure 3 shows some examples of good and poor gradient situations.

Crossing angle. The crossing angle is the angle at which the loran-C TDs cross each other. If you have a choice, you should use lines that cross as close to 90 degrees as possible. Where you have no choice of lines to use, be especially wary of the accuracy of your fix as the crossing angle approaches 30 degrees.

Figure 4 shows the potential for error in such a situation. At position 1, the probability of an error in your fix is fairly low, while at position 2, the probability of an error is quite high, because of both crossing angle and gradient.

TD biases. After you account for the limitations on accuracy imposed by gradient and crossing angle, there remains one aspect of loran-C signal

257

propagation that you can use to increase the absolute, as well as repeatable, accuracy of your fix—and that is the determination of the TD biases for your operating area.

The problem is that the theoretical TD lines, which the government printed on your chart, are going to be different, in many areas, from the actual TDs you'll encounter. This accounts for the difference between the *absolute* accuracy of about 1/2 mile, versus the *repeatable* accuracy of about 100 feet, that loran-C users can expect. One solution to this problem is to determine the specific error for your operating area and use it as a TD bias value that you can add or subtract from your receiver display to come up with a more accurate fix.

For example, here's what you could do to determine the TD biases for your area:

1. Monitor the TDs of the stations you normally use at a few known geographic points — such as your dock, mooring, harbor breakwater, and other fixed structures.

2. Write down the numbers you obtain at each spot, and plot your actual location on the chart. The differences between your geographic location and the TD-indicated location tells you your TD bias for each station you are using.

Figure 5 shows an example of this technique, using a hypothetical location of 40° 01.2′ N 73° 36.3′ W and some hypothetical loran-C lines. Because you are at your dock, which is accurately charted, you have an excellent fix of your position. Your loran-C receiver, however, displays numbers that are about −0.6 and −1.5 microseconds off. These are the TD biases for your area on the stations you are using. If you now add these values to other loran-C readings in the same general area,

the absolute accuracy of your fix will improve to a corresponding degree.

You should avoid using floating aids to navigation for this calibration procedure, as they can swing a substantial distance around their anchors, depending on wind and sea conditions. At the same time, if you have logged the loran-C coordinates of your harbor's entrance buoy, you ought to be able to get pretty close to it in almost any weather conditions. That's what makes the repeatability of loran-C so useful.

Loran-C without charts. Many areas — especially harbors, bays, and estuaries — do not yet have detailed charts with loran-C lines printed on them. Also, you may be able to receive signals from a loran-C station that isn't normally considered useful in your area, so it isn't plotted on your chart. You can still use your receiver in these situations in two ways:

1. You can make up a log of loran readings at various points in your harbor such as turning marks, entrance buoys, and so on. Then, no matter what the weather, you can find your way home using your preselected reference points.

2. You can make your own detailed loran-C chart of the area using a couple of methods. One way is simply to extend the existing lines from your coastal charts into the harbor area you want covered. By noting the precise geographical points that the lines pass through, you can transfer them to your large-scale chart.

A more accurate way, however, is to use the loran-C tables published by the Defense Mapping Agency (DMA), which are available at major chart supply stores or directly from the DMA. A detailed description of how to use the tables is provided in each volume.

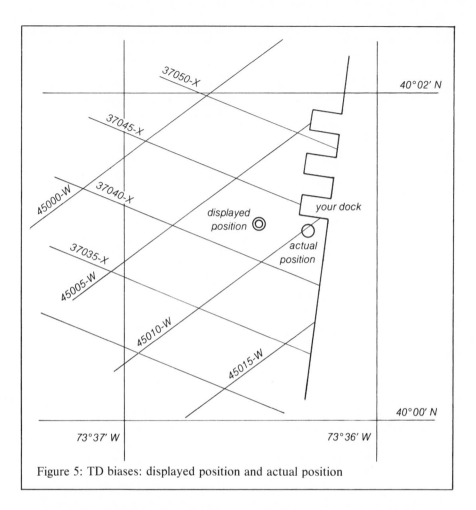

37050-X

40°02′ N

37045-X

45000-W   37040-X

displayed
position ◎

your dock

37035-X

actual
position

45005-W

45010-W

45015-W

40°00′ N

73°37′ W   73°36′ W

Figure 5: TD biases: displayed position and actual position

Navigating with loran-C. Now that you know what the loran-C numbers are telling you, here are a couple of ways you can use your receiver:

1. Offshore, a loran-C fix every couple of hours will give you all-weather knowledge of your position and tell you how you are doing on your course.

2. Coastwise, in thick weather, you may want to keep your receiver running continuously to track your progress along a stretch of coastline. Many of the newer receivers draw less than one amp of current at 12 volts dc, so the battery drain isn't so great as you might think.

While sailing along a printed (or other constant) loran-C line is one obvious way to use the numbers, another technique you should consider is one I call "action points." Action points are locations at which you need to perform some action, such as:

• Tack to avoid a reef, ledge, or other obstruction.
• Stop to listen for a whistle, bell, or horn.
• Change course to a new heading, just as if you had come to a turning mark.

To establish these points, you simply plot the locations at which you want to take the action on your chart, interpolate the loran-C TDs, and jot the numbers down someplace handy. As you sail along, the TD displays change, telling you how close you are to your action point. When the right numbers show up in the loran-C display, you've arrived at your action point, and can do whatever needs doing.

The one thing you should not do with your loran-C is depend on it to the exclusion of other navigation tools — compass, depthsounder or lead, watch, log, and sextant. Loran-C is a superb navigational aid, but it is just that; your receiver can malfunction, stations can go off the air, and you can misinterpret what you see in the display. But if you use it wisely, loran-C will help guide you safely home well into the 1980s.

7

CALCULATORS

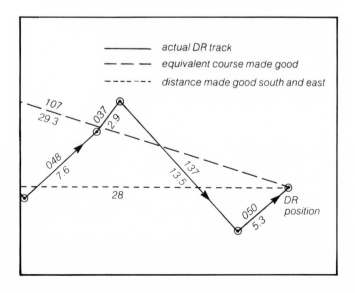

actual DR track
equivalent course made good
distance made good south and east

107
29.3

037

2.9

048
7.6

137
13.5

28

050
5.3

DR
position

Try a Programmable Calculator

By Jim Abbott

The last two decades have seen a real revolution in the art of sailing. Fiberglass and aluminum in hulls, extruded aluminum in spars, and synthetics in sails have changed the whole picture in a very short time. Less obvious are recent advances in electronics that have revolutionized instrumentation to the point where now we have available more reliable numbers than we know what to do with. But even that is changing. Hand-held calculators have come aboard and are able to eat up numbers faster than the other machines can generate them. The whole art of navigation, which until now was the province of the mathematically and scientifically minded, is rapidly becoming available to a neophyte who majored in art history just to get away from trigonometry and numbers.

Today you can make a quantum jump in the form of the *programmable* calculator. In essence, a programmable calculator, in contrast to the old-fashioned kind, does a whole series of operations at the push of a single button. You don't have to find the sine of the apparent wind and add it, and so forth. All that has been done for you by the mathematician who wrote the program. All you have to do now is enter the apparent wind, your course speed, and the machine does the rest. These new marvels can have as many as 30 different programs on a single chip that sits easily on a one-cent postage stamp, and they'll do practically any problem that the most demanding skipper can dream up. I won't try to describe in detail what each of these machines can do. For one thing, any comments I make now could be obsolete by the time you read this. I do want to make you aware of some of the fantastic program possibilities that exist today. I also have good news for the hard-pressed skipper trying to keep up with the price of last year's boat; for once deflation is here and for under $100 you can buy many times the calculator capabilities that were available three years ago for over $200!

I am a lifelong professional mathematician, and it might sound like heresy to talk you out of learning trigonometry. But at the Naval Academy we learned long ago that having mathematicians teach spherical trigonometry was not the real way to produce navigators. You *teach* mathematics, but you *train* navigators. You train him or her by telling him or her what numbers from what publications to put on which lines on what forms. I was weaned on *Bowditch* in high school and spent many years teaching *Napier's* rules to future naval officers, but I must confess that I cannot, for the life of me, remember today what *Napier's* rules were! My point is that you don't really have to know all the theory to get the answer the skipper wants. Besides, who can remember the law of sines for spherical triangles when someone is pouring a bucket of water down your neck and the skipper is yelling at you to get up on deck and help pull in a blown-out spinnaker?

Most mathematics students learn someplace, sometime, that the sine of 30 degrees is one-half. But I suspect that my wife's answer (she's not a mathematician) that "it's cold," is far closer to the point — especially if you're into frostbiting. The main reason that a student remembers such a fact is that the professor knows it, and the student knows he is going to put it on a test sometime.

A calculator can accept an apparent wind angle of 28 degrees just as easily as it can 30 degrees, and my point is that now you no longer need to know sine 30°, or even how to solve triangles, or to remember specific formulae. Of course it is nice to know these things, but as long as the machine works, it is not necessary. The reason is that the mathematicians have already built that sort of thing into these machines. So without going into the specifics of any particular calculator (which you can get from the manuals that come with them), here are a few of the many things you can expect from your new piece of equipment.

One of the first things I realized after using my calculator for a while was that it is frequently easier to use the *Light List* than it is to use a chart to compute courses and distances. I always did have a hard time drawing lines on a soggy chart, three feet by four feet, folded in two, on a 12-inch chartboard with a 16-inch parallel rule, especially when I had one foot in the sink! But now I can crawl into a quarterberth with my *Light List* and my trusty little black box and call out the courses and distance as

they appear on the calculator. In seconds. How do I do it? I enter latitudes and longitudes from the *Light List* tables and I get courses and distances directly. There's a program to do that.

Before the start of a race I make a list of the positions (latitude and longitude) of all the possible marks in the race circular and then, when the course is announced, I simply enter those marks in the order of rounding. Similarly, when I'm getting a radio direction finder (RDF) fix, first I enter the latitude and longitude of the stations from the tables. Next I put in the bearings from the RDF and I get a fix that I can then plot for the skipper's edification. The RDF stations don't have to be on the chart.

A second use that I have become aware of is getting the calculator to help in tactical decisions. For example, before the start or even while sailing on a leg, the skipper may want to find the true wind without having to come head to wind to find it out. I enter the compass course, the boat's speed, the current's drift and set, and the apparent wind, speed and direction. The machine then gives me the true wind. I punch a few more buttons and I have the time to the lay line and the time to the mark. If the skipper tacks ahead of time, the calculator gives me the new distance and bearing to the mark and updates the time to the lay line on the new tack. Then, as we approach the mark I'm asked where the wind will be on the next leg, and I announce (dramatically) that it will be on the port side at 60 degrees. Now everyone knows which spinnaker to set or even if it is possible to carry a spinnaker.

At sea you can be off watch, but if the helmsman has kept a half-hour log of speed made good and estimated course made good with extra entries for any tacks, you simply enter all of them and you can get a dead reckoning (DR) position without further fuss. You can plot all of these things directly on the chart, but how many of us really need to?

When it comes to celestial navigation, very few small-boat sailors do enough to keep in practice, and they forget things like whether to add height of eye to semi-diameter or to subtract it. But this is all outlined in the calculator manuals, and there are programs to correct the sextant, compute azimuths and intercepts for sun lines, and even give you direct latitude and longitude of a position without the use of any plotting sheets. It's all done in minutes, even with a time-out on deck to help with a quick tack.

I feel the result of all this is that now you are more disposed to *practice* your celestial navigation than you may have been before when you had to work through all the details. I suspect that many navigators will be doing more, not less, navigation when they learn about the potential of these little helpers.

Most navigators know how to work a current vector diagram. But under the pressure of listening to an RDF for a null, watching the depth-sounder, or listening for a bell in the fog, they just don't get around to

actually computing the effect of the current on the boat's position. Content with a "guesstimate" they end up either being swept into the mark or missing it entirely in the fog.

But it is so easy to do with the machine that the computation becomes automatic. And that's probably the real secret of their success; use the little devils until they become second nature and you'll soon find yourself getting much more out of all those other navigation instruments spread around the boat. It's easy to drop back into old habits like drawing the course on a chart or using the speed-time-distance slide rule for speeds made good. Try "overusing" the calculator for one season, and I believe it will pay off for you over the years.

My trouble is that I'm really a traditionalist and I still think in terms of points. And the younger generation can't follow my orders to steer *north northeast a quarter east*, and that bothered me. But now I have to tell *my* machine that I really mean 25.3125 decimal degrees! But I guess I'd better get with it if I want to sail on a boat with aluminum spars, Dacron sails, electronic instruments — and minicomputers. Because that's the next step.

Dead Reckoning without Having to Plot

By Joe Consolmagno

With an electronic calculator that can cost $20 or less, you make the old-time art of traverse sailing (tracking courses and distances when you are beating to windward) become a valid practical navigation tool for even the smallest boat.

The usual method of dead reckoning (DR) is to plot, directly onto the chart, the direction and distance run for every course you have steered from the last known position. In a small sailboat that has little space, you are less inclined to spread out charts, and maintaining a useful dead reckoning plot on the chart is difficult even under the best of conditions. It can border on the impossible in a situation such as a search pattern where there are frequent course changes. Yet this is *precisely* the kind of condition that most urgently calls for a good DR track.

Traverse sailing eliminates the need to plot each and every track or course steered, requires minimum record keeping at the helm, and reduces a whole series of courses and distances you have run to a single rhumb line that you can put on the chart at a convenient time if a plot does become necessary. The helmsman's written log can be as simple as a notebook divided into three columns: *watch time; compass heading;* and *indicated speed* or *distance* (this entry depends on the boat's instrumentation). Entries need only be made at each significant change in course or speed to enable a navigator to come up with a solution, if he has the information on course and distance traveled that is basic to all dead reckoning.

Traverse sailing converts the distance you have traveled on each course into two components: the distances made good *north or south;* and those traveled *east or west.* You then add the N-S and E-W distances for courses algebraically and convert them back into a single equivalent distance and course. In effect, you combine a series of small right triangles into one large right triangle in which the net distances (north or south and east or west) are the two legs, the equivalent distance traveled is the hypotenuse, and the equivalent course angle is the acute angle adjacent to the N-S leg.

The math involved is customarily handled by using traverse tables which can be confusing and time consuming. Some 90 pages of HO 9 *(American Practical Navigator)* are taken up by traverse tables, and another 12 are devoted to explaining their use. But eliminating the need for these tables by using a pocket calculator makes traverse sailing practical for any small-boat navigator.

The calculator model needs to be only moderately advanced, providing keys for the trigonometric functions of *sine, cosine,* and *tangent.* If you are a part-time navigator, you don't even have to know trigonometry to use them. You only have to know when to tap the right key that will convert a course to its *sine* or *cosine*, information that can be cued right onto the worksheet. After that, the operation is all simple arithmetic.

There are two equations involved to convert each rhumb line into its component N-S and E-W legs:

- The cosine of the course sailed multiplied by the distance run on that course equals the distance made good north or south. If the answer comes up a positive number in the calculation display, the direction is north. If it comes up negative, the direction is south.
- The sine of the course times the distance equals the distance made good east or west. If it is positive, the direction is east. If it is negative, it is west.

When you have performed this operation for each course sailed, total up the N-S and E-W distances. If you want to make a plot at this point, you need no further calculation. With these two sums, you can locate the dead reckoning position on the chart merely by measuring off the net distances made good, north or south and east or west, from the point of departure. Then you draw a line from the point of departure to the DR position. This represents the equivalent course and distance made good through all the course changes.

You can also find this line mathematically. Because the N-S and E-W net totals are the legs of a right triangle, you have a choice of calculator solutions.

Dividing the E-W total by the N-S total produces a number which then becomes the *course angle* when you press the inverse tangent key, which might be labelled either tan^{-1} or *arc*

tan on your calculator. If the direction you traveled nets out north and east, the course angle is the actual course. For the other directions, you have an additional step to make to arrive at the actual course:

- For south and east, subtract the course angle from 180 degrees.
- For south and west, add the course angle to 180 degrees.
- For north and west, subtract the course angle from 360 degrees.

The net distance you traveled, east or west, divided by the sine of the course angle gives you the equivalent distance made good for all courses sailed. There are other formulae which will give you this distance, as right triangles are like that. But in any case, a calculator can make short work of whatever formula you do use.

To demonstrate what I mean by traverse sailing with pocket electronics, take your calculator in your hand and let your fingers do the walking through the following exercise.

You want to find your DR position after you have sailed these courses and distances: 142 degrees for 12.1 miles; 048 degrees for 7.6 miles; 037 degrees for 2.9 miles; 137 degrees for 13.5 miles; 050 degrees for 5.3 miles.

Taking the first leg, step by step: Enter the first course into the calculator (142). Press the *cosine* key. Press the *multiply* key. Enter distance traveled (12.1). Press the *equals* key.

The number that appears in your display can be rounded off to -9.5 miles. This is the distance made good on the north/south axis: The minus sign indicates it is to the south.

Enter the same course again, but press the *sine* key this time and multiply it by 12.1 once more; you get 7.4 miles as the rounded-off distance made good on the east/west

Calculator steps	1st leg	2nd leg	3rd leg	4th leg	5th leg	Distance made good
Enter course	*142*	*048*	*037*	*137*	*050*	*N(+) or S(−)*
Press cosine *and* multiply *keys*						*E(+) or W(−)*
Enter distance	*12.1*	*7.6*	*2.9*	*13.5*	*5.3*	
Press = key for distance made good (N or S)	*−9.5*	*5.1*	*2.3*	*−9.9*	*3.4*	*−8.6*
Re-enter course	*142*					
Press sine *and* multiply *keys*						
Re-enter distance	*12.1*					
Press = key for distance made good (E or W)	*7.4*	*5.6*	*1.7*	*9.2*	*4.1*	*28*
To find equivalent course						
Enter total distance E or W	*28.0*					
Press divide *key*						
Enter total distance made good N or S \	*−8.6*					
Press = key and inv. tang *keys (course angle)*	*−72.9*					
To find equivalent distance made good						
Enter total E or W	*28.0*					
Press divide *key*						
Enter course angle	*−72.9*					
Press sine *and = keys (distance made good)*	*29.3*					

if N S + and E W +,
    Actual course = course angle
if N S − and E W +,
    Actual course = 180 − course angle
if N S − and E W −,
    Actual course = 180 + course angle
if N S + and E W −,
    Actual course = 360 − course angle

therefore here; 180 − 72.9 = 107 (actual course) and 29.3 is distance made good

Figure 1: Sample worksheet for taking computations from deck log (course and distance) and converting to equivalent course and distance sailed

axis. It is a positive number, indicating the direction is east.

Follow the same procedure for each of the five legs (Fig. 1). Then add up the distances, north and south, and east and west. The example in Figure 1 shows a net distance made good of 8.6 miles south and 28 miles east from the point of departure.

Now you can plot your dead reckoning position directly on the chart by measuring off 8.6 miles due south (magnetic) from your point of departure and 28 miles due east (magnetic)

from that southern terminus. A straight line drawn between the point of departure and the DR position will represent the equivalent course and distance made good. The plotting done in Figure 2 shows this equivalent course line in relation to the actual dead reckoning track: one line does the work for five.

You can find the equivalent course and distance made good by adding a few more steps on the calculator, as shown again in Figure 1.

For the equivalent course angle: Enter total distance made good east

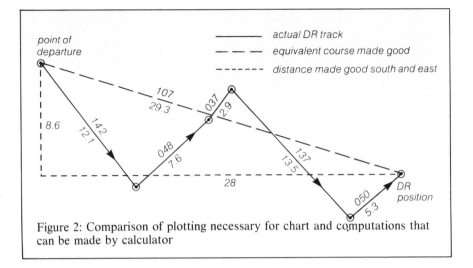

107
29.3

037
2.9

8.6

14.2
12.1

048
7.6

137
13.5

28

050
5.3

DR position

Figure 2: Comparison of plotting necessary for chart and computations that can be made by calculator

or west (28 (E)). Press the *divide* key. Enter distance made good north or south (−8.6 (S)). Press the *equals* key. Press the *inverse tangent* key.

The number appearing in the display, −72.9, is the course angle. Since the direction of travel is south and east, you must subtract the number from 180 degrees to give the true course. While −72.9 is still in the calculator displayed as a minus figure, pressing the *add* key, entering 180, and pressing the *equals* key will complete the transaction and display a figure that rounds off to 107 degrees. That is the equivalent actual course.

For the equivalent distance made good: Enter the E/W distance (28). Press the *divide* key. Enter the *course angle* (−72.9). Press the *sine* key. Press the *equals* key. The distance made good rounds off to 29.3 miles.

Describing calculator operations is more tedious than actually doing them. Once the method I've described becomes familiar, you can solve the traverse sailing exercise I've illustrated here in three to five minutes on the calculator.

One note of caution for the first-time dead reckoner. Marine dead reckoning measures course and distance *through the water*, not over the bottom, and it does so without reference to leeway, tide, or current. It differs in this regard from aerial navigation, which makes *drift* an integral part of its dead reckoning. So to convert a marine DR position to a workable *estimated position*, you must make allowance for these deflecting forces, which you can lump together as *current* for a convenient label.

One way to do this is to consider *current* as an additional leg in the DR track. The direction toward which the current flows is taken as the course. The current's speed, multiplied by the time the boat is in it, is the distance. Treat this data like the course and distance data for all the other legs when you are working out the traverse sailing problem.

The big advantage of traverse sailing by calculator for any small-boat navigator is that vital dead reckoning information can be kept as a back-up navigation system at all times without ever having to plot it on the chart unless the need arises — when visibility closes down, for example. All that is required is that the written log accurately show every change in course and speed and the time of each change, starting from the last known position. When you determine a new position or fix by bearing or arriving at a marker buoy, you can abandon the original track, start another series, and not use a pencil to make even a single mark.

But if the weather closes down or you need a DR position for an emergency situation, a few minutes spent with the deck log and the calculator will do the trick.

With practice, it's about as painless a system for navigating small craft by dead reckoning as you can find.

Another Way to Solve the Navigational Triangle

By M.A. Schultz

Bowditch, in his *American Practical Navigator*, lists approximately 70 variations on the solution to the basic celestial navigational triangle. While it hardly seems useful to propose still another solution, new equipment has become available, and it is conceivable that the method I propose will be helpful in some circumstances, for no tables are required for the solutions. The technological advance is the advent of the pocket calculator. These mini-computers do call for a return to the basics of solving for latitude and longitude from celestial sights.

As is well known, early navigators solved the navigational triangle directly by means of the cosine-haversine method. The exact solution was tedious and cumbersome, and dozens of tables of various forms sprung up that precalculated hundreds of thousands of situations. A problem solution merely involved looking up the nearest values of the given estimated parameters and interpolating between tabular values when the inputs did not coincide with the tables.

An exact solution to the spherical triangle was not possible without having an exact latitude or longitude, or more specifically its derivative, the Local Hour Angle (LHA). As

neither of these parameters could be gained from dead reckoning calculations with high accuracy, a later navigational method was generally adopted, the line of position method.

This scheme involved calculating altitude and azimuth from an estimated latitude and longitude. The azimuth angle was laid out on the chart, and a line of position drawn at right angles to the azimuth line by comparing observed altitude (h_o) with calculated altitude (h_c) and making suitable corrections. (Those not familiar with the method should see either Bowditch or *Celestial Navigation for Yachtsmen*, by Mary Blewitt). An *exact* position was not obtained; only the knowledge that the true position was probably on the line of position. If sights on two or more celestial bodies could be obtained, the intersections of the lines of position could give the real point position with greater certainty.

When using the pocket calculator, all the preliminary sightings, corrections to sextant altitude, timing and *Almanac* gyrations are still required. It is necessary to obtain the GMT (Greenwich Mean Time) from the local time of sight and hence the declination from the *Almanac*. (The pocket calculator does have enough power that I suppose the purist could obtain declinations from empirical astronomical formulae if he were so

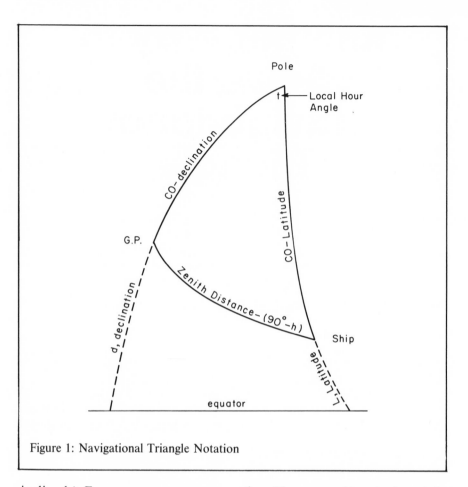

Figure 1: Navigational Triangle Notation

inclined.) For our purposes, we assume an up-to-date *Almanac* is aboard, but no tables.

We can now proceed to solve the navigational triangle by any of several means. For reference purposes, the navigational triangle notation used is given in Figure 1. The conventional table notation for the relationship between latitude and declination of "same name" or "contrary name" is not used as such, but it is necessary to know whether the latitude and declination are north or south in order to draw the correct triangle.

Let us use the pocket calculator in the conventional altitude-azimuth calculation to obtain a line of posi-

tion. The assumed longitude and the latitude are known from dead reckoning calculations. It is not necessary to select the nearest even number of degrees as is required in some of the tabular methods. The LHA (Local Hour Angle) is obtained from the GHA (Greenwich Hour Angle) and longitude. For calculator usage, all angles must be converted to *decimal* degrees, minutes and seconds; a very simple task for the calculator. The general formula for conversion to decimal degrees is:

decimal degrees =

$$\text{degrees} + \frac{\text{minutes} \times 60 + \text{seconds}}{3600}.$$

For example, 30°30'30" converts to

$$30 + \frac{30 \times 60 + 30}{3600} = 30.50833333°$$

in a trivial few seconds for the calculator.

The LHA, the latitude and the declination are then converted to decimal degrees, and listed for easy availability.

These numbers are then punched into the following formula for h_c:

h_c = arc sin
[sin L sin d + cos L cos d cos t].

The keyboard punching sequence for the HP-35 is:

L sin d sin X L cos d
   cos X t cos X + arc sin

This punching sequence is in the so-called reverse Polish notation which is the same as is used in common desk type adding machines and calculators.

To punch in this sequence of numbers and function keys takes about 60 seconds. The sequence can be listed ahead of time in tabular form and a few seconds saved if desired.

The answer (h_c) is now available to 10 significant figures.

The azimuth angle is then obtained from the formula:

$$Z = \text{arc sin} \left[\frac{\sin t \cos d}{\cos h_c}\right],$$

a short 30 second exercise for a 10 digit answer.

The azimuth angle is then plotted on the chart, h_c subtracted decimally from h_o, the difference converted back from the decimal notation to minutes (decimal × 60) and used as a correction factor toward or away from the celestial body to plot the line of position. Note that with 10 digit accuracy, the accuracy of the calculation has been removed from the process. No tables or interpolations have been used and the same numbers are obtained each time in contradistinction to a slide rule solution.

If you are an aging, partially blind navigator who can't see the tables well enough to make a simple interpolation, and you have a few extra minutes of time on your hands on the wide ocean, punching large numbers into a small calculator can be a great deal of fun.

Calculators: Keeping Them Going

By Ed Bergin
and Jack Buchanek

Over the years we've written a lot about the advantages of the pocket calculator and how it can make short work of many piloting and celestial navigation problems. We know they are very handy instruments indeed.

Unfortunately, the marine environment can make short work of your calculator and render it useless if you are not careful. Fortunately, there are some things you can do to protect your instrument from those rigors, and we are going to share with you some of the things we've learned. Because there is really nothing you can do to repair the instrument once you are at sea, there are some important steps you can take to get the most out of your device — and you can take them even before you step onboard.

First, select a reliable calculator. By that we mean a known instrument from a company with a good reputation. Ask around. Scientific calculators have been going to sea in large numbers for at least five years, and like sailmakers and yacht designers, they now have a track record. If other sailors are saying good things about a firm's products, you should take that into consideration.

Second, before you go sailing, use your calculator for several hours. In the calculator industry there is a rather well-kept secret involving the *infant mortality rate* of microcircuit products. Simply stated, this refers to the tendency of calculators to "fail young" if they are going to fail at all. Once your calculator survives its initial break-in period, the chances are it will give you a normal useful life.

During this test period review and practice the types of problems you will be working at sea. You should take with you worksheets containing complete sample problems. That way, if you ever think the calculator is malfunctioning you can run a test problem to check it.

If you have a magnetic-card programmable calculator, make sure you take an extra set of program cards with you. I know one skipper who put his mag-card programs in a drawer that also contained a hand-bearing compass. The result? The compass's magnets scrambled his mag-card programs.

If you're using a solid-state programmable such as the Texas Instruments or Tamaya NC series, be prepared with some kind of back-up system. With the TI calculators, for example, you could carry a spare Nav-Pac. Incidentally, when you are changing solid-state software packs, always touch a piece of solid metal first (e.g., galley stove or table leg) in order to dissipate any static electricity you may have built up. Static electricity can damage the solid-state software modules.

If your primary calculator is one of the more expensive, programmable types, you could carry an inexpensive basic slide-rule calculator for use as a back-up. In any case, no matter how you solve your problems with a calculator, before going to sea you should also know how to solve the same problem without using a calculator.

In piloting, this means developing skill with the maneuvering board and nautical slide rule; in celestial, this means carrying (and knowing how to use) a set of sight reduction tables.

Aboard your boat, you face two basic problems: how do you keep the calculator charged; and how do you keep it working?

The problem of keeping the calculator charged varies with the instrument itself. Some calculators, such as the Tamaya NC series give you a choice. You can equip them either with rechargeable battery packs or throwaway penlight batteries. Given this choice, we prefer throwaway batteries, but you may decide otherwise. If you are going to far-away places such as the South Pacific, take a big handful of batteries with you. On a long trip of, say, several years, pay attention to the shelf life of the batteries and replace new for old as you go whether or not the "old" batteries were actually used.

When you are using replaceable batteries, we recommend that you purchase the more expensive *calculator* type that are designed to minimize the chance of battery leaks which might damage the calculator. You should also remember to remove replaceable batteries from the calculator any time the calculator is not being used for any length of time, say more than three to four weeks. Again, this will cut down the chances of damage from battery leaks.

One of the easiest (and often overlooked) ways to preserve your batteries is to get into the habit of using your calculator economically. For example, if you are working a celestial problem, first make sure you have all the information at hand before switching the calculator on. This means you have already looked up your *Almanac* data, worked up your dead reckoning (DR) position, corrected your sextant reading and organized your data for quick and easy entry into the calculator. Then, once you have worked the problem, remember to turn the calculator off.

While some calculators are equipped with automatic shut-off switches to guard against total discharge because of operator forgetfulness, most calculators used in navigation require you to turn the instrument off.

Calculators that come only with rechargeable battery packs and standard 110-volt converter-chargers (such as the Texas Instruments and Hewlett-Packard scientific and programmable models) pose a different set of problems. Of course, if your boat is equipped with a 110-volt generator, about all you would need is an extra rechargeable battery pack as a spare.

If, like most boats, your electrical power source at sea is limited to the ship's 12-volt battery system you'll have to decide between buying additional charge packs or buying a 12-volt converter. These converters, now available for the Tamaya, Hewlett-Packard and Texas Instruments calculators, let you charge your calculator from a 12-volt power source. Along with the converter, you must also buy a cigarette lighter receptacle which is wired into your boat's 12-volt system.

To charge the instrument, you plug one end of the 12-volt converter into the cigarette lighter and the other into the calculator. If you're making a short trip, say a five-day run to Bermuda or a 12-day trip to the Virgin Islands, you can probably get by with a spare rechargeable battery pack or two.

By carefully conserving our calculator time we were able to work all our sights on a 10-day trip from Morehead City, North Carolina, to St. Thomas on one rechargeable battery pack using a nonprogrammable basic slide-rule calculator. A colleague of ours, using throwaway batteries, went through two sets of batteries on a 33-day passage from the East Coast to the Azores.

You must make sure, though, to charge the calculator and all of the battery packs carefully before leaving port. Just because the calculator or battery pack is new, you should not assume it is fully charged. It would be a good idea if all scientific calculators came equipped with battery condition indicators. However, since those most popular with navigators don't have this feature, be alert to the signs of low battery power: dim display, erratic performance, wildly wrong answers.

You should know that when the batteries are low, a calculator can give you some goofy answers. If your DR places you northeast of Bermuda and your calculator puts you in Rarotonga, check your batteries.

Whenever the batteries get low on a mag-card programmable unit, the mag cards themselves can stick part way through the calculator. We know of one case where this sticking even scrambled the program card. Therefore, users of these calculators should be particularly careful to keep their instruments fully charged. In any case, whenever we work a problem — particularly if it is a complex celestial problem — we run a test problem first to make sure the calculator is operating correctly. Anytime we get a calculator answer

that appears way off, we run the test problem as a check against calculator malfunction.

Because most scientific calculators solve the celestial triangle with three variables, Local Hour Angle (LHA), Declination and DR Latitude, you can use the following variable to test your calculator. You should know, however, that slight, but non-navigationally significant, variations of up to a tenth or two in the answer can result from the way different types of calculators round off the numbers:

- DR Latitude   42°30′North
- LHA   51°42.4′West
- Declination   8°10.1′North

In the test problem, the Latitude and Declination are entered as positives to indicate that they are both north; the LHA is entered as a negative to indicate that it is west.

The answer to the test problem is:

Computed Altitude   33°14.8′
Azimuth   111.439 or 112°

The enemies of a calculator at sea are the same enemies that attack all your ship's electronic gear. They include water, shock, vibration, and extreme temperatures.

Whereas most good calculators have a moisture barrier sealing off vital components (it seems engineers were forever spilling coffee on their calculators) the best way to deal with water damage is through prevention. Obviously, you must keep your calculator away from salt water. We have a rule that no one takes the calculator on deck to work a sight, no matter how nice the weather. Since moisture through condensation can also be a problem, we recommend storing your calculator with a couple of small bags of silica gel.

You should also store the calculator in a safe dry place near the navigator's station. At a minimum, I would put the instrument in a waterproof plastic bag, even a sandwich bag if nothing else is available. For even more protection you can buy special plastic bags, which seal the calculator in a water-tight compartment surrounded by another bag which inflates to form a shock-absorbing layer of air. These are available at most well-stocked camera shops.

Every skipper should arrange a secure place to use his calculator at sea. The key word here is *secure*. When a boat is rocking in a seaway you need virtually three hands to juggle the *Almanac,* the plotting sheet, and the calculator. The best thing to do is to glue a couple strips of Velcro to the chart table and a couple more strips to the back of the calculator. Then when you are under way the calculator will stay in one place on the navigator's table.

While at sea we also occasionally spray the battery compartment of the calculator with silicone spray or WD-40.

Since the speed of the calculator enables you to solve complex celestial problems in a few seconds, you should also get in the habit of working each problem twice. You should also *reality* test each calculator answer, evaluating it in light of all the other information you have available including your DR position, radio direction finder bearings or loran fixes.

By following these common-sense practices your calculator, as the Timex people like to say, will be "spared a licking and should keep on ticking" for a long time. If you treat it well, it will do the right thing when you ask it to.

8
CONTRIBUTORS

Jim Abbott is a professor of mathematics at the U.S. Naval Academy and has been navigating for more years than he would like to admit. Abbott has sailed many of the Academy's bigger boats, including the 90' *Freedom,* the 72' yawl *Royono,* and the famous 60' cutter *Highland Light.* After years of navigating by traditional methods, he has "discovered" the programmable calculator, which proves, so he says, that you can teach an old dog new tricks.

Alan Adler is a consulting engineer in Palo Alto, California, and has sailed, primarily in that area, for more than 25 years. He has written numerous articles and technical papers on sailing topics and has designed his own yacht, a *Fast-40* — a 40', ultra-light, 3,600 pound keelboat.

Edwin J. Bergin has been writing about navigation for more than 10 years. He is a frequent contributor to SAIL Magazine and is the co-author of *Piloting, Navigation With the Pocket Calculator.* He is one of the founders of the Navigation Institute, Inc., in Arlington, Virginia, and also has co-authored three programmed learning courses in navigation. These courses range from basic piloting to celestial navigation. He has cruised extensively on his 35' Hallberg-Rassy sailboat.

Parker Boggs pursues the "electronics" beat as one of SAIL Magazine's associate editors. He has been messing around in boats since childhood and holds a U.S. Coast Guard Ocean Operator License. He has coastal and offshore navigating experience in a variety of boats, both racing and cruising.

Jack Buchanek, along with Ed Bergin, authored *Piloting, Navigation With the Pocket Calculator,* which is published by Tab Books. These two have served as consultants to Texas Instruments and are the founders of the Navigation Institute, Inc., in Arlington, Virginia.

Joe Consolmagno was an aerial navigator in the Army Air Corps during World War II, flying patrol missions in the Pacific Theatre and convoy escorts over the North Atlantic. He has served as commodore of the Bark Shanty Sail Club in Michigan, as director of the Lake Huron Yachting Association, and as council member of the North American Yacht Racing Union. Mr. Consolmagno has written for national sailing publications for the past twenty years and was formerly responsible for the public relations activities of the Chrysler Marine Division. He currently resides in Florida.

Paul Dodson sailed the New England coast extensively as a child. After college he entered the Navy, where he developed his navigation skills during nine years of sea duty on small ships and patrol boats. He served as navigator aboard a destroyer and an ocean minesweeper. Mr. Dodson taught Advanced Navigation at the U.S. Naval Academy as well as serving as an ocean racing safety officer and heading up the plebe summer sailing program. He assisted in the editing of a seamanship text published by the U.S. Naval Institute and was technical editor of a text on practical navigation.

Richard du Moulin is Vice President of Ogden Marine, Inc., New York. He began racing in 1955 on Long Island Sound in Lightnings and Blue Jays and in his family's sloop *Lady Del.* At Dartmouth College he was sailing team captain, and from 1969-1972 he was ocean racing coach at the U.S. Naval Academy, where he was also skipper of its 54-foot yacht *Rage.* As navigator or skipper, he has participated in numerous Transatlantic, Bermuda, and SORC races aboard yachts such as *Charisma, Infinity,* and his family's Carter 39 *Blaze.* As navigator, he has crewed aboard several 12-Meters including *Mariner, Intrepid,* and *Enterprise.* For excitement and an occasional midwinter swim, he races a frostbite dinghy with his wife, Ann.

John Ellsworth learned navigation while serving as a quartermaster aboard a U.S. destroyer in the mid-sixties. In 1970, he received a degree in journalism and then went to work as a technical writer for N.A.S.A. in the Apollo Program. He also worked for Pan American World Airways writing flight manuals and training programs. In 1978, he earned a masters in communication studies, and since then he has been teaching these subjects at a community college in New York. He has also delivered boats throughout Long Island Sound and has taught sailing, most recently as skipper-instructor for Sail Caribbean Voyages. Besides teaching sailing, photography, and writing, Mr. Ellsworth enjoys playing the guitar and singing forlorn love songs and songs of the sea and travel while at anchor in a secluded harbor.

Michel Emmanuel was born and raised in the sponge-fishing village of Tarpon Springs on the west coast of Florida, and today is a practicing lawyer in Tampa. He has cruised the Gulf coast from the Yucatan to the Dry Tortugas, Cuba, the Bahamas and the Mediterranean. Mr. Emmanuel is currently serving on the Fales Committee at the U.S. Naval Academy. This committee plans and supervises the sailing program and Mr. Emmanuel is a coach for offshore racing and cruising. He is between boats now, as he and his wife are looking for a 38' boat they can handle themselves. He enjoys filling in as navigator on ocean racers and is a frequent participant in the SORC.

Ray Fletcher has taught offshore and coastal navigation and sailing in the California Adult Education Program for seven years. For the past four years he has also conducted a school that teaches navigation and sailing at the Channel Islands Landing in Oxnard, California. He has written articles for several nautical publications and writes a weekly column on navigation and sailing for a local newspaper. Mr. Fletcher holds a U.S. Coast Guard Ocean Operator License for power and auxiliary sail.

Robert H. Gulmon was a retired Navy Captain who lived in Kailua, Hawaii, until his death in 1978. He received the Silver Star for his service in World War II while serving aboard a submarine. His Navy career was spent serving on and commanding submarines and submarine tenders and being part of the Antisubmarine Warfare Force at Ford Island, Hawaii. His sailing experience was primarily on a 23' catamaran. Mr. Gulmon taught celestial navigation at a community college after his retirement from the Navy.

C. Louis Hohenstein is an engineer and offshore navigator. He has navigated in three Newport-Bermuda Races and for ten years in the SORC. He has owned and skippered several sailboats and has cruised extensively as well as raced in the Bahamas and Florida

Keys. Mr. Hohenstein, a former naval officer, holds the highest navigational grade awarded by the U.S. Power Squadrons. He has written numerous articles on navigation, technical, and business subjects, and is the author of four books.

James B. Kane first became interested in sailing at the age of 18 while serving as an apprentice seaman on a three-masted schooner and later as a cadet on a three-masted bark. After graduating from King's Point in 1943, he began going to sea on cargo ships. Today, he holds an unlimited Master's License with first-class pilot endorsements for many of the East Coast ports of the U.S. and is now the captain of one of the largest sandsuckers owned by the Army Corps of Engineers for dredging harbors and inlets. Because of his life at sea he has never had enough time for a boat of his own, but has chartered boats in many ports throughout the world, adapting navigational practices used on large ships as well as those methods used by ancient mariners, such as the Polynesians.

William V. Kielhorn's first sea-going experience was as a cabin boy aboard a destroyer during the "rum war" of the 1920's, and he later served as a seaman aboard various ships engaged in the Bering Sea Patrol during the 1930's. Immediately after Pearl Harbor he was commissioned in the Coast Guard and served as a ship's officer on a dozen or more craft ranging in size from 100' schooners to 300' cutters and destroyers and up to a 20,000-ton transport. Mr. Kielhorn has a master's degree in oceanography and during his career he has been affiliated with the International Ice Patrol, the Woods Hole Oceanographic Institution, the U.S.N. Hydrographic Office, and the Office of Naval Research, and he was manager of Lockheed's Oceanics Division. He has also held teaching positions at the U.S. Coast Guard Academy and at U.C.L.A. Mr. Kielhorn is now retired and is living in Naples, Florida, where he is active with the U.S. Coast Guard Auxiliary and the Civil Air Patrol.

William R. Knowlton was a lieutenant commander in the U.S. Naval Reserve from 1942 to 1945. He taught celestial navigation and wrote navigation manuals for the U.S. Naval Air Corps and flew as navigator on "flying boats" for the Naval Air Transport Service. After retiring from farming in 1970, he spent a great deal of time sailing a Cape Cod Goldeneye that he moored in Marion, Massachusetts. He raced it successfully until his death in 1977.

Murray Lesser is an ex-aerodynamicist turned computer engineer. Since 1964, he and his wife, Jean, have been spending their vacations cruising the northeast coast from Long Island Sound to Mount Desert Island. During that time he has examined much of sailing's "conventional wisdom" in the light of his professional training and experience, and he has written a number of thoughtful essays about the pleasures — and the pains — of sailing.

Charles Mason has been either in or around boats virtually all his life. A founding editor of SAIL Magazine, he is presently its executive editor.

John Mellor has been sailing since the age of 13 and served as a junior officer in the Royal Navy for five years. During this time, he received professional training in navigation and seamanship and did a lot of cruising in Navy yachts. He resigned his commission in 1968 and became a professional yacht skipper, working in the Mediterranean and doing deliveries. Besides numerous magazine articles, he has had two books published in Britain by Souvenir Press: *Sailing Can Be Simple* and *Cruising Safe and Simple*. A further volume on seamanship is currently underway. Mr. Mellor has owned three boats and is a qualified RYA Yachtmaster Examiner.

Ralph Naranjo has spent the past five years circumnavigating the world with his wife and children on their 41' sloop *Wind Shadow*. His boating experience began in a skiff on Long Island Sound. Later surfing and diving captured his interest, and ultimately cruising became the culmination of these aquatic activities. *Wind Shadow* and crew are currently in Oyster Bay, New York, where Mr. Naranjo is captain of the Seawanhaka Yacht Club. The Naranjos have compiled a slide/lecture series, "Across Three Oceans — A Family Cruising Adventure," which depicts both the techniques as well as the aesthetics of extended cruising. Shorthanded cruising is the Naranjos' preference, as well as the focus of many of Mr. Naranjo's articles.

Jack Nelson began sailing as a boy in Florida. During World War II he entered a U.S. Navy Officers' Training Program where he learned coastal and celestial navigation. He has cruised and raced on the East and West Coasts and the Bahamas, and he has made a passage from San Francisco to Hawaii. In 1978, Mr. Nelson discovered a way to use ordinary pocket calculators for celestial navigation

computations, developed other innovations, and began "Celestial Navigation Weekend Workshops" in Southern California, Seattle, and Fort Lauderdale. He is currently preparing a videotape cassette for home and group learning.

Dag Pike built his first boat, a canvas-covered kayak, as a child in wartime Britain. He went to sea as a deck apprentice at age 16 and spent five years in the British Merchant Marine. This was followed by a ten-year spell as deck officer with the British Lighthouse Authority. He then spent another ten years as an inspector of lifeboats with the Royal National Lifeboat Institution. Part of this time was used in developing and testing new designs of lifeboats, particularly inflatables. He is a freelance writer and undertakes boat deliveries to maintain experience. He has published several books, including *Electronic Navigation for Small Craft;* he also has a couple of books pending. Mr. Pike is qualified as a Master Mariner and is a member of the Royal Institute of Navigation, an Associate of the Royal Institute of Navigation, and an Associate of the Royal Institute of Naval Architects.

Earl Rubell practiced medicine in California until his retirement in 1979. He has extensive cruising experience along the California coast, and he has chartered boats in such places as the Virgin Islands, the Hawaiian Islands, and the Grenadine Islands, and in 1977 he was the skipper and navigator on a boat delivery from California to Hawaii. Since his retirement, Dr. Rubell has been cruising full time in a 30' sloop.

Burt Sauer was born in Iowa in 1923 and was a "dry land" sailor from age 14. He read accounts of early small boat voyagers, great voyages of discovery, and the famous sea battles. He also made a study of square rigger sailing and the design, lofting, and construction of modern sailboats, as well as piloting and celestial navigation. He owned a sextant before he ever saw the ocean. In 1962, he moved to California. He bought his first boat, a Cal 25, with the particular objective of testing some theories for self-steering arrangements. He gained a lot of experience in singlehanding and is a member of the Pacific Singlehanded Sailing Association. Early in his sailing career Mr. Sauer was a regular around-the-buoys racer and still participates occasionally. He has worked in his spare time as a sailboat rigger and delivery skipper. He is also the inventor of "Complete Traverse

Tables for Sailing Ships" and other precomputed navigational aids for the small boat sailor.

Michael Saunders was born in South Africa and brought up in Mozambique, where most of his free time was spent in a variety of little boats, from trading dhows to stitched-bark canoes. After obtaining an engineering degree in England, Mr. Saunders returned to Africa. In 1972, as a result of the political scene and other circumstances, he gave up his job, sold all his possessions, and bought an old 33' ketch, named *Walkabout*. With his wife and four children, he set sail around the Cape of Good Hope to St. Helena, South America, the West Indies, the Azores, and finally to England. The voyage took two years and is related in Mr. Saunders' book, *The Walkabouts*. Since then the Saunders' life and livelihood have revolved around boats; they have lived on them and built them. Mr. Saunders writes for a living and provides a highly specialized design and consulting service which rests heavily on the experience gained in the many craft he has delivered professionally over thousands of miles. He is a Royal Yacht Association Oceanmaster and a yacht surveyor.

M.A. Schultz is a professor emeritus in the Nuclear Engineering Department at Pennsylvania State University. Prior to working at the university, he was employed as an engineer at Westinghouse where he designed navy radar and sonar equipment. He also was involved in the design and construction of the instrumentation and control system for the first nuclear-powered submarine, the USS *Nautilus*. His first sailboat was an early O'Day Sailer (#296), and his sailing ambitions grew to the ultimate ownership of a Morgan Out Island 41

based in the Caribbean charter fleet. Professor Schultz's interest in celestial navigation is mostly theoretical as most of his sailing is done in sight of land.

Robert Silverman has been sailing for more than 20 years. He has crossed the Atlantic several times and has cruised extensively on both sides of it. He is a dentist by profession, and his wife is a nurse. For the past three summers, the Silvermans have been in the Azores, where Dr. Silverman has run a sail repair business for the yachts that pass through there each year. Both Silvermans are contributors to SAIL Magazine.

Bill Thomte grew up in a family boatyard in New York, and by the time he was 18 years old he was qualified in all phases of construction and repair of wooden and steel boats. He spent over 22 years in the U.S. Navy, moving up through the ranks to chief petty officer before being commissioned an ensign in 1956. He retired from the Navy in 1966 and since then has been a marine surveyor. Over the years he has owned 17 sailboats. The latest is a 30' yawl named *Vivacious* on which he and his wife have cruised for many years along the East and Gulf coasts and the Bahamas. Mr. Thomte is a member of the National Association of Marine Surveyors and the American Society of Naval Engineers.

Crocker Wight's interest in celestial navigation stems from his days as a naval aviator in World War II. He taught navigation for both the Civilian Pilot Training Program and for the U.S. Navy. He is well known in yachting circles for his work in preparing East Coast Consolan Charts while that navigational aid was still in operation.